Buffy to E

Buffy to Batgirl

*Essays on Female Power,
Evolving Femininity and Gender Roles
in Science Fiction and Fantasy*

Edited by JULIE M. STILL
and ZARA T. WILKINSON

Foreword by Katharine Kittredge

McFarland & Company, Inc., Publishers
Jefferson, North Carolina

LIBRARY OF CONGRESS CATALOGUING-IN-PUBLICATION DATA

Names: Still, Julie, editor. | Wilkinson, Zara T., 1985– editor.
Title: Buffy to Batgirl : essays on female power, evolving femininity
  and gender roles in science fiction and fantasy / edited by Julie M. Still
  and Zara T. Wilkinson ; foreword by Katharine Kittredge.
Description: Jefferson : McFarland & Company, Inc., Publishers, 2019 |
  Includes bibliographical references and index.
Identifiers: LCCN 2019032617 | ISBN 9781476664460 (paperback : acid free paper ∞)
  ISBN 9781476637259 (ebook)
Subjects: LCSH: Science fiction, American—History and criticism. | Fantasy fiction,
  American—History and criticism. | Science fiction films—United States—
  History and criticism. | Fantasy films—United States—History and criticism. |
  Sex role in literature. | Sex role in motion pictures.
Classification: LCC PS374.S35 B835 2019 | DDC 813/.0099287—dc23
LC record available at https://lccn.loc.gov/2019032617

BRITISH LIBRARY CATALOGUING DATA ARE AVAILABLE

ISBN 978-1-4766-6446-0 (softcover : acid free paper)
ISBN 978-1-4766-3725-9 (ebook)

Front cover illustration by Andrea Pittori (Shutterstock)

Printed in the United States of America

McFarland & Company, Inc., Publishers
  Box 611, Jefferson, North Carolina 28640
  www.mcfarlandpub.com

Acknowledgments

Working on the Buffy to Batgirl conference was a tremendous experience. We are grateful to all who participated, attended, spoke, and supported it in any way. Bea Santos came up with our logo. Chancellor Phoebe Haddon and events coordinator Kristin Walker at Rutgers University–Camden provided financial and institutional support. Library director Gary Golden (now retired) and colleagues at the Paul Robeson Library pitched in and were patient with the disruption to work schedules that the conference caused. Our families were also very understanding of disruptions to daily schedules. The McFarland staff have been very receptive to the project and helpful in preparing the manuscript. Special thanks to McKenna Britton for her proofreading skills.

Table of Contents

Foreword

Punk Academe: The Rise
of the Rule-Breaking, Boundary-Shaking
DIY Conference

KATHARINE KITTREDGE

It started as a rude gesture directed at The Keepers of the Canonical Keys. "Pippi to Ripley" was hatched up by a disgruntled senior scholar and three merry prankster students[1] huddled in a vaguely mid-apocalyptic professor's office in upstate New York. We were having one of those wildly cycling conversations which rapidly evolve from a gripe session to building castles in the air: we would throw away the rules and create a new event, not a fan-con, not an academic conference, but something that borrowed what was best from both, with elements of film festivals, community arts events, and all-night bull sessions thrown in.

Even though we were working within an academic framework (we use Ithaca College facilities, staff, print and publicity resources), there was good reason to reject the prevailing model of academic conferences. Academic conferences, as they exist in the twenty-first century, fall roughly into two categories: (1) enormous events sanctioned by a long-established group of scholars constructed to reward work in well-trodden areas of study and to perpetuate the old-boy-networks that control prestigious academic positions and opportunities for publication; and (2) professional organizations like CUR (Council on Undergraduate Research) which charges members over $700 for an individual conference, making tens of thousands of dollars for both the organization and the hosting institution. What makes these developments even more egregious are trends in the academic job market that compel graduate students (and faculty in non–tenure track positions) to do extensive conference presentations in order to be considered for teaching

1

jobs even while many institutions are cutting back on the funding that would support these activities. At the other end of the spectrum, undergraduates are being pressured to do "professional level" research to compete for spots in graduate school, but the only venues that are open to them are either the prohibitively expensive events like NCUR or graduate-student organized conferences that give them little exposure to mature scholars.

Our vision for the event we christened "Pippi to Ripley" (named for Pippi Longstocking and the character Ellen Ripley from the *Alien* films) was to create a space in which fans, media creators, and scholars of all ages and stages could meet and exchange ideas. The first conference, held in April of 2011, was truly a do-it-yourself affair, with undergraduate volunteers creating websites, designing posters, and baking brownies for the mid-morning snack break. Since then Ithaca College has stepped up to support the event, helping to underwrite its expenses in return for the opportunity to promote it as community outreach, and to market it as a way that our undergraduates gain valuable experience in a number of different intern/volunteer capacities. Over the years, we have also been fortunate to find generous keynote speakers who waived or reduced their speaking fees in support of our non-profit, highly inclusive model.

In addition to providing creative workshops for local kids and pedagogical panels and workshops for teachers and librarians, we have succeeded in putting together a program of high-quality academic presentations delivered by equal numbers of professors, graduate students, and undergraduates. We are adamant about the need to include, nurture and support our youngest scholars because they often take our discussions in creative directions unexplored by more seasoned scholars.

Over the years we have refined our system for mentoring first-time presenters: it begins with intense feedback on their proposals, a personal contact person to answer questions, and detailed instructions about what to expect and how to conduct themselves at the actual conference. We also begin each conference with a 10-minute "conference etiquette" talk which provides ground rules both for first-time presenters and for community attendees (who range from long-time comic book fans to local middle school children and their teachers). The public—and all of the presenters' guests—attend for free, and the presenters pay a minimal registration fee of less than $50 to cover printing and custodial expenses as well as to provide them with meals during the conference (well-fed presenters are not only more articulate, they also tend to be nicer to each other).

Our choice to focus the conference on gender and imaginative fiction arose out of the interests of the four people who dreamed it up: three scifi geeks and a professor of women's studies. Since then, we have spun off three "daughter conferences" that have adapted our model to emphasize areas of particular interest to their coordinators: "Catwoman to Katniss: Villainesses and Heroines of Fantasy and Science Fiction," sponsored by Middle Tennessee State University in 2012, reflected that program's strength in young adult literature. "Buffy to Batgirl: Women and Gender in Science Fiction, Fantasy, and Comics" held in 2014 at Rutgers–Camden emphasized comics, a field which the program's coordinators knew from their support of local comic book conventions. "Beauty to Black Widow: Exploding Gender Barriers in Children's Literature, Fantasy, Science Fiction and Comics" was held at Mansfield University in 2018 and will be run a second time in 2020. It is our hope that future years will see the creation of additional daughter conferences which will adapt the Pippi to Ripley model to reflect their own strengths and interests.

The creation of this book—ably edited not by professors concerned with elongating their CVs but by two librarians who are deeply committed to the serious consideration of popular culture—is both a testament to the success of the beyond-academic ultra-inclusive model of critical engagement and an extension of it into a new realm. The essays are wide-ranging and insightful, focusing their critical gaze on texts that have never been closely analyzed, and providing new insights into familiar texts which benefit from discussions which extend beyond traditional academic discourse. The overall effect is one of intellectual renewal. It stands as a potent reminder of the benefits of stepping outside of the walls of the ivory tower and taking seriously the beauty, diversity and rich ideas that are waiting to be discovered in unexpected places.

NOTE

1. Ryan Ende, Giovanni Colantoni, and Adam Ellerson. I would also like to mention my co-coordinator and muse, Elizabeth Bleicher, who joined us in 2013.

Katharine Kittredge is a professor of English at Ithaca College in Ithaca, New York. Her areas of interest are 18th-century British literature, children's literature, science fiction, and gender studies. She has organized or co-organized all of the Pippi to Ripley conferences at Ithaca.

Introduction

JULIE M. STILL *and* ZARA T. WILKINSON

It is possible that angels have feared to organize conferences, and certain that fools have rushed in to do so. In our case, so have librarians. Organizing an academic conference is a serious undertaking, and we certainly had no idea what we were getting into when we set about creating Buffy to Batgirl: Women and Gender in Science Fiction, Fantasy, and Comics, a two-day international conference held on the campus of Rutgers University–Camden in May 2014.

How did we get here? Well, as befitting any odyssey, it all started in Ithaca. In May 2013, we both attended Pippi to Ripley: The Female Figure in Fantasy and Science Fiction, a conference held on the campus of Ithaca College in Ithaca, New York. The conference was small but comfortable, with thoughtful panels that brought together both faculty and student presenters. A casual conversation with Katharine Kittredge, the professor of English who organized Pippi to Ripley, revealed that the conference had been held once before in 2011, and was intended to occur every other year. (It has since been held in 2015 and 2017.)

We wondered if anyone had proposed a "sister" or "daughter" conference in the even-numbered years in between. There had been one in 2012, we learned, in Tennessee. That, and the memory of a recent email from our campus administration seeking proposals for large events, led to the glimmer of an idea. "Could we plan one?" we wondered aloud. We were both life-long fans of science fiction, both interested in the topic. It would be exciting, we thought, but a lot of work. At the end of the drive home, we were left with one question: *Why not?*

After mulling it over for a bit longer and coming to the same conclusion, we sought the blessing of both Katharine Kittredge and our library director to propose a conference, Buffy to Batgirl, at Rutgers–Camden. When it was approved as a Chancellor's Signature Event and offered both funding and support from the campus, we were elated. Audacious optimism in our own abilities, the support of our colleagues, and an excellent campus events and communication staff allowed us to pull off a successful conference. Although we both had attended academic conferences, we were neither experienced conference organizers nor seasoned event planners, so the planning process was a meaty professional challenge. While working on conference planning, we were temporarily sharing a windowless basement office due to a construction project, so the entire process was slightly surreal—we were out of our usual environment in more ways than one.

On May 2 and 3, 2014, more than 150 people attended Buffy to Batgirl, coming from across the U.S. and from four different countries. Our attendees were professors, graduate students, independent scholars and even some diligent and promising undergraduate students. The presentations delivered at the conference were so thought-provoking and engaging that we knew we needed to find a way to share them with a broader audience. The next logical step was to pull together an edited volume, which you now hold in your hands. The time gap between the conference and the completion of the book is in no way reflective of the essay authors, but instead charts the bumpy path of the editors. We appreciate the patience of the McFarland editorial staff and are pleased to, finally, share with you some of the wonderful papers from Buffy to Batgirl. The book consists of twelve essays arranged in three sections: Images of Female Power, Evolving Femininity, and Re-Framing and Re-Forming Gender Roles.

The five essays that make up Section I, Images of Female Power, explore the multitudinous ways that science fiction and fantasy depict powerful women and the sources of their power. In "Something Wicked This Way Comes? Power, Anger and Negotiating the Witch in *American Horror Story*, *Grimm* and *Once Upon a Time*," Alissa Burger and Stephanie Mix examine the figure of the witch, itself an ancient archetype of female power, as it is represented in those three television series. In "Witches, Mothers and Gentlemen: Re-Inventing Fairy Tales in *Buffy the Vampire Slayer*," Kerry Boyles describes how *Buffy the Vampire Slayer* subverts fairy tale tropes in order to celebrate female empowerment and emphasize the dangers of the patriarchy. Alice Nuttall, in "Selfish Girls: The Relationship Between Selfishness and Strength in the *Divergent* and Tiffany Aching Series," locates selfishness as a source of female power in the teenage girls depicted in the popular *Divergent* book trilogy and Terry Pratchett's *Discworld* series. Patricia Isabella Schumacher also addresses female empowerment in "'Have good sex': Empowerment Through Sexuality as Represented by the Character of Inara Serra in Joss Whedon's *Firefly*," focusing on the ways that Inara's extreme femininity and sexual agency casts her as a powerful woman with the trappings of third-wave feminism. This section concludes with another look at Buffy in "Girl Power and Depression in *Buffy the Vampire Slayer*," as Shyla Saltzman tackles the other side of female empowerment by examining the toll that constantly playing the postfeminist hero takes on Buffy Summers.

Section II, Evolving Femininity, features three essays that trace the development of the female hero. In "Girl Rebooted: Transforming *Doctor Who*'s Sarah Jane Smith from Sidekick to Hero," Sheila Sandapen follows the development of Sarah Jane Smith, who traveled with the Doctor in *Doctor Who* and, decades later, became the star of her own spin-off show. Sandra Eckard continues the focus on a single character in her essay, "The Evolution of Lois Lane: Reflections on Women in Society," which documents Lois Lane's journey from Superman's girlfriend to independent woman, ruminating along the way on how the character has reflected the changing role of women in society. Each of these essays provides a fascinating look at how a single long-running female character has changed in both characterization and the centrality of her role. In "Alternate, Not Arrested Development: Bryan Fuller's Female Protagonists," Trinidad Linares continues the theme of evolving femininity by focusing on the female protagonists of the TV shows *Dead Like Me*, *Wonderfalls*, and *Pushing Daisies*. Linares argues that the science fiction settings of these recasts their underachieving female characters as new, third-wave feminist models of femininity and female agency who are allowed to enjoy the unrestricted, undefined path that is often a luxury reserved for men in popular media.

The four essays in the final section, Re-Framing and Re-Forming Gender Roles, look at how science fiction and fantasy can depict, dismantle, and reframe the roles of women in society. In "Vampires Who Go to High School: Everyday Women's Culture in *Twilight*, *Dracula* and *Fifty Shades of Grey*," Caolan Madden locates the popularity of *Twilight* and *Fifty Shades of Grey* in their investment in and foregrounding of the banality of everyday life. In "Using the Animator's Tools to Dismantle the Master's House? Gender, Race, Sexuality and Disability in Cartoon Network's *Adventure Time* and *Steven Universe*," Al Valentín examines how science fiction and fantasy cartoons can lay the groundwork for new understandings of not only gender and sexuality but also race and disability, centering and normalizing all types of differences. Peregrine Macdonald then returns to *Firefly* in "'Little Geisha Dolls': Postfeminism in Joss Whedon's *Firefly*," focusing on how Inara exemplifies postfeminism as well as its limitations and shortcomings. Lastly, in "Beyond the Monomyth: Yuriko's Multi-Mythic Journey in Miyabe Miyuki's *The Book of Heroes*," Eleanor J. Hogan turns to the fantastical *The Books of Heroes* as she proposes a "multi-mythic" model of the heroic journey as an alternate to the monomythic (male) journey described by Joseph Campbell in *The Hero with a Thousand Faces*.

The authors who contributed to this volume use science fiction and fantasy to examine, explore, and question the depiction of women and gender in contemporary society. We invite you to take a closer look at the essays in this book, and to join us in both celebration and critical examination of some of your favorite characters—whether on a spaceship or in Sunnydale.

I.

Images of Female Power

Something Wicked This Way Comes?

Power, Anger and Negotiating *the Witch in* American Horror Story, Grimm *and* Once Upon a Time

ALISSA BURGER *and* STEPHANIE MIX

The figure of the witch is a familiar one, from the earliest fairy tales to contemporary fiction, film, and television. As Jack Zipes writes of the witch's complicated history in *The Irresistible Fairy Tale: The Cultural and Social History of a Genre*, "We are not certain of the witch's origins because we do not have written records of early pagan periods, only artifacts … that indicate women were often depicted as goddesses and were worshipped because they had extraordinary powers that allowed them to perform miraculous acts such as making people and environments fertile, or destroying people and environments" (57). As far back as those pagan times to which Zipes refers, witches have hovered at the boundaries of our cultural dreams and nightmares. Their power haunts fairy tales, where the witch often uses those abilities for evil purposes, like the wicked queen who attempts to poison Snow White so that she herself can once again be *"the fairest of us all"* (Grimm and Grimm 329, emphasis original). The 1939 MGM film *The Wizard of Oz*, adapted from L. Frank Baum's classic children's story, featured two witches, one good and beautiful while the other is evil and ugly, dichotomously pitted against one another over a little girl from Kansas and a pair of magic shoes. The White Witch ruled over Narnia with cruelty and an ice-cold iron fist in C.S. Lewis's *The Lion, the Witch, and the Wardrobe*. The Sanderson Sisters of *Hocus Pocus* (1993) stalked through the night, hunting the lives of children, while *Sabrina the Teenage Witch* (ABC, 1996–2000; WB, 2000–2003) tried to balance her everyday life as a normal American teenager with her magical heritage, with hijinks frequently ensuing. J.K. Rowling's *Harry Potter* series transported readers—and with the film adaptations, viewers—to Hogwarts School of Witchcraft and Wizardry and the magic that lay just behind the façade of real-life England. These are only a handful of the witches—both wonderful and wicked—who have captivated readers and viewers, and as the contemporary popularity of the witch figure shows, they continue to cast a powerful spell in popular culture.

The witch is about much more than spells and incantations and the very word "witch is memetically loaded" (Zipes 56). As Linda Baughman, Allison Burr-Miller, and Linda Manning argue, "Depictions of witches are a way by which our culture thinks about and grapples with the idea of brilliant women. After all, at some points in our history, intelligent women were thought to be as unlikely (and as potentially dangerous) as witches" (104). This intelligence and power are shown as simultaneously empowering and threatening, often seen as potentially hostile and unpredictable, as well as uncontainable. As Julie D. O'Reilly argues in *Bewitched Again: Supernaturally Powerful Women on Television, 1995–2011*, "Superpowered women on television serve as an important site of negotiation for determining the social and cultural acceptability of female power both on and off screen, as the representations of such characters both overtly challenge (through the characters' innate abilities) and subtly reinforce (through the characters' limited agency) hegemonic power structures" (11–12). As a result of negative perceptions of women's power, witches are at the central point of perpetual contestation and ongoing negotiation, with these representations reflecting the real-world contexts and tensions that surround them. In "Why Witches on TV Spell Trouble in Real Life," Jennifer Latson explains that "depictions of American witches have been a pop-cultural fixture. Often, their story serves as an allegory for persecution, injustice, and the dangers of mob mentality." At her very core, the witch figure is a litmus test of cultural perceptions of and responses to women's power and, particularly in the case of wicked witches, women's anger.

The representation of the witch is an inherently feminist one, in its negotiation of witchcraft as a power which enables its users to exercise their agency and influence the world around them through alternative and non-patriarchal avenues. From this perspective, while witches have historically been "depicted as cruel, exotic, devious, and evil figures in popular culture" (Zipes 77), the witch can also be read from a range of multiple positive perspectives, including "as a fantasy of a 'superwoman' and … as an archaic mother" (Sempruch 9). Contemporary discourses of the witch center on notions of the magically gifted woman as independent, competent, and almost always in complete control of her powers, using them to her own advantage. These positive representations of strong witches are significant because they highlight the intelligence, power, and agency of these women. While the contemporary witches of book, film, and television series like *Harry Potter, Buffy the Vampire Slayer* (WB, 1997–2001; UPN, 2001–2003), and *Charmed* (WB, 1998–2006) use their magic as a form of agency, a dichotomy of good and evil continues to influence these representations. This makes even the positively empowered witch suspect, a tension perhaps best epitomized by the transformation of Willow Rosenberg (played by Alyson Hannigan) into "dark Willow" in *Buffy the Vampire Slayer*, who wreaks vengeance in the aftermath of her girlfriend Tara's (Amber Benson) murder and whose rage threatens to literally destroy the world. No matter how benevolent and socially-integrated the witch may be, she is to be feared unless and until she can be effectively contained or, if that proves impossible, destroyed. As Marion Gibson points out in *Witchcraft Myths in American Culture*, "The problem with undomesticated [witches] is the threat they pose to the omnipotence of the American male, and women are particularly dangerous because they are so 'fascinating,' 'bewitching,' and 'enchanting'" (197).The tension surrounding the witch's power, and the dual discourse of this female figure as simultaneously empowered and dangerous, creates a conflicting and contested space around the witch in which she is generally categorized within the traditional dichotomy of good and wicked witches.

The recent critical debate about readers' and viewers' expectations of female characters' "likability" is also central to the interaction of this popularity with the negotiation surrounding witches' power and its containment (or lack thereof). As Roxane Gay points out in her essay "Not Here to Make Friends," "even from a young age, I understood that when a girl is unlikable, a girl is a problem" (84). Turning her attention to literature and popular culture, Gay explains that "unlikable is a fluid designation that can be applied to any character who doesn't behave in a way the reader finds palatable" (85), generally in ways that situate the woman in question outside the scope of traditional gender norms. This is a standard of evaluation to which male characters are seldom held, and never to the same degree of rigorous enforcement. Literature and popular culture are bursting at the seams with male antiheroes—men who can be difficult, if not impossible, to like. However, "An unlikable man is inscrutably interesting, dark, or tormented, but ultimately compelling, even when he might behave in distasteful ways" (Gay 88), a luxury very few similar female characters are afforded. Vanity, insensitivity, ruthlessness, a penchant for control, a coldness or calculation in her relationships with others: these are characteristics that, while potentially acceptable or even admirable in a male character, are likely to brand a female character as "unlikable," deviating as they do from the nurturing, sensitive passivity that traditional feminine gender roles prescribe. Finally, likability is often a performance, a role played to win acceptance and approval. As Gay reflects, "In many ways, likability is a very elaborate lie, a performance, a code of conduct dictating the proper way to be. Characters who don't follow this code become unlikable" (85). These powerful female characters are thus doubly damned: first, for deviating from traditional gender role expectations and second, for refusing to pretend to be someone or something they are not, eschewing the lie to instead embody the truth of themselves, their identities, and their unapologetic strength. These expectations of female characters' likability have a real-world correlation in the lives of women, as Chimimanda Ngozi Adichie discusses in *We Should All Be Feminists*, where she reflects on "how invested [women and girls] are in being 'liked.' How they have been raised to believe that their being likable is very important and that this 'likable' trait is a specific thing. And that specific thing does not include showing anger or being aggressive or disagreeing too loudly" (23–24). Echoing the double standard of "unlikable" female characters versus their compelling male antihero counterparts, Adichie points out that women face this same duality in their daily lives, where "We spend too much time telling girls that they cannot be angry or aggressive or tough, which is bad enough, but then we turn around and either praise or excuse men for the same reason" (24).

In recent years, the "season of the witch" has come around again, with high-profile prime time television witches in *Grimm* (NBC, 2011–2017), *Once Upon a Time* (ABC, 2011–2018), *Sleepy Hollow* (FOX, 2013–2017), *American Horror Story: Coven* (2013), *The Witches of East End* (Lifetime, 2013–2014), and *Salem* (WGN, 2014–2017). There are even more witches on the horizon, including a reboot of the 1990s series *Charmed*. As Latson notes, witches' "mainstream popularity has … to do with our personal fantasies of power," especially for those who are often denied it. Megan Gibson (2013) furthers this argument in her consideration of the current shift in popularity from vampires to witches, explaining:

> For nearly a decade, the undead ruled pop culture. Now, witches are getting another crack at dominance. And I think that's a good thing—particularly for the young girls and women who are the primary audience for these shows. Unlike the female leads in most vampire stories, women in witchcraft stories are typically depicted as strong, capable characters. They might not always be noble, but they're certainly not weak or passive characters who sit on the sidelines while the men take charge.

In addition to this increased level of power and agency in the representations of these women, the witch figure also creates potential space for the embrace and celebration of difference. Melissa Maerz, looking specifically at *American Horror Story: Coven*, comments on the fact that these representations "[take] people who don't have much of a voice in this country—older women, African Americans, social outcasts—and turns them into almighty creatures, able to prey on the young and entitled, and occasionally kill white boys with their vaginas" (54). But along with this strength, agency, and difference, there is a continuing ambivalence in responding to women's power, a demand that women whose power cannot be contained must be exiled or destroyed.

However, today's television witches are refusing to be contained, to restrict or reign in their power to placate the more normative culture surrounding them. Despite this refusal to surrender—or perhaps because of it— these magical women continue to be compelling and irresistibly popular among audiences, if not necessarily sympathetic, as seen in *American Horror Story: Coven*, *Grimm*, and *Once Upon a Time*. The contested balance between these women's individualism and their essential—if at times horrifying— humanity against the dehumanizing "wicked witch" label is particularly significant. The primetime witches of *American Horror Story: Coven*, *Grimm*, and *Once Upon a Time* negotiate the dual, intertwined debates of women's power and likability, highlighting cultural discomfort with the former and a steadfast demand for the latter.

American Horror Story: Coven

The third season of the FX show *American Horror Story* (subtitled *Coven*) introduces viewers to both good and wicked witches, and every shade in between. Within the confines of Miss Robichaux's Academy for Exceptional Young Ladies in New Orleans, there is a group of young women being trained to hone their magical skills under the tutelage of the school's headmistress, Cordelia Foxx (played by Sarah Paulson). Included in the "students" at Miss Robichaux's Academy are Madison Montgomery (Emma Roberts), Zoe Benson (Taissa Farmiga), Nan (Jamie Brewer), Queenie (Gabourey Sidibe), and Misty Day (Lily Rabe). Serving as the coven's "Supreme" is Cordelia's mother Fiona Goode (Jessica Lange), who possesses all the possible powers of a witch and is therefore biologically ordained to lead.

Cordelia is a solid example of the "likable" witch. She is married at the outset of the season, and is tasked with raising and training the young witches into their roles within the coven. She negotiates the outbursts of the girls, and continually impresses upon them that controlling their power is crucial to the survival of the coven. Again, we see the familiar idea of containing a witch's power to satiate the outside world by maintaining a low profile. In addition to a commitment to suppressing power, Cordelia embodies the concept of loyalty, especially to the coven. While she does end her marriage to her husband Hank (Josh Hamilton), it is not in deference to the constant Endora-like insistence from her mother, but as a result of his infidelity. When she learns after his death that their entire marriage was initiated as a ploy of his father to gain access to the coven, her heartbreak seems to stem more from her unwitting betrayal to her fellow witches than from any remaining romantic feelings.

Cordelia's dedication to the coven is poignantly shown in her reaction to the deaths of the witches. She is furious when she learns that her mother has murdered Madison, just as she is later furious with Madison for refusing to resurrect Zoe from the dead. She is shown sobbing and still holding Misty Day as she disintegrates after her failure to return from Hell during the Seven Wonders (the test to discover who will become the coven's new Supreme.) However, it is the second death of the coven's student-finder and Cordelia's mother figure, Myrtle Snow (Frances Conroy),that is the most personally devastating to her. In choosing to bring her surrogate mother to the coven's brand of justice by having her burned at the stake, Cordelia proves herself to be self-sacrificing almost to a fault. She is willing to give up the woman who raised and loved her to maintain the reputation of the coven. In the most graphic and disturbing display of her devotion, she goes so far as to gouge out her own eyes with gardening shears in order to regain the gift of second sight in hopes of using it to protect the coven from future attacks. Cordelia's self-sacrificing disposition serves as a sharp contrast to her mother, Fiona. Where Cordelia is "likable" and a more generally acceptable image of a witch and a woman, Fiona Goode is the polar opposite. Following in the tradition of the wicked witch as unclean and a source of chaos and desecration, "Constituted as hysterical and disordered in relation to logocentric structures, the 'witch' is suspended at the point of crossing into the unspoken or forbidden. Her speech perverts the language of philosophers; laughter, spells, and evil incantations flow from her grotesque and filthy mouth" (Sempruch 2). Vain, selfish, and ruthless, Fiona serves none but herself. Any fleeting glimpses of humanity we see in Fiona—from her outrage at her daughter being blinded by acid and cheated on by her husband to her love affair with the murderous ghost known as the "Axeman" (played by Danny Huston) and her professions of true love—are overshadowed by her darker nature.

Fiona represents all those characteristics that denote villainy within a witch. An older woman, she is shown in her first few scenes of the series visiting her doctor's office and discussing the possibility of undergoing experimental treatment with a youth serum he has created. Upon his refusal to administer it, she takes his life from him, drawing it into herself to restore a bit of vitality, a common theme in representations of witches, as seen in films from *Hocus Pocus* (Kenny Ortega, 1993) to the more recent *Snow White and the Huntsman* (Rupert Sanders, 2012) and *The Wicked* (Peter Winther, 2013), in an echo of the traditional "fairest of them all" desire for youth and beauty. When she is diagnosed with cancer and faces her own mortality, Fiona's powers begin slipping away from her and transferring to the young witch that will be the next Supreme. Rather than relinquish her power and bow out gracefully as other Supremes have done, Fiona begins to target the girls individually as she suspects them of gaining power, beginning with Madison. This is a complete reversal of Cordelia's near worshipful view of the power structure. In Cordelia's mind, power is something to be respected and revered in those who hold it. To Fiona, it is something to take and control for one's self.

A combination of all these qualities is likely what leads to the eventual discovery that Fiona literally has no soul. She has been deemed beyond saving by the Voodoo Loa Papa Legba (Lance Reddick), and this judgement is largely deserved. After all, she is incredibly selfish. When asked if she would give anything for immortal beauty and power, she answers almost immediately that she would, showing her willingness to damn her own daughter and everyone else that she loves. She has become accustomed to vast amounts of power, and has done nothing constructive with it for the good of the coven and those around her, choosing instead to squander it on notoriety and wealth for herself. She also clearly demonstrates that she has little regard for human life, and no problem with committing heinous acts of murder. She is shown happily burying an ax in the neck of an enemy, slitting the throat of the witch who was the Supreme before her, and at one point defending Nan's innocence to Papa Legba by rationalizing that "she killed the neighbor, but that bitch had it coming" (Episode 3.10, "The Magical Delights of Stevie Nicks").

However, there are moments in the series when we are given glimpses of humanity within Fiona: her initial return to the coven being prompted by an instinctual defensiveness after seeing coverage of Misty's burning at the stake on the news, her outrage at Hank's betrayal of her daughter, and her subsequent dismissal of Cordelia in anger for putting the coven in danger all lead to the conclusion that, despite how self-centered she may be, she does hold the coven in high regard and displays an aptitude for swift and brutal retribution to those who seek to destroy it. Likewise, she clearly lacks the compassion and attentiveness required to be a parent, but there are moments when it is clear that she cares greatly about her daughter. It is real anguish we see when she finds that Cordelia has been blinded, and it is real regret that she displays in her last encounter with her daughter when she admits that any disapproval she may have shown for her only stems from the fact that Cordelia serves as a constant reminder of her own mortality.

It should be noted that, as with most narratives involving the wicked witch, Fiona dies. She does so not in a blaze of glory, not at the hands of an enemy, but in the fashion that she would find most distasteful. In the end, she has become a haggard woman, devoid of her former beauty and without enough power to light a cigarette. Similarly, the other "wicked witches" within the show also meet untimely ends. The fictionalized version of voodoo queen Marie Levaux (Angela Bassett) finds herself doomed to an eternity in hell, forced to repeatedly murder the innocent daughter of the brutally sadistic and racist Delphine LaLaurie (Kathy Bates) as Delphine is forced to watch. Madison is strangled to death by the boy she thinks she may have loved and is buried in the yard with no ceremony and with almost no acknowledgment that she is even gone. This is a particularly painful end to the girl who was raised as a child star, then lived under the assumption that she would become the next Supreme. The cruelest twist of Fiona's personal Hell, however, is the complete mundanity of it. This formerly all-powerful woman who has been accustomed to a life of luxuries and casual sex is doomed to spend the rest of eternity married to one man, living in a cabin and frying up catfish day after day. It is intensely symbolic that the strongest witch of her generation meets her punishment in the form of domestication.

In addition to exploring themes of racism and women's fear of aging, *American Horror Story: Coven* depicts a rather visceral instance of rape. Each of the four seasons of the show used rape as a plot point, and the use of rape as a way to convey a very personal brand of fear and injustice has been criticized as clichéd and insensitive. As Karen Valby points out in her article "TV's Tiresome Assault on Women," "it seems whenever a female character needs a juicy arc or humanizing touch, writers fall back on the easy, awful crime of rape," continuing on to note that these rape storylines are often used as "a cruel device to trigger viewer compassion for a woman it isn't always easy to like" (55). *Coven*, however, uses the familiar threat of rape against women to build a rape-revenge narrative using the women's magical gifts. This depiction of women using their powers to avenge themselves on those who have attacked them helps to subvert the popular narratives of rape culture, and runs against the grain of other uses of rape as a plot point in popular culture. Though the women of *Coven* have been attacked, sexual assault has done nothing to diminish their personal power. There is no male hero figure who avenges them; their anger is instead focused through their powers to punish those who have abused them.

In the very first episode of the season, viewers are introduced to Madison Montgomery, the entitled and narcissistic young movie star who has been sent to Miss Robicheaux's after using her telekinetic powers to murder a director who criticized her on set. Madison is nearly the spitting image of coven Supreme Fiona: blonde, beautiful, arrogant, vain, and on occasion quite cruel. She is the epitome of the Mean Girl. When she meets Zoe, she press-gangs her into being her new "best friend" and drags her to a frat party. We are shown the members of another fraternity attending the party in a scene where the head of the group, Kyle, is laying down rules for the other members, which include no public vomiting, no public exposure, and generally no behavior that might endanger their charter. This trope of heavy drinking, heavy partying frat boys is familiar to anyone who has seen the quintessential college movie *Animal House* (John Landis, 1978). At the party, the young men witness the dramatic entrance of Madison and Zoe, and their tropes are likewise immediately set before us. Madison's first words are to haughtily ask where she can find a drink. Zoe is presented as the uncomfortable, more modest friend, tugging at the short hemline of the tight dress that Madison has let her borrow for the night. While Madison is comfortable in flaunting her body, Zoe is generally shown in looser, more substantial styles. Upon catching the attention of Kyle, Zoe begins a flirtation with him, finding him apparently more sensitive and sweet than his macho friends. At the same time, Madison is segregated from the rest of the party in a mostly abandoned stairwell when she is found by the loudest of Kyle's frat brothers. Her image as an unlikeable, "bitchy" woman is furthered when she asks him if he will be her slave, and upon being asked what he would get in return, she retorts that as a slave, he will not get anything. It is at this point that we see the boy slip something into Madison's drink. After this, viewers are subjected to a fairly graphic scene in which the "slave" in question and his frat brothers have brought the drugged Madison to an empty bedroom. The "slave" boy is raping Madison while the other boys film it with their phones. Things only stop when Zoe and Kyle barge in, and Kyle attempts to fight the rapist. Once Kyle and his frat bothers flee the party for the safety of the party bus on which they arrived, they immediately start getting rid of the evidence. The recordings of the events are deleted, and the lead rapist insists that Kyle keep quiet about the entire incident to keep the fraternity from being disbanded.

This jarring scene follows a common narrative in rape culture. The "bitchy" girl gets her comeuppance after drinking at a party at which she arrived in a short skirt. It is an image that has played out in countless college stories, both in film and real life. Events only change in a conceivably positive way when Madison and Zoe's powers come into play. When Zoe and Madison follow the boys into the street only to see them fleeing in the bus, Zoe breaks down. Madison, however, steels herself and channels her telekinetic powers to flip the bus over, killing nearly every boy in the vehicle. This reversal in the power structure that rapists usually find after committing a sexual assault is a refreshing, if violent, one to witness. Without her status as a witch, Madison may have been forced to accept what happened to her as another unpunishable occurrence. Without any evidence or witnesses willing to testify against the rapists, she may not have found recourse within the legal system. Her magical abilities allow her to focus her anger and reap her own vengeance.

Zoe later uses her own powers to bring final justice upon the actual rapist. Upon finding that Kyle was not one of the survivors of the crash, she discovers the rapist undefended and alone in his hospital bed. In her own fit of anger at his assault on her friend and the sheer fact that he managed to live when Kyle had not, Zoe climbs into his bed and unleashes the vagina dentata-esque powers that sent her to Miss Robichaux's in the first place. When she has sex with him, the boy suffers an aneurism that causes blood to pour from his nostrils, as Zoe literally kills him with her vagina. This is another powerful example of a woman's very femininity and the fear of what her sexuality can do to a man—in this instance bringing down a sexual predator through her own act of rape. In bringing attention to, and striking back against rape culture, it is questionably admirable, depicting sexual assault as a weapon, even if it is in possibly "justifiable" circumstances.

Grimm

NBC's *Grimm* is a buddy-cop series with a supernatural twist, "mixing horror, mystery, fantasy, drama, and police procedural" (Schwabe 304). In addition to solving murders in Portland, Oregon, homicide detective Nick Burkhardt (played by David Guintoli) discovers that he is a "Grimm," a familial legacy that allows him to see supernatural creatures invisible to almost everyone else. While the Grimms operate on a foundation traced back to the Brothers Grimm and the stories they transcribed—revealed in *Grimm* to be fact rather than fiction—this connection remains relatively tangential throughout the series, which sets up a discourse of ability and responsibility that frequently echoes that of the Slayer in *Buffy the Vampire Slayer*, with the distinguishing difference that though there aren't many Grimms, Nick is not the only one. Just as Nick's actual connection to the Brothers Grimm is quite loose, so are the creatures he sees and, when necessary, fights or destroys. Referred to within the series as "Wesen," these creatures are "new creations in a vaguely Germanic-Nordic vein" (Hale), including Blutbad (translated as "blood + bath," and a version of the canonical werewolf figure), Fuchsbau ("fox hole" or "burrow"), and Hexenbiest ("witch beast").

While *Once Upon a Time*'s fairy tales enter the real world through the intersection and overlap of these two distinct worlds, "the magical in *Grimm* not only coexists with the nonmagical but also originates in the human world" (Schwabe 303). While Nick has a hereditary gift for seeing Wesen, because the magical and fantastic are an integrated part of the presented reality, "anyone can potentially perceive the magic within the real world" (Schwabe 296). This is especially true when the Wesen or humans encountering them are under stress or engaged in intense conflict, which is an issue for Nick's partner Hank Griffin (Russell Hornsby) and another cop, Sergeant Wu (Reggie Lee), both of whom briefly think they are suffering from hallucinations and impending madness before Nick shares the truth with them. Just as the line between reality and fantasy is permeable in *Grimm*, perception and truth are similarly slippery propositions. As Claudia Schwabe argues in "Getting Real with Fairy Tales: Magic Realism in *Grimm* and *Once Upon a Time*," the "juxtaposition of the supernatural and the natural, and the fact that they cross paths multiple times throughout the story lines, creates an intriguing tension between the familiar and the unfamiliar as well as between the apparent and what lies hidden beneath the surface" (294). In short, things are not always what they seem, and time-honored roles are in a state of constantly shifting negotiation. For example, in the pilot episode of *Grimm*, a red hoodie-clad runner disappears on her jog through the forest and when Nick sees a wolfish Blutbad in the vicinity, he's sure he has his man (or, more accurately, his Wesen). However, not only is this particular Blutbad innocent, he turns out to be a reformed Blutbad named Monroe (Silas Weir Mitchell), committed to vegetarianism and pilates, and quickly becomes one of Nick's closest friends, a rich source of Wesen lore, and a kind of unofficial investigator when Nick's cases veer into the land of fantasy. The issue of perception works both ways, with Nick frequently challenging the Wesen community's expectations of him. Historically, Grimms have been committed to eradicating Wesen, whether guilty or innocent, but Nick treats them instead as individuals, very rarely killing any of these creatures and only when they pose an otherwise unstoppable threat to others, the community, or the world. As Kristiana Willsey explains in "New Fairy Tales Are Old Again: *Grimm* and the Brothers Grimm," "Nick comes to occupy a more ambiguous place between the human and the supernatural worlds" (211), a fluidity which disrupts the demarcations between reality and fantasy, as well as between perceptions of canonically good and evil. With this new interaction between Grimm and Wesen, cross-species collaboration begins to disrupt what has previously been constructed as a hard and fast, "us versus them" duality, as Nick, Hank, Wu, and Nick's girlfriend Juliette (Bitsie Tulloch) develop close friendships and solve cases side by side with Monroe and his Fuchsbau girlfriend and later wife Rosalee (Bree Turner).

The representation of magic, witchcraft, and women's power is under frequent negotiation throughout the series as well, with the two main witch characters—referred to in the *Grimm*-verse as "Hexenbiests"—being Adalind Schade (played by Claire Coffee) and in the fourth season, Nick's girlfriend Juliette, who is transformed into a Hexenbiest as a side effect of a magic spell. The volumes of Grimm lore left to Nick by his Aunt Marie (Kate Burton) define these creatures in an early episode, a "Hexenbiest [is a] a witch-like creature that somewhat resembles a demon or goblin. They work at the behest of royalty and are identifiable by a dark birthmark under their tongues" (Episode 1.3, "BeeWare"). In the pilot episode of *Grimm*, the first Wesen that Nick sees "woge" (physically shift from human to Wesen) is the Hexenbiest

Adalind Schade: as he watches a beautiful, blonde professional woman walking down a city street, she transforms, briefly revealing the rotted, monstrous face of the witch within, before changing just as quickly back to her human appearance.

Adalind is a recurring character over the course of the series' first five seasons, though her power and allegiance are constantly shifting. In the first-season episode "BeeWare," Adalind is a victim, under police protection, though as soon as the threat passes, she becomes a danger herself, as she seduces Nick's partner, Hank, cultivating a destructive obsession and putting him into a coma. Nick is able to release Hank from Adalind's spell but only by robbing her of her powers, which must be done with "the blood of a Grimm," a feat Nick achieves by kissing Adalind as they struggle, causing her to bite his lip and accidentally ingest his blood (Episode 1.17, "Love Sick"). Adalind is willing to sacrifice anything and anyone to get the power she craves, using sex, magic, and often a combination of the two to get what she wants. When she finds herself pregnant with Sean Renard's (Sasha Roiz) baby—Renard's mother is a Hexenbiest, making him half-Zauberbiest (or male witch); Renard is also a member of the Royal Family, as well as Nick's police captain—she goes to the Royal Family in Vienna and begins negotiating the baby's value, setting a price on the unborn child's head, and leveraging the baby as a bargaining chip to regain her powers. In the opening episodes of the third season, Adalind performs a grueling ritual, the Contaminatio Ritualis, to become a Hexenbiest once more, with tasks including the murder and desecration of another Hexenbiest's body, a sacrifice and penance that must be cosmically "accepted" (Episode 3.1, "The Ungrateful Dead"; Episode 3.2, "PTZD"). As calculating as Adalind is with her baby's life when cutting this deal, however, once the baby is born, Adalind's ferociously protective maternal instinct kicks in, and with her powers restored and her baby in her arms, she switches sides once more, going back to Portland, Renard, and unwittingly, putting herself under Nick's protection.

Nick and Adalind's relationship is incredibly volatile, with each taking from the other that which matters most. After Nick robs Adalind of her powers, she takes Juliette away from him, casting a rudimentary spell that puts Juliette in a coma and causes selective amnesia, with Juliette unable to remember anything of Nick or their life together (Episode 1.22, "Woman in Black"). Nick, Renard, Hank, Monroe, and Rosalee collaborate to take Adalind's child Diana, protecting the girl from the designs of the Royal Family, and sending her away in secret with Nick's mother, another powerful Grimm (played by Mary Elizabeth Mastrantonio). Adalind, not in on this larger plan, is understandably devastated by the loss of her child, desperately searching for Diana, willing to cut any deal that will get her daughter back, and with her powers restored, raining vengeance and destruction on those who have taken her child (Episode 3.18, "The Law of Sacrifice"). Adalind uses sex and magical power once more when she transforms herself into Juliette and has sex with Nick, which causes him to lose his powers as a Grimm (Episode 3.22, "Blond Ambition"), and inadvertently results in Adalind becoming pregnant with Nick's child. While Adalind occasionally helps Nick and the others, in the series' first four seasons she is largely featured as a wicked witch, morally suspect and not to be trusted, even when she claims to be on their side.

A much more complex negotiation of the Hexenbiest's power in *Grimm* is with Juliette's transformation in the series' fourth season. Throughout the first three seasons of the series, Juliette makes the bumpy transition from not knowing anything about Wesen and Grimms to struggling with this new knowledge and finally, accepting and supporting Nick, and even participating in investigations as part of the larger human/Wesen hybrid team. When Nick loses his power as a result of Adalind's spell, though Juliette understandably struggles with Nick's (albiet unknowing) infidelity, she volunteers to make the sacrifice necessary for him to regain his powers, with a direct reversal of the spell, in which she has to take a potion to transform herself into Adalind and have sex with Nick (Episode 4.6, "Highway of Tears"), with the regaining of Nick's ability inextricably tied to this betrayal, Juliette's pain, and Nick's uneasy combination of guilt and desire. The true punishment comes later, however, when Juliette discovers that she has now been transformed into a Hexenbiest herself and, tapping into this newfound power, she finds an outlet for her rage and previous powerlessness that soon overshadows and then destroys her love for Nick and their lives together. While Juliette is originally anxious to get rid of these powers, she soon embraces them, turning against her friends and loved ones. She reflects on the irony of their role reversal, telling Nick that she understands now why he likes being a Grimm and having a power that so few others have, reflecting on her own power that "now I know and I understand and I don't want to give it up…. Once you're in it and you've tasted it and lived it, you can't go back. Everyone else just seems blind. I like this power, Nick" (Episode 4.18, "Mishipeshu"). This disconnect as Nick struggles to accept Juliette's new abilities is also echoed by Henrietta (Garcelle Beauvais), a Hexenbiest with whom Juliette consults. As Henrietta tells Nick, "There's only one way to deal with your Hexenbiest: kill her. Or accept her for who she is, just like she accepted you being a Grimm. And while she's discovering what she's capable of, I would suggest you keep a safe distance" (Episode 4.14, "Bad Luck"). While Juliette has frequently been ignorant of, and powerless to protect herself from, some of the more violent and vengeful Wesen who have come after Nick—and in several cases, come after her as well, positioning her as a damsel in distress in need of Nick's rescue. With her new abilities she no longer has to be afraid. Newly powerful, she starts to use her new abilities in destructive ways, aligning herself with the Royal Family against Nick and the others, destroying the trailer that holds all of Nick's Grimm books and accoutrement, attacking her friends, and attempting to kill Nick.

It is here that Juliette and Adalind are brought into direct conflict, fighting head to head as Juliette discovers just how volatile her own powers are, as she pursues and attempts to kill Adalind, first as revenge for what Adalind has done to her and later, as a result of her discovery that Adalind is pregnant with Nick's child as Nick protects Adalind, the final betrayal. Juliette literally becomes dehumanized in these final episodes of the season and following an especially violent attack in Rosalee's spice shop, Monroe says, "Whoever that was, I'm done trying to help it" (Episode 4.21, "Headache"), stripping Juliette of not just her individual identity but her very humanity, the monstrosity of her power and rage demoting her from a "she" to an "it." Conversely, just as Juliette becomes more monstrous, Adalind becomes increasingly human. Reaching out to Nick to enlist his help in protecting their unborn child, she makes a great sacrifice to create a potion that will suppress Juliette's powers. Creating the potion through the desecration of another Hexenbiest's corpse, echoing the abjection of the earlier Contaminatio Ritualis, Adalind tests it on herself, losing the vast majority of her powers in a desperate attempt to suppress Juliette's, though it is all for naught when Juliette refuses and destroys the potion. In the end, Juliette is ready and willing to kill Nick, who refuses to fight against her, fatalistically accepting her power and his own imminent destruction before it, only saved when Juliette is stopped by another Grimm, a young woman named Truble (Jacqueline Toboni). But even when Juliette and Adalind are pitted directly against one another, they still transcend a good/evil dichotomy, as each struggles to come to terms with her power. The series' fifth season finds Adalind contemplating a permanent sacrifice of her powers for the good of herself, Nick, and their child (Episode 5.2, "Clear and Wesen Danger") and horrified by her powers' return (Episode 5.12, "Into the Schwarzwald"), while the presumed-dead Juliette returns in a new permutation as "Eve," part of an elite resistance team, stronger and more in control of her powers than ever before (Episode 5.6, "Wesen Nacht"), back on Nick's side, but ruthless, calculating, and cold.

The witches of *Grimm* are never as wholly monstrous as *Coven*'s Fiona and their emotions, motivations, and essential humanity are foregrounded, though they are still quite clearly marked as inherently dangerous. Their power is rarely viewed for its own intrinsic merits but rather, viewed and evaluated based on the benefit or harm it can cause the larger and in some ways, patriarchal structure of the greater good, whether in its threat to a Grimm, its undermining of the social group and proxy family created by Nick and the others, or the large-scale power plays between the Royal Family and the Wesen resistance movement.

Once Upon a Time

Once Upon a Time taps into a rich vein of fairy tale discourse, specifically within the Disney tradition (ABC is a property of the immense Disney corporation), putting familiar and fantastic characters into the anachronistic setting of the contemporary small town of Storybrooke, Maine. This transition from fantasy to reality, from an imagined past to a real life present, creates myriad opportunities for negotiating the fairy tale and its impact on contemporary culture and media. The world in *Once Upon a Time* is what Claudia Schwabe refers to as a "reality fairy tale … [where] magic crosses over into the real world" (297). As Schwabe explains, in *Once Upon a Time*, "the primary world, reflecting contemporary reality, is paralleled by a secondary magic world; fantasy characters and magic cross into the primary world and converge with reality; and the main protagonist experiences the fantastic within an ordinary, realistic setting" (307). This dualism allows the series to engage with the larger fairy tale tradition in an anachronistic setting, playing on and subverting the uncanny combination of fact and fiction, fantasy and reality. As Rebecca Hay and Christa Baxter argue in "Happily Never After: The Commodification and Critique of Fairy Tale in ABC's *Once Upon a Time*," through its emphasis on "personalizing and internalizing, the show suggests fairy tales are more reality than fantasy" (318). As a result, while the series embraces magic in the wide range of fairy tale elements and foundation upon which it builds, the intersection with the real also makes those characters relatable, creating powerful opportunities for self-identification and empathy.

Witchcraft, women's power—and the larger responses to it—vary significantly between *Once Upon a Time* and *Grimm*. As Mike Hale explains in "The Enchanted Forest, in Sunshine and Shadow," "In *Grimm* our world needs protection from mostly frightening supernatural forces; the stars are men. In *Once Upon a Time* our world is a frightening prison from which the mostly innocent supernatural characters must escape; the stars are women." Like *Coven*'s Fiona, Regina Mills (played by Lana Parrilla) in ABC's *Once Upon a Time* is a less than exemplary image of a woman in power. Referred to as "The Evil Queen" in the fantasy land of the Enchanted Forest, she is the live-action embodiment of the wicked stepmother from the animated Disney movies most viewers have grown up with. Generally clad in shades of black, blood red, and deep purple and wielding her vengeance like a sword, Regina is clearly marked as the antagonist to the wholesome yet feisty Snow White (Ginnifer Goodwin). Where the show diverges from previous fairy tale depictions, however, is in its willingness to display character growth. While she is unabashedly wicked, Regina is a villain for villainy's sake. As Schwabe explains, "insight into the villains' background stories, feelings, and personal motivations in *Once Upon a Time* explains why the evil queen and Rumpel-stiltskin became malicious. For both, the loss of a loved one plays a pivotal role and can evoke in the viewers a strong sense of compassion for these mis-creants" (311). Viewers are given a nuanced vision of a woman who has gained and kept her powers through less than savory means. Where Fiona is driven almost purely by self-interest, Regina has been hardened by lost love, an over-bearing mother bent on gaining power, and a deep sense of betrayal and lone-liness. Where Cordelia was essentially removed from her mother's influence for the majority of her formative years, Regina was held tight under her mother's thumb to the detriment of any relationships she may have fostered. Regina "is authoritative and monstrous in positions of domesticity (adoptive mother to Henry) and political power (the evil queen and mayor) alike" (Hay and Baxter 324) and her use of magical power is less self-serving than it is a tool of self-preservation. It does, however, reinforce Rumpelstiltskin's favorite adage that "magic comes with a price." Regina's rise in power directly corre-lates to her loss of her more human aspects, namely compassion.

After her mother Cora (played by Barbara Hershey) uses magic to kill her low-born fiancée, Regina is forced into a loveless marriage to a man whose daughter she already blames for her lover's death. This, in combination with her mother's assertions that gaining rank is the most worthwhile pursuit in life, pushes Regina to rebel against not only her husband the king but against her mother as well. By training with the dark being known only as Rumpel-stiltskin (Robert Carlyle), she gains the power she needs to exact her vengeance against Snow White for her perceived betrayal, along with the ability to hold her status as queen and the faintest possibility of returning her love, Daniel (Noah Bean), to the living. As Regina gains more and more power, however, we see her lose more and more of her gentle nature. When she begins her training, she staunchly refuses to cause any physical harm. This stance slips little by little as her story progresses, and we watch her trans-formation from the girl who saved Snow White on a runaway horse to a woman who can tear the still beating heart from the chest of a foe to manip-ulate or kill them as she sees fit. From plotting and carrying out her husband's murder to her growing obsession with having her revenge on his daughter, Regina travels further and further down the road to becoming the angry, ruthless witch viewers are introduced to only as The Evil Queen. Finally, at what may be the height of her villainy and the lowest she can seemingly scrape in the name of vengeance, she finds the curse she will use against Snow White, Prince Charming (Josh Dallas), and the entire kingdom to plunge them into an alternate world on Earth with no magic or recollection of who they are or what they have been through, a world without time. However, the curse requires that she sacrifice the heart of the thing she loves most, her last apparent link to humanity, her own beloved father, King Henry (Tony Perez).

Reassuringly, however, Regina also differs from *Coven*'s Fiona in her ability to redeem herself. While Regina has tortured, murdered, and manipulated as The Evil Queen—and to some extent as the mayor of the town of Storybrooke—she finds solace in the form of her adopted son, Henry (Jared Gilmore). In this way, *Once Upon a Time* subverts the age-old image of a cold-hearted witch who cannot love, a character trajectory also explored in Disney's 2014 feature film *Maleficent*. Henry becomes Regina's new focus in her life in Storybrooke and it is through her relationship with him that she slowly begins to accept that she cannot control his love through magic, as she has attempted to do with others since Daniel's death. It is also because of Henry that she comes to accept his other family, including Emma (Jennifer Morrison), Rumpelstiltskin, Snow White/Mary Margaret, and Prince Charming/David. This displays not only a complicated upheaval of the idea of wickedness by showcasing a formerly two-dimensional character's motivations, but offers a much rosier outlook of redemption than the "wicked" women of *American Horror Story* receive. Instead, within the complex structure of the long-arc serial narrative, viewers are asked to continually reflect upon, reexamine, and dynamically negotiate their understanding of Regina. As Hay and Baxter argue, Regina's

> backstory questions the fairy-tale conventions of good and evil. Could the apparently loveless queen have loved someone so much that his loss numbed her heart? And if Regina truly deserves sympathy, how can audiences cheer on her impending demise, even if it is necessary to a traditional happily ever after? When even traditional villains become relatable, how can traditional endings become similarly realistic? [324].

Over the course of the series' four and a half seasons, this question remains a common refrain, both for Regina personally and for the larger, oft-questioned dichotomy of heroes and villains. As Regina tells the others, according to the storybook in which their lives are chronicled, villains don't get happy endings, no matter how much they have changed or how justly they may deserve them. However, just as this narrative pattern and moral prescription is recognized and addressed, the series underscores the true reality beyond the good and evil dichotomy. As Mary Margaret/Snow White tells Regina, "You are not all evil and I am not all good. Things are not that simple" (Episode 4.9, "Fall"). While she begins the series as a relatively flat character, the Evil Queen who is capable of all manner of heartless acts of cruelty, as it continues, *Once Upon a Time* tells "a new tale with a dynamic, empathic Regina" (Hay and Baxter 324). In coming to know herself, opening herself up to others, and charting her own path toward becoming a hero, Regina is sympathetic, likeable, and human, an erstwhile Evil Queen that viewers can relate to and invest with their hopes for a new kind of happy ending.

In its complexity and capacity for significant change, *Once Upon a Time* offers the most hopeful representation of magically gifted women of the series presented here. In addition to this challenge of the good/bad moral dichotomy, *Once Upon a Time* also complicates the threat of the powerful woman by showing magically gifted women from a wide range of opposed and constantly negotiated moral identifications. For example, Storybrooke has been visited by other iconic fairy tale witches, including Oz's Wicked Witch of the West, here called Zelena (played by Rebecca Mader) and *Sleeping Beauty*'s Maleficent (played by Kristin Bauer van Straten). While both are willfully and admittedly evil, with a goal of destroying the happiness of others, they are also both given traumatic backstories, delving further into why these villains have become villainous in the first place, with Zelena rejected and abandoned by her mother and Maleficent enraged by the loss of her child. Further complicating matters and disrupting the good versus evil conflict, Storybrooke's heroes are implicated in both of these tragedies: Zelena is Regina's half-sister, who was denied the family and the future that Regina had—however complicated and traumatic that was in its own right—and Maleficent's child was taken by Snow White and Prince Charming, used as a sacrifice to siphon the potential for darkness out of their own unborn child. As a result, rather than being the diametric opposite of one another—good guys and bad guys, heroes and villains—the heroes carry their own guilt, bearing some responsibility for the evil that has been allowed to grow within the villains, and who now turn to these heroes to seek their vengeance, a retribution which in most cases, is at least partially justified. With no "winner" in this scenario, the heroes and villains must instead work together to dismantle this "us versus them" scenario, engaging with one another instead through regret, apology, and hope.

Another discourse of the magically gifted woman in *Once Upon a Time* is the woman with uncontrollable powers, which is explored in Season Four through both *Frozen*'s Elsa (Georgina Haig) and Emma's recognition, fear, and eventual embrace of her own formidable powers. Echoing the narrative in Disney's 2013 blockbuster *Frozen*, Elsa and Anna (played by Elizabeth Lail) are separated and Elsa comes to Storybrooke looking for her sister. Upset over not being able to find Anna, Elsa struggles to control her powers, surrounding Storybrooke with a wall of ice and nearly killing Emma when the two of them are accidentally trapped inside with no means of escape (Episode 4.2, "White Out"). Elsa is able to take control of her own powers through the support and acceptance of those around her, including her discovery of her lost Aunt Ingrid (Elizabeth Mitchell), who has the same powers as Elsa, and who has her own tales of learning to master her power and being rejected by her sisters. Emma also struggles with her own powers as she learns to control them, fearful of hurting those she loves. When she is upset, much like Elsa, Emma's power breaks the bounds of her control and she accidentally hurts both David and Henry (Episode 4.7, "The Snow Queen"; Episode 4.8, "Smash the Mirror"). While her first instinct also echoes Elsa's in *Frozen*, as she removes herself from Storybrooke and isolates herself in the forest where she can't hurt anyone, this proves ineffectual and Emma only regains control of her power and herself by working side by side with those she loves, as well as learning from and sharing her experiences with Elsa.

Emma is also a dynamic combination of darkness and light. Prophesied as "The Savior," her magic is perceived as light, good, and useful for the protection and welfare of the larger community in Storybrooke. However, when Snow White was pregnant with Emma, she received an ominous fortune from Maleficent: that while Emma would indeed have the power and potential to be a great hero, there was also a chance that she could become a great villain, "darker than any this realm has ever seen" (Episode 4.14, "Enter the Dragon"). To protect Emma, Snow White and Prince Charming stole Maleficent's child, in the form of a dragon egg, and had Emma's potential for evil magically channeled into that egg, which was then transported to another realm, saving Emma. However, Emma's safety is assured at the cost of Maleficent's child, as well as Maleficent's last vestiges of love and humanity, and when Emma learns the truth, their choice jeopardizes the ideal heroic vision she has of her parents. While Emma faces many challenges that tempt her toward darkness, including having to kill to protect Henry (Episode 4.19, "Lily"), in the end her darkness comes not from temptation or failure, but through sacrificing herself to save others. In the fourth season's finale, when the power of the Dark One is loosed from Rumplestiltskin's failing body, Emma draws it into herself, serving as a vessel and a prison, choosing darkness for herself to protect those she loves (Episode 4.22, "Operation Mongoose, Part 2").

Season Five of *Once Upon a Time* furthers this blurring of the line between savior and villain, as we see the consequences of Emma's turn as the Dark One. While she has been the hero of the story thus far and indeed only took the darkness inside of her to continue protecting the people she loves, that darkness manipulates her largest weaknesses, most notably her need for independence. As a woman who gave her own child up the moment he was born, who lived most her life without family and was abandoned by the only man she had loved, Emma has an arguably understandable need to be self-reliant borne of constant loneliness.

It is interesting to see this self-sufficiency turned against her in her bout as the Dark One. Her son goes so far as to say that he cannot trust her to perform magic if she refuses to trust in her family's ability to help her. After becoming the Dark One purely to save her family, and shortly thereafter being forced to make a life-altering decision that may jeopardize the world to save the life of the man she loved, Emma's willingness to pay any price for love has been amply demonstrated. To then have this self-sacrificing nature turned into a flaw suggests an impossible choice as a woman: there is a societal pressure to give everything for one's children and family, but making decisions independent from that family in order to protect them is punished. Having magical abilities does nothing to alleviate the stereotypical pressures of womanhood. If she had included everyone in her plans rather than wiping all their memories, it may have led to her lover, Captain Hook/Kilian (Colin O'Donoghue), once again succumbing to the darkness that the curse of being a Dark One had laid upon him. She is essentially trapped in a no-win scenario. By excluding everyone from her plan, she has driven away her family, and caused the doubt to bloom within Kilian that eventually leads him to stray down a dark path once again.

It should be noted, however, that Emma's exercise of independence does not compare to that of Fiona, and Emma's actions after Kilian's death do not compare to those of Regina. Her self-reliance comes at the expense of her own interest, not to the advantage of it. Where Fiona abandoned Cordelia throughout her adolescence while she went to live a decadent life as the Supreme elsewhere, Emma works alone to preserve the safety of her family. Likewise, even with the burden of darkness already within her, Emma does not retaliate in vengeance upon King Arthur (a villain in this retelling), or Merlin, or anyone connected to the legend of Excalibur. She does not let Kilian's death completely stain her the way Daniel's death blackened Regina's heart. Instead, when Kilian is killed by Excalibur, Emma does the only thing she can think to do and magically tethers him to the sword, thus turning him into another Dark One. It is, however, merely a temporary solution, one that leads to the deeper question of manipulation.

Emma's use of magic to tether Kilian to Excalibur, though done in an attempt to save his life, removes his agency, and endangers both him and those around him. Kilian has lived centuries as Captain Hook, and has delighted in murder and thievery. Though he has changed for Emma's sake, it is not hard to push him back into a vengeful, violent mindset. Unfortunately, this is precisely what his new identity as a Dark One provokes. He handles the transformation marginally well at first, but when he discovers that she has controlled him by using Excalibur, he loses trust in her and reverts to his old ways. When Emma sees how her actions have affected him and the implications they have had for everyone else (including causing Merlin's death) she again does the only thing she can think of and uses her magical abilities to erase the memories of Kilian and anyone who had knowledge of his change. On a much less graphic scale, one can see the same perilous issues of manipulation and consent presented by Zoe's fatal rape of the fraternity brother who had in his turn raped Madison in *American Horror Story: Coven*. While in both series the women felt their actions to be justified, their use of magic to manipulate and remove the will of others—no matter how altruistic their intentions—shows an abuse of power that bears unsettling resemblances to truly evil characters.

While the premise of *Once Upon a Time* is built upon a fairy tale foundation of heroes and villains, the series almost immediately upsets these dichotomies, complicating the easy understanding of good and evil, including in its representation of magically powerful women. From Regina's redemption to a new understanding of what made Zelena and Maleficent into wicked witches, the question of agency and control engaged by Elsa and Emma, and Emma's own long-arc narrative negotiation of her power and potential, *Once Upon a Time* offers a wide variety of magical women who are both good and evil, sometimes both at the same time, and undeniably human.

Conclusion

Fiona, Cordelia, and their *Coven* of witches, Adalind and Juliette of *Grimm*, and *Once Upon a Time*'s Regina are just a few of the witches who have made their way to primetime television in recent seasons. While on the surface we can identify them as easily fitting within the good witch or wicked witch paradigm, these representations also move beyond that simple dichotomy, giving us nuanced, fallible, and three-dimensional women. They may still have their moments of monstrosity, such as Fiona's attacks on the young witches of the coven to retain her own slipping power or Regina's sacrifice of her father, but we can also see the witch as a woman, as an individual, even within this evil. These witches are, in some ways, a female incarnation of the male antihero that has seen a recent explosion in primetime popularity, as they eschew the demand to be sympathetic or "likable" to instead pursue their own desires and claim their own power. As Gay points out, there's a double standard that presents unlikable men as complex and compelling, while unlikable women are seen as aberrant, deviating as they do from the expectations of traditional femininity (88). Against this popular culture backdrop that often criticizes and contains women's power, the witches of *American Horror Story: Coven, Grimm,* and *Once Upon a Time* are arguably revolutionary, refusing to be bound by these expectations or constrain themselves by enacting more acceptable feminine roles. The growing complexity of these representations of witches is significant because, as Elizabeth Pearson Plummer points out, while "the powers which women have been afforded have been restricted to the impossibly good or perfect woman, the power of the evil temptress, or the power of the scapegoat, women need their new mythmakers to open the portals to a more complex vision of what their femininity can mean" (82). Popular culture often serves as a mirror, reflecting the anxieties and tensions of its surrounding society, serving to pinpoint the conflicts that most trouble their sociocultural moment, and as these and other examples show, the magically gifted woman is one of these key tensions. These witch figures have the potential to be part of the new body of myth-making Plummer discusses, creating innovative possibilities for women's power and identity, by embracing and exercising their abilities, resisting the urge to be categorized, and refusing to be contained.

Works Cited

Adichie, Chimimanda Ngozi. *We Should All Be Feminists*. Anchor, 2014.

American Horror Story: Coven. Created by Brad Falchuck and Ryan Murphy. Perf. Jessica Lange, Sarah Paulson, Emma Roberts, Taissa Farmiga, Jamie Brewer, Gabourey Sidibe, Lily Rabe. FX, 2013–2014.

Baughman, Linda, Allison Burr-Miller, and Linda Manning. "Back to the Future: The Brilliant Witches of *Bewitched*." *Geek Chic: Smart Women in Popular Culture*. Palgrave Macmillan, 2007, pp. 103–119.

Gay, Roxane. "Not Here to Make Friends." *Bad Feminist: Essays*. Harper Perennial, 2014, pp. 83–95.

Gibson, Marion. *Witchcraft Myths in American Culture*. Routledge, 2007.

Gibson, Megan. "Witches Are the New Vampires—and That's a Good Thing." Time.com (2013): n.p. *Academic Search Complete*. Web. 7 Aug. 2015.

Grimm. Created by Stephen Carpenter, David Greenwalt, and Jim Kouf. Perf. David Guintoli, Russell Hornsby, Silas Weir Mitchell, Bree Turner, Bitsie Tulloch, and Claire Coffee. NBC, 2011–present.

Grimm, Jacob, and Wilhelm Grimm. "Snow White and the Seven Dwarves." *Grimm's Complete Fairy Tales*. Barnes and Noble, 1993, pp. 328–336.

Hale, Mike. "The Enchanted Forest, in Sunshine and Shadow." *New York Times*, 21 Oct. 2011. https://www.nytimes.com/2011/10/22/arts/television/grimm-on-nbc-and-once-upon-a-time-on-abc-review.html. Accessed 29 Oct. 2015.

Hay, Rebecca, and Christa Baxter. "Happily Never After: The Commodification and Critique of Fairy Tale in ABC'S Once Upon a Time." *Channeling Wonder: Fairy Tales on Television*. (Series in Fairy-Tale Studies). Wayne State UP, 2014, pp. 316–335.

Latson, Jennifer. "Why Witches on TV Spell Trouble in Real Life." Time.com (2014): n.p. *Academic Search Complete*. 29 Oct. 2015.

Maerz, Melissa. "American Horror Story: Coven." *Entertainment Weekly* 1281 (2013): 54. *Academic Search Complete*. Web. 7 Aug. 2015.

Once Upon a Time. Created by Adam Horowitz and Edward Kitsis. Perf. Jennifer Morrison, Ginnifer Goodwin, Lana Parrila, Josh Dallas, Colin O'Donoghue. ABC, 2011–present.

O'Reilly, Julie D. *Bewitched Again: Supernaturally Powerful Women on Television, 1996–2011*. McFarland, 2013.

Plummer, Elizabeth Pearson. *Mermaids, Monsters and Madwomen: Voices of Feminism and Feminine Consciousness*. Diss. Pacifica Graduate Institute: 2002. ProQuest, 6037643, 2002.

Schwabe, Claudia. "Getting Real with Fairy Tales: Magical Realism in *Grimm* and *Once Upon a Time*." *Channeling Wonder: Fairy Tales on Television*. (Series in Fairy-Tale Studies). Wayne State UP, 2014, pp. 294–315.

Sempruch, Justyna. *Fantasies of Gender and the Witch in Feminist Theory and Literature*. Purdue UP, 2008.

Valby, Karen. "TV'S Tiresome Assault on Women." *Entertainment Weekly*, vol. 1301, 2014, pp. 54–55.

Willsey, Kristiana. "New Fairy Tales Are Old Again: Grimm and the Brothers Grimm." *Channeling Wonder: Fairy Tales on Television*. (Series in Fairy-Tale Studies). Wayne State UP, 2014, pp. 210–228.

Zipes, Jack. *The Irresistible Fairy Tale: The Cultural and Social History of a Genre*. Princeton UP, 2012.

Witches, Mothers and Gentlemen

Re-Inventing Fairy Tales
in Buffy the Vampire Slayer

KERRY BOYLES

In the opening scene of "Welcome to the Hellmouth," a pair of teenagers break into the deserted Sunnydale High School at night. The girl, a pretty blonde, acts nervous, but is coerced by her more dominating male partner. She seems anxious, fretting about strange noises until he assures her that they are alone. Reassured, the scared girl reveals her true face, complete with fangs, and drains the boy of his blood. She is actually Darla, an old vampire with a penchant for dressing as a naughty schoolgirl.

This scene begins *Buffy*'s subversion of horror tropes, as it plays on audience expectations of what should happen and very self-consciously does the opposite. In her discussion of *Scream* (1996), the postmodern slasher satire that premiered only months before *Buffy*, Valerie Wee explains that the teen slasher film genre established by films like *The Texas Chainsaw Massacre* (1974) "featured imperiled, sexually attractive women being stalked by a knife-wielding serial killer and included scenes of unexpected and shocking violence and brutality" (52). A self-proclaimed fan of horror films, *Buffy* creator Joss Whedon has explained in interviews that he wished to create a blonde girl that monsters would fear. Thus, Darla and Buffy are two sides of the same coin: Buffy, a teen who penetrates with a stake instead of fangs, and her vampiric counterpart are both reimagined versions of (blonde) female victims who appear again and again in horror movies and who are usually dispatched quickly by the bloodthirsty (male) horror villain. This is what show creator Joss Whedon has called "genre-busting," which he says is at the heart of both the film and the TV show (qtd. in Hagelin 6).

33

However, less obvious than this subversion of horror tropes is the show's dismantling of fairy tale elements and messages. Scholar Kim Snowden commented at the Buffy to Batgirl conference on the way the show uses references to Red Riding Hood to reflect the evolution of Buffy and Riley's relationship, and much has been made of Buffy's obvious feminist messages in everything from popular articles like Emma Dibdin's "9 Reasons Buffy Summers Is TV's Greatest Feminist" to Patricia Pender's "'Kicking Ass Is Comfort Food': Buffy as Third Wave Feminist Icon." Yet no one has fully examined how the show's use of fairy tale elements—specifically the evolution of those elements—contribute to the show's overall feminist messages.

In "Whose Side Are You On, Anyway?" Sarah E. Skwire analyzes "Killed by Death," "Gingerbread," and "Hush" to show that *Buffy*, like fairy tales, is didactic and that these episodes are fundamentally about disconnections between children and adults. For Skwire, these episodes subvert the usual subordination of the child to the adult's better understanding and skill, as "Killed by Death" and "Gingerbread" "serve to distinguish uncomprehending adults who are blind to, and foolishly trapped by, demonic dangers from the wise children who see what adults cannot see and who understand the reality of these 'imaginary' evils" (196). She calls this a "brilliant inversion of the generally accepted dynamic of fairy tales both as tales and as pedagogical devices" (196). While Skwire looked at these episodes as promoting children as knowledgeable and powerful, the episodes can also be deconstructed as fairy tale adaptations. Through this, we can evaluate how the series reconfigures fairy tale elements to promote feminist messages. This essay analyzes "Gingerbread" and "Hush," as well as Season Two's "Ted" and Season One's "Witch," and their use of fairy tale elements as part of the show's larger "genre-busting" feminist point of view.

Literary fairy tales by Giambattista Basile, Charles Perrault, and Jacob and Wilhelm Grimm often present anti-feminist messages, celebrating young, passive maidens while condemning older, powerful queens and witches. In his introduction to *Fairy Tales and the Art of Subversion*, Jack Zipes describes the "patriarchalization" of fairy tales, explaining that oral folk tales lost their "matriarchal mythologies" by the Middle Ages: "the goddess became a witch, evil fairy or step-mother; the active young princess was changed into an active hero; [and] matrilineal marriage and family ties became patrilineal" (7). Zipes argues that the tales increasingly began to present the "concerns of a monarchist, patriarchal, and feudal society" and notes that "power and oppression [are] the key concerns of the folk tales" (8). In this way, *Buffy* reverses this process, returning to power to an active female hero.

Even as they dismantle horror tropes, Joss Whedon and company subvert fairy tale narratives to create an empowering, pro-feminist discourse that is in sharp contrast with the conservative, patriarchal messages of many fairy tales. While fairy tales often punish willful, powerful women for rebelling against patriarchy, *Buffy* re-interprets fairy tales in order to celebrate and promote female empowerment and emphasize the dangers of patriarchal oppression. This seems most apparent in three episodes: Season Two's "Ted," a cybernetic Bluebeard tale; Season Three's "Gingerbread," a critical commentary on witch-hunting and "Hansel and Gretel"; and Season Four's "Hush," a Whedon-created tale with a female hero. In the first two episodes, the show distorts a classic fairy tale to either promote a feminist message or to criticize the original message of the tale. This feminist twist on fairy tales becomes more overt and more sophisticated in "Hush," which presents its own original heroine-centric fairy tale.

Fairy Tales, Patriarchy and Buffy the Vampire Slayer

Maria Tatar describes the various elements of fairy tales or magic tales in *The Hard Facts of the Grimms' Fairy Tales* (1987), noting that these tales often include a victimized hero who rises from humble beginnings, familial conflict, and disruption of the home, all of which appear in *Buffy*. Tatar explains, "Fairy tales chart the rise of a single, central hero as he moves through a magical foreign realm from an oppressed condition in the drab world of everyday reality to a shining new reality" (61). Tatar calls these heroes "victims and seekers" because magic tales are propelled by villainous acts that harm the heroes or losses that put the heroes in positions of need. For example, in some versions of the tale, Hansel and Gretel's parents decide to leave their children in the forest to die (villainy), or the parents simply die or are stolen away by a dark cloud (loss). These acts or losses force the victimized hero on a quest that eventually leads to a rise in fortune. Tatar notes, "The main body of fairy-tale plots is … devoted to hardships, struggles, and narrow brushes with death both at home and on the road" (71). Rather than show desires, these tales reflect and represent fears and phobias as tangible objects, much as horror and Gothic narratives do. The home, which should be a center of tranquility and safety, is often invaded by sinister forces: evil stepmothers, men who kill their snooping wives, neglectful parents, and even the Devil himself.

Not only does *Buffy* use fairy tale elements as the basis for several monster-of-the-week episodes, the series as a whole can be examined as a modern-day fairy tale. *Buffy* begins with a disruption and (literal) expulsion for the heroine when she must move to Sunnydale after having burnt down the gym of her previous school. The rest of the series follows Buffy as she attempts to find her footing and adjust to ordinary teenage problems, even as dark forces threaten her. The disruption of the home is central to the episodes discussed in this essay, as the episodes all feature some kind of invasion, whether it is of Buffy's actual home or the town of Sunnydale.

Buffy is similar to the fairy tale in structure because it uses fantastical elements as metaphors for the mundane. In fairy tales, ordinary events of adolescence like menstruation or sexual awakenings are represented through tales like the Grimms' "Little Red Cap" and "Little Briar Rose" and Perrault's "The Sleeping Beauty in the Wood." In *Buffy*, issues of adolescence are dealt with in similar ways: school gangs become principal-eating hyenas; Buffy's college roommate is actually a soul-sucking demon; fraternity brothers drug and sacrifice young virgins to a snake-demon that blesses men with material wealth and patriarchal power. As Sara Magee notes, Whedon's model for the series is the idea that high school is literally hell, and "[t]he show prided itself on portraying important high school issues in ways that had not been done before, using demons and vampires to illustrate problems with relationships, peers and sex" (885).

Moreover, as with tales like "Sleeping Beauty" or "Snow White," destiny plays a major role as a ruling hand for the Buffy, who is also called the "Prophecy Girl." Many early episodes remind viewers: "In every generation there is a chosen one. She alone will stand against the vampires, the demons and the forces of darkness. She is the Slayer." Throughout the series, Buffy grapples with her destiny as the "Chosen One." Once a Slayer dies, often while she is still young, another is "called" to replace her. When Buffy drowns in "Prophecy Girl" (1997), the dedicated and disciplined Kendra becomes a Slayer. Kendra appears in several episodes in Season Two until she is killed by Drusilla and succeeded by Faith, a defiant and sometimes rogue Slayer. This system of death and replacement recalls the replacement motif of many fairy tales. In fairy tales, younger women replace older women in positions of power; animals are substituted when evil characters want to cook or kill good ones; and villains often meet the horrible ends intended for their victims. In Perrault's "Sleeping Beauty in the Wood," the fairy that opens the tale by cursing the Sleeping Beauty is not punished, but is replaced by an ogress mother-in-law who torments the young bride and her children once she awakes. The ogress later throws herself into a vat of toads and vipers (meant for her daughter-in-law), another instance of substitution or replacement. In the tale, sleep is substituted for death (by the good fairy), animal meat is substituted for human flesh, and an evil woman takes the place of a good one in death. The steady process of Slayers replacing one another evokes the substitution or replacement motif that appears in many tales; however, Buffy emphasizes that these young women are not interchangeable, but offer many different shades of femininity: dark and light; good and evil; obedient and rebellious.

Thus, *Buffy* seems to echo many of the narrative and thematic elements of fairy and magic tales. Nevertheless, as critics like Jack Zipes, Sandra Gilbert, and Susan Gubar have shown, fairy tales are fundamentally conservative in nature. Tales like "Little Snow-White," "Cinderella," "The Sleeping Beauty in the Wood" or "Little Briar Rose," and "Hansel and Gretel" reinforce patriarchal and class hierarchies and demonize women who try to usurp male authority. This is shown again and again in the fair maiden/evil witch dichotomy, as the tales celebrate passive (often unconscious) women and punish unmaternal evil stepmothers, witches, or fairies. For example, at the end of Basile's "Sun, Moon, and Talia" (1634), a precursor to Perrault's "Sleeping Beauty in the Wood" (1697), the shrewish wife—who has previously attempted to eat the mistress and son of her errant husband—is burned alive. In Perrault's tale, this character becomes an ogress mother-in-law who is devoured by a tub of vipers and snakes. Similarly, "Hansel and Gretel" includes an evil old witch who is shoved into an oven by the child she attempted to cook. Snow White's evil stepmother, who refuses to allow a younger woman to replace her, is forced to dance until she dies in flaming hot shoes. These women are often characterized by their unnatural hunger for beauty, wealth, power, and even human flesh. Though there are monstrous figures like the Devil or Bluebeard who appear in tales by the Grimm brothers and Perrault, patriarchy is often represented by paternalistic, benevolent rulers who overcome and crush these errant women as well as bloodthirsty men like Bluebeard or Robber Bridegroom.

Though several episodes of *Buffy* include fairy tale elements from these tales or other fairy tales, these elements are subverted and distorted, creating an empowering, pro-feminist message that is in sharp contrast with the conservative messages of many fairy tales. It does not seem coincidental that in *Buffy*, patriarchy is often the foe that Buffy must fight and overcome. These villains include the Master, Ted, the Mayor, and (to some extent) the Initiative and Caleb. In the first season, patriarchy is personified by the Master, whose name indicates his hierarchical authority and whose age, Old World language, and customs are juxtaposed with Buffy's youth and cheeky wit. Buffy destroys him physically by way of giant stake and linguistically by pointing out his "fruit-punch mouth," telling him to go to hell, and calling him a "loser." In Season Two, patriarchy meets science fiction in the form of Joyce's gentleman caller Ted, a cybernetic android whose mission is to collect women and bring them back to his 1950s lair of traditional values. Like Ted, Mayor Richard Wilkins III appears to be an ordinary man, but is really a supernatural killer. The Mayor, Season's Three's "big bad," is a paternalistic, mini-golf-loving, and self-proclaimed "family man" who adopts the rogue slayer Faith and ascends into a demon on graduation day, attempting to devour the class of '99.

Although the Master, Ted, and the Mayor are all quite different, they reflect the way that patriarchy and misogyny can be both individual and institutional. While the Mayor is a single individual at the top of a corrupt political system (in Sunnydale), the Initiative is a collective enterprise that prizes conformity, uniformity, and obedience. Though run by Dr. Maggie Walsh, the militaristic Initiative is an underground organization of (male) super soldiers whose approach is immediately at odds with Buffy's individualistic, low-tech methods and her refusal to look "all 'Private Benjamin'" by adopting their uniform. Though not evil itself, the Initiative is destroyed by its own creation, Adam, a "cybernetic *Übermensch*" made of fused human, demon, and machine parts (Bishop 350). Kyle Bishop explains that Buffy's methods are those of "self-reliance" and "human spiritualism" which ultimately defeat the cold, emotionless reason and technology represented by Adam (350). As Bishop suggests, the conflict between Buffy and Adam is that of good and evil, man and woman, Satan and Christ, and humanity and technology.

Buffy deals with these patriarchal figures and institutions in different ways, but through her victories over them, the show produces a pro-woman, pro-feminist, anti-conformity, and anti-establishment message. Like the Mayor and the Initiative, the Watchers' Council, a mostly male organization that coaches, controls, and punishes the slayers, represents structural, political, and bureaucratic patriarchal power. As J.P. Williams notes, "The Council represents male-dominated hierarchy caring less about any particular girl who happens to be the Slayer than about exercising control over the power she represents" (62). When a Slayer comes of age, the Council subjects her to a "rite-of-passage" in which her Watcher depowers her and forces her to fight a vampire without any of her supernatural abilities. Shortly following this traumatic experience, Buffy quits the council, and when they approach her again in Season Four's "Checkpoint," the Council pedantically forces her to undergo a review of her skills to determine if she is worthy of significant information. Quentin Travers, director of the Watchers' Council, attempts to "remind" Buffy of the "resolute status of the players in [their] little game," saying, "The Council fights evil. The Slayer is the instrument by which we fight. The Council remains, the Slayers change. It's been that way from the beginning." When Giles exclaims that Buffy is not their "bloody instrument," Travers threatens to close down Giles' magic store and have him deported, saying, "Now perhaps you're used to idle threats and sloppy discipline, Miss Summers, but you're dealing with grownups now." This scene is significant in reading the Watchers' Council as a representation of subjugation of women, as their institutional authority allows them to bully even Buffy. Travers's abuse of his power and use of patronizing and objectifying language seem calculated to suppress Buffy's rebellion and reinstate the Council's authority over her. However, Buffy triumphantly re-asserts herself and her power at the end of the episode, reminding the Watchers that "without a Slayer, [they're] pretty much just watchin' *Masterpiece Theater*" and that they have no ability to defeat evil without her. Once again, Buffy rejects the Council's attempt to control and subjugate her, not only physically, but through her language.

In *Buffy*, patriarchy is often associated with authority or tyranny, lack of individualism, and conformity, all of which the show criticizes. Not only is this in sharp contrast with the messages of many fairy tales, it is important to consider how the show uses and inverts fairy tale narrative elements to create its overall feminist message.

Ted, "Bluebeard" and the Feminist Utopia

Though it could never be called a "fan favorite" episode, Season Two's "Ted" (1997) offers a unique spin on the classic "Bluebeard" tale. In Perrault's fairy tale, a young woman marries a man with a blue beard because of his enormous wealth. She is given keys to every room in the house but instructed not to enter one chamber. Defying his order, she enters the forbidden room and discovers the bodies of his previous wives. She nearly meets the same gruesome fate, but is ultimately saved at the last minute by her brothers. Similarly, in the Grimms' "Robber Bridegroom," a young woman discovers that her wealthy suitor is really a murderer and a cannibal. As Nicholas Ruddick explains, "There is a large body of fairy tales about a male villain who serially murders his wives and stores their mutilated bodies in a secret chamber in his own house" (346). These tales seem to reflect anxieties over marriage, and "encourage young women to trust their instincts about prospective husbands, to learn as much as possible about them before marriage, to take care not to be blinded by their own desire for matrimony, and to resist when parents, impressed by a suitor's wealth, seek unwittingly to hand over their daughters to a monster" (Ruddick 346).

"Ted" takes the story of the serial killer beau and moves it more clearly into the home. As Tatar explains, "Family conflicts, rather than the class of conflicts folk tales set on farms and in villages, lie at the heart of" magic tales or "wondertales" (61). She continues: "As the tale unfolds, the intrafamilial conflict escalates; parents and siblings become ever more vindictive, and the hero's sufferings multiply" (61). Buffy, our suffering hero, is at odds with her mother, Joyce, and Joyce's new boyfriend, Ted Buchanan (John Ritter), a computer software salesman. Like the mysterious suitors of similar fairy tales, there does not appear to be anything amiss about Ted except for Buffy's sense of foreboding and distrust. Buffy's best friends, Xander and Willow, are easily swayed with mini pizzas, cookies, and software updates, dismissing Buffy's misgivings about her mother's new beau. Yet just as the young women in the earlier fairy tales must learn to trust their instincts, so must Buffy, as her suspicions are ultimately validated. Early in the episode, Buffy explains: "I'm pretty good at sensing what's going on around me, and there is definitely something wrong with this Ted." Like the original tales, the episode seems concerned with presenting the pitfalls of dating and relationships while encouraging young women not to dismiss misgivings about mysterious men. Though Buffy's distrust makes her impolite and unpleasant and escalates the conflict in the home, it ultimately saves her mother's life and protects the domestic space from invasion.

Ted's pleasant demeanor slips when Buffy and her friends join Ted and Joyce for a game of mini-golf and, finding Buffy has cheated, Ted lectures her, calls her "little lady," and threatens to "slap that smart-ass mouth of [hers]." The conflict between them escalates until she finds Ted in her room, having read her journal and threatening to "out" her as slayer if she fails to submit to his authority as the man of the house. When Buffy attempts to keep him from leaving the room with her diary, and therefore using it to control her, he attacks her, giving her "permission" to use her slayer superpowers against him. Ted falls down a flight of stairs and seemingly dies. Although the episode touches on the moral issue of Buffy killing a human, it is revealed that Ted is actually a wife-killing cyborg. The original Ted, whose wife left him, created the cybernetic Ted to bring back his wife and keep her hostage until she died. Ted continued to do so with more women until he finally met Joyce. Here is another iteration of the fairy tale replacement motif, as each successive woman acts as a substitute for Ted's original wife, even going home with an upgraded version of Ted. Ted eventually returns from the "dead," hoping to claim Joyce and bring her back to his underground lair, but Buffy finishes him off with a skillet to the face.

The struggle for power between men and women is at the forefront of "Ted." The episode opens with a lighthearted and seemingly irrelevant debate between Xander and Willow on which member of the popular husband-wife singing duo, the Captain and Tennille, had more power in their relationship. Xander calls the Captain a "puppet," and this exchange sets up the battle for power between Buffy and Ted or between Joyce and her predatory boyfriend. The female utopia of Buffy's single-mother household is threatened by the invasion of Joyce's new suitor. Ted is a model of 1950s patriarchy, as he was built by the original Ted Buchanan in the 1950s, and he wants to run the household, calling Buffy's mother "Joycie" and saying, "I don't take orders from women," "You're going to find that I don't like being disobeyed," and "You don't have to worry about anything, Daddy's here." Rather than the ever-present evil stepmother of many fairy tales, this episode features an evil (potential) stepfather. Ted's attempts to subjugate Buffy are unsuccessful, and, like the young wife in the original tale, she overcomes him; however, she does so with her own supernatural strength, eventually defeating Ted by attacking him first with a nail file and finally the cast-iron skillet, symbols of femininity and domesticity. Ted's penchant for baking, which gives him a kind of queer domesticity at times, really works as a way for him to drug (with tranquilizers) and overpower Joyce, Buffy, and her friends. Ted swears by his cast-iron skillet, and Buffy reclaims this object as she reclaims her own domestic space from the interloping patriarch. In response to Ted demanding she show herself, exclaiming, "I don't stand for this kind of malarkey in my house!" Buffy nails him with the skillet, saying triumphantly, "This house is mine!"

Clearly this scene represents Buffy, as a young woman, overpowering the patriarch that attempts to subjugate her, transforming the house and domestic objects into sources of power. The defeat of Ted harkens back to fairy tale heroines like Gretel pushing the witch into the oven or the young woman triumphantly revealing a severed finger that marks her betrothed as a murderer in "Robber Bridegroom." Ultimately, Whedon and co-writer David Greenwalt seem to emphasize the importance of motherhood and female bonding in the absence of controlling masculinity, as Buffy and her mother end the episode by planning to watch *Thelma and Louise* again. Ted represents "traditional American" values: he says Grace at dinner, he intends to take his "rightful" place as head of household, he is an exceptionally successful salesman, and he advocates a rigid morality ("right is right and wrong is wrong") that does not allow for moral ambiguity. Even as Ted represents patriarchy, so is he essentially fake, constructed, old-fashioned, and out-of-date enough to be silly. In the '90s, Ted's 1950s conservative values are just so passé. Yet just as the show presents the weird as ordinary and outsiders as heroes, so does it conversely represent the familiar, the traditional, and the privileged (white, male, middle-class, Christian) as monstrous. Sunnydale is a place where outsiders and monsters can be heroic, but insiders, and anyone who likes mini-golf, are usually monstrous. "Ted" in particular presents the monstrous nature of patriarchal values and highlights Buffy's role in fighting them as our heroine.

"Gingerbread," Witches and Mothers

While "Ted" retells the "Bluebeard" tale with a cybernetic twist, Season Three's "Gingerbread" (1999) uses "Hansel and Gretel" as a framework in order to subvert the original tale's anti-witch messages. In "Gingerbread," Sunnydale embarks on a twenty-first-century witch hunt when the bodies of two murdered children are found with occult symbols carved into their bodies. However, the children themselves are really illusions created by a demon that incites mass hysteria and violence against women. The episode serves as a commentary on authoritarianism; persecution of outsiders, including goths (this was the '90s); misogyny; and the role that texts play in promoting sexism and the persecution of outsiders. However, in order to fully understand the evolution of the witch figure in *Buffy*, from villain to victim, it is necessary to consider Season One's "Witch" (1997) in contrast with "Gingerbread."

The first two episodes of the series, "Welcome to the Hellmouth" and "The Harvest," operate as a two-part pilot and introduce the major characters and villains of the first season of the series. However, the third episode, "Witch," is the first stand-alone monster-of-the-week episode. It finds Buffy in the midst of cheerleading tryouts, where potential cheerleaders are plagued by several mysterious accidents. It is revealed that a witch, Catherine Madison, has possessed her daughter Amy's body in an attempt to re-live her cheerleading wonder years, which are glorified in a display case in the high school. Catherine has been using her powers to attack her competition so that she can make the squad despite her daughter's more clumsy body.

The episode has a pretty straightforward take on witches, complete with bubbling cauldrons, youth-stealing, voodoo Barbies, and intense female competition. Through these elements, it evokes the Grimm tale "Little Snow-White" (1812), in which a queen, learning from her enchanted mirror that she is no longer fairest in the land, attempts to have her stepdaughter killed. The huntsman tasked with killing the girl allows her to escape, and Snow White takes refuge in a house of dwarves, where the queen (in disguise) attempts to murder her three times: first with cursed bodice laces, next with a poisoned comb, and finally with the ubiquitous poisoned apple. It is ultimately Snow White's "death" that causes the Queen's downfall. Because of her great beauty, the dwarves fashion a glass coffin for Snow White, and she is found by a prince, who becomes enamored with her. The prince convinces the dwarves to give Snow White to him, and when he has her body moved to bring home to his castle, the apple is dislodged. Snow White awakens, they marry, and the evil witch queen is made to dance in hot slippers until she dies. As Gilbert and Gubar note in *The Madwoman in the Attic*, the tale rewards female passivity and punishes a woman who perversely refuses to let a younger version replace her.

Like the evil queen of the fairy tale, Catherine Madison attempts to replace her daughter, which is shown as unnatural and a violation of laws that dictate that younger women replace older women. The episode emphasizes Catherine's obsession with her appearance, as Willow explains that she would go on a "broth binge" whenever she gained any weight, forcing herself to eat only broth. Like the villainous Queen in "Little Snow-White," the mirror represents each woman's patriarchal "self-evaluation" and Catherine too "becomes maddened, rebellious, witchlike" when her husband, here a Homecoming King rather than an actual king, leaves her for "Miss Trailer Trash" (Gilbert and Gubar 38). Both "Little Snow-White" and "Witch" represent villainous women who have lost value in a patriarchal society, and whose desperation to become valuable again leads to violent acts against younger women. As Christina Bacchilega explains, the mirror in "Little Snow-White" acts as a metonym for patriarchal culture that glorifies and fetishizes teen girls and "which defines the very identity of Snow White ('the fairest of all') and her stepmother (the ex-'fairest of all') and the nature of their relationship (rivalry)" (2). In "Witch," the trophy and picture of Catherine in the display case performs this metonymical function. The cheerleading trophy represents valuable feminine qualities: youth, beauty, and popularity as indicated by cheerleading, which allows the girls to put their youth and beauty on display.

As Gilbert and Gubar explain, the witch, or woman-monster, "as a representative of otherness … incarnates the damning otherness of flesh rather than the inspiring otherness of the spirit, expressing what … men consider her own 'presumptuous' desires rather than the angelic humility and 'dullness' for which she was designed" (28). Like that of Cordelia, Catherine's shallowness, or what makes her "of the flesh" rather than "of the spirit," is indicated by her obsession with apparently superficial things like popularity, beauty, and cheerleading, even as an adult woman. Yet it is not her superficiality that makes her monstrous, but her "presumptuous" desire to re-live her youth and to do so at any cost. These desires are presented as monstrous, and the witch and "the monster-woman, threatening to replace her angelic sister, embodies intransigent female autonomy" (Gilbert and Gubar 28). Like Snow White's evil stepmother, Catherine perversely refuses to accept her fate as an aging woman who must be replaced by the younger model(s). Nevertheless, in both tales, the villainous women are responding to cultural cues that they are no longer valuable because they are no longer young.

The episode literalizes one major element of "Little Snow-White": that "the Queen and Snow White are in some sense one: while the Queen struggles to free herself from the passive Snow White in herself, Snow White must struggle to repress the assertive Queen in herself" (Gilbert et al. 41). Gilbert and Gubar posit that the fairy tale Snow White disobeys the protective dwarves several times, admitting the Queen in disguise several times despite their warnings, suggesting that Snow White's desires are reflected in the feminine objects that ensnare her. Snow White and the Queen are two sides of femininity, represented in the red and white apple or the body-swapping mother and daughter. Like the evil Queen, it is her own power, and her own subversion of the natural order, that dooms Catherine. Giles is able to reverse Catherine's body-switching spell, and in the confrontation that follows, Catherine explains that she is going to "put [Amy] where [she] can't make trouble again," a spell she ultimately attempts to use on Buffy. As Catherine aims the curse at Buffy, the Slayer protects herself with a mirror, causing the curse to rebound on Catherine, trapping her inside her prized cheerleading trophy. As with the Queen, the mirror is Catherine's undoing, and like Snow White, Catherine is objectified and put on display in a glass case. Catherine is depowered, and in her symbolic "death," she becomes an inanimate object, or what Gilbert and Gubar call "the eternally beautiful, inanimate objet d'art patriarchal aesthetics want a girl to be" (40). The mirror transforms Catherine into an object such that even a powerful woman becomes silent, still, and powerless. The message of "Witch" is not unlike that of the original tale: that aging women ought to not act out, and that to be obsessed with "superficial" appearances can be destructive, even if these are shown to dictate a woman's social value.

Like her mother, Amy becomes trapped by her own spell in "Gingerbread," and is stuck as a rat for several years. This, too, can be linked with the Snow White's imagined future. Significantly, Gilbert and Gubar note that there are no good role models for Snow White once she has married, as

> surely, fairest of them all, Snow White has exchanged one glass coffin for another, delivered from the prison where the Queen put her only to be imprisoned in the looking glass from which the King's voice speaks daily.... And if Snow White escaped her first glass coffin by her goodness, her passivity and docility, her only escape from her second glass coffin, the imprisoning mirror, must evidently be through 'badness,' through plots and stories, duplicitous schemes, wild dreams, fierce fictions, mad impersonations. The cycle of her fate seems inexorable [42].

Amy, the ostensible Snow White of this episode, eventually fulfills this predicted fate by becoming much more like her mother than may be expected at the end of "Witch." She only appears in a few episodes following "Witch," including Season Two's "Bewitched, Bothered and Bewildered," in which the love spell she attempts for Xander backfires, making every woman in love with him except for Cordelia, the one for whom the spell was intended. Amy later turns herself into a rat to avoid being burned at the stake in "Gingerbread." However, once she is de-ratted in Season Six's "Smashed," Amy becomes a much darker witch, getting Willow "hooked" on magic and casting darker spells on Willow (even turning her into Warren, the man who killed Willow's love Tara) as revenge for spending years as a rat. Thus, the episode "Witch" works as a thematic re-interpretation of "Little Snow-White," even beyond what is apparent within the episode itself.

Though the series overall has some ambivalence about witches and magic, even if it ends with Willow empowering potential slayers as a kind of witch-goddess, the messages of Season Three's "Gingerbread" are in sharp contrast with the anti-witch messages of "Witch." In many ways, "Witch" provides a straightforward repetition of many of the same themes and messages of "Little Snow-White," and warns of older women who go against the natural order in the absence of male control. In this way, the episode maintains many of the problematic messages about women that are present in the source material. In sharp contrast with this, Season Three's "Gingerbread" overtly criticizes the anti-witch and anti-women messages of fairy tales like "Little Snow-White" and "Hansel and Gretel." The episode's title refers to the witch's house in "Hansel and Gretel" and the episode draws loosely from the Grimm fairy tale, one which also employs evil women as villains.

In the tale, a mother (or stepmother) convinces her husband, a poor wood-cutter, to leave the children in the woods so that they can avoid starving themselves. On their second attempt, they rid themselves of their children, who become lost in the woods. The children are drawn to a house made of bread, or gingerbread, with a roof of cake and windows made of sugar that is inhabited by an old child-eating witch. The old witch attempts to cook and eat them, but a quick-thinking Gretel tricks her into the oven and cooks her alive. In this tale, the men are blameless or without agency while the women are evil, hungry, and witch-like. Even Gretel emerges from the gingerbread house with newfound powers, and Verena Kast notes: "Gretel appropriates the witch's intentions and uses them against her—in that way, she annihilates her. This of course presupposes that Gretel also has witchlike qualities, otherwise she never would have been able to guess what the witch intended" (31). Thus, "Hansel and Gretel" is another tale that is about female wickedness and, to some extent, punishing that wickedness.

Like "Witch," and by the same token "Little Snow-White," "Gingerbread" and "Hansel and Gretel" are about motherhood and the way women have been depicted in literature. However, rather than participate in the demonizing of powerful women, as it did in "Witch," "Gingerbread" overtly criticizes the way strange, powerful, or eccentric women have been vilified through the witch figure in fairy tale narratives. "Gingerbread," like "Ted" and "Witch," focuses on domestic and familial conflict, once again between mothers and daughters. Buffy "outs" herself as a slayer at the end of Season Two, and in an attempt to better understand her daughter's life, Joyce surprises Buffy on patrol but is profoundly disturbed when they find the bodies of two young children with apparent occult symbols carved into their bodies. Joyce becomes obsessed with the children's deaths, holding a vigil and forming MOO (Mothers Opposed to the Occult), whose lobbying leads to the confiscation of "offensive material" from the library, locker searches, and harassment of goth teens. The sign—revealed to be a protection sigil for Buffy—is harmless, but Amy and Willow are implicated in the locker search. The dead children appear to Joyce, telling her to hurt their murderers and warning about the "bad girls." The Scoobies, or Buffy and her friends, realize that the same children's bodies have appeared in towns since the seventeenth century and were originally named Hans and Greta, or Hansel and Gretel. Giles explains, "There is a fringe theory held by a few folklorists that some regional stories have actual very literal antecedents," or that, as Oz translates, "fairy tales are real." However, these events are not the work of witches, but a demon in disguise:

> GILES: Some demons thrive by fostering hatred and persecution amongst the mortal animals. Not by destroying men, but by watching men destroy each other. Now, they feed us our darkest fear and turn peaceful communities into vigilantes.
> BUFFY: Hansel and Gretel run home to tell everyone about the mean old witch.
> GILES: And then she and probably dozens of others are persecuted by a righteous mob. It's happened all throughout history. It happened in Salem, not surprisingly.

The mob attempts to burn Amy, Buffy, and Willow at the stake, but Giles forces the demon to show its true face and it is killed by Buffy, ending the hysteria in Sunnydale.

The episode transfers the role of villain from fairy tale witch and mother to those who persecute women, though here they are inspired by a demon. Significantly, however, the demons simply feed on the "darkest fear" that already exists within the townspeople, which means that the episode reflects and comments on the ways fears of women result in the persecution of women. This episode points out the way fairy tales, especially those like "Hansel and Gretel," demonize women. It does so by making literal the messages of fairy tales: punish or destroy the "bad girls," which the fairy tale "children" repeat over and over again throughout the episode. The "bad girls" targeted by Sunnydale are outsiders; they are different, powerful, and strong. While the exchange between Buffy and Giles does not specifically discuss women as the primary target of the "righteous mob," "Gingerbread" seems fundamentally concerned with women, conflict between women (specifically mothers and daughters), and the way women are vilified. Michael, a goth boy who also participated in the protection spell for Buffy, is attacked but is not targeted as a witch for burning. Though Michael explains that the mob has pulled others out of their homes, some of whom may not be young women, these other victims of the hysteria are never shown. The children's emphasis on "bad girls," that only young women are nearly burned alive, the machinations of MOO, the introduction of Willow's mother in order to focus on mother-daughter relationships, and the use of the "Hansel and Gretel" narrative elements makes the episode less about larger hysteria and more specifically about historical and contemporary anxieties about "good" and "bad" women.

"Gingerbread" overtly criticizes the way powerful women are often depicted as "bad," while "good" girls must be compliant. In *Buffy*, distinctions between "good" and "bad" girls go all the way back to "Welcome to the Hell-mouth," when Joyce calls Buffy a "good girl" who "just fell in with the wrong crowd." In Season Two's "When She Was Bad," Buffy acts out as she deals with the trauma of dying and defeating the Master at the end of Season One. In "Gingerbread," as Sheila ties Willow to the stake, she tells her to "be a good girl" and "hold still." Here, the series questions what makes a girl "good" or "bad" and how these distinctions have been used to control and suppress women; here, a "good girl" is one who is tied up. Though she is the lighter Slayer, in contrast with the hyper-sexual, violent, and rebellious Faith, Buffy is neither a "good girl" nor a "bad girl," but something else entirely. This is yet another way that *Buffy* inherently distances itself from fairy tales, which so often categorize women as "good" or "bad" and reward or punish them based on these distinctions. Buffy, as a composite of both light and dark, is more human, real, a role model rather than a rehashed character for viewers to recognize and condemn or applaud accordingly.

Even as it overtly condemns the hysteria around witches engendered by fairy tales, "Gingerbread" preserves one major thematic element of "Hansel and Gretel": conflict between mothers and daughters. The mother's attempt to rid herself of the children is the act of villainy that opens the story, and though Hansel seems the natural hero of the tale, it is really Gretel who defeats the witch, a re-iteration of the hungry mother figure from the opening. Hansel, locked away, is not present when Gretel, pretending she does not know how to climb into the oven, tricks the witch into doing it herself, and pushes the witch into the oven, cooking her alive. The witch's death scene is a distorted version of a usual domestic ritual: a mother teaching her daughter to cook. In *Buffy*, Joyce's instincts for protecting children are distorted by the demon, leading to her near sacrifice of her own daughter and other girls in Sunnydale. Ironically, the adults who are so concerned with protecting children in the abstract ultimately prove harmful to their real children.

The witch in the house of gingerbread does not make an appearance in "Gingerbread"; rather, the episode focuses on the evil mother (or stepmother) character. Amy's presence in the episode, and the emphasis on witchcraft throughout, naturally evokes her mother's previous exploits. In "Witch," Catherine's attachment to her daughter, or her involvement in her daughter's life, is contrasted with Joyce's more healthy detachment and fulfilling career life. This is inverted in "Gingerbread," where Joyce is the more attached parent. Sheila Rosenberg provides a foil for Joyce's more clingy parenting style: as Willow explains, Sheila is not involved in either her curricular or extra-curricular activities. Sheila calls Buffy "Bunny," does not notice Willow's hair-cut for months, and dismisses her interest in Wicca as a "classic adolescent response to incipient adulthood." If language is key to understanding *Buffy*, the ways adults and teens speak differently in "Gingerbread" is part of the episode's exploration of conflict between teens and adults. The academese of Sheila and Giles and the absurd acronyms of Joyce (MOO) are in opposition to the clear, straightforward speak of the teenagers. The exchange between Giles and Oz clearly juxtaposes their two "languages," as Oz translates Giles's academic language to the much more straightforward "fairy tales are real." Yet Sheila and Joyce are the real "bad girls" of "Gingerbread" because they place their trust in the wrong things: demons in disguise, academia, the Mayor, and parenting tapes and books. In a speech, Joyce declares that it is "time for the grownups to take Sunnydale back"; however, the episode makes clear that the grownups and their institutions are the problem, not the solution. In "Gingerbread," the witch-hunt metaphor not only serves as a critique of depictions of women in literature and myth, but as a critique of parent's policing of "offensive material" for adolescents and children.

"Hush," the Gentlemen and the Fighting Princess

Finally, in the Season Four episode "Hush," one of the most famous and beloved episodes of the series, Sunnydale is once again beset by evil, this time in the form of grinning, grotesque, skeleton-like Gentlemen. Their inability to speak causes some confusion and miscommunication, but the Scoobies eventually identify them as monsters from a fairy tale. After several young people are murdered by The Gentleman, Giles, using a book of fairy tales rather than his usual archaic tomes, provides the full explanation of The Gentlemen, writing and illustrating the story on overhead transparencies. Giles explains that The Gentlemen come to a town, steal the inhabitants' voices so no one can scream, and kill seven people to collect their hearts. According to the tale, they cannot be killed by any weapon, but "the brave princess screamed once and they all died." Using her strength and Slayer clairvoyance, Buffy regains her voice and kills The Gentlemen, once again saving the town from an invading evil.

"Hush" does not draw from an existing fairy tale, but invents its own female-centric tale. The Gentlemen are introduced in the opening of the episode, in which Buffy dreams of kissing Riley as a demonstration during her psychology class. Their kiss causes the sun to set and the lecture hall becomes deserted. She hears a faint voice, and comes upon a young blonde girl holding a box, singing:

> Can't even shout, can't even cry;
> The gentlemen are coming by.
> Looking in windows, knocking on doors
> They need to take seven, and they might take yours.

Can't call to mom, can't say a word;
You're gonna die screaming but you won't be heard.

Buffy's dream is prophetic, and the girl's lines introduce the central issues of
the episode: that The Gentlemen are on their way, they will attack people in
their homes, they will attempt to steal seven hearts, and that, robbed of
speech, the townspeople will be helpless. Examining the way adults are often
clueless in contrast with more knowledgeable teens and children in fairy tale
episodes of *Buffy*, Skwire explains, "the stereotypical method of delivery for
a fairy tale is a top-down model" where the knowledgeable adult "tells the
tale to a child" (196). Here, the child, perhaps Buffy's inner child, appears as
the one most knowledgeable and provides the first account of The Gentlemen,
though it is cloaked in the uncanny song lyrics. In contrast with the child
who provides this warning, The Gentlemen are sophisticated, adult male
monsters. As Skwire notes, they glide above the ground, they wear formal
black suits, and, unlike our heroes, their nonverbal communication is clear
and elegant, as they speak through "graceful gestures" (202). In contrast with
their flailing and bandaged minions, "their suits, their height, and their ele-
gance all serve not only to accent the horror of their bloodthirstiness but also
to contribute to the very sophisticated, adult appearance of The Gentlemen"
(Skwire 202–203). Skwire uses this as evidence that yet another fairy tale
episode of *Buffy* is clearly concerned with distinctions between adults and
children.

However, this can be pushed further by considering how The Gentlemen
are horrific, uncanny revisions of other grown-up patriarchal figures. In
"Hush," once the town has lost their voices, a man in a black suit sits despon-
dently in the middle of the street. He holds a briefcase, which is of similar
shape to those The Gentlemen use to carry their scalpels. While this man
may simply work as part of the scene of chaos that erupts after the town's
voices are stolen, he may serve as a human parallel for the otherworldly monsters. Always polite and well dressed, The Gentleman epitomize sophisticated,
and deadly, patriarchal codes of conduct. Even the name "The Gentlemen"
seems meant to convey their grotesque politeness and seeming sophistication.
They use flourishing gestures to show deference or modesty and polite clap-
ping to congratulate one another. They are relentlessly smooth and quiet.
The brute work of overpowering victims is done by their apish minions.
These lackeys, or footmen, are never explained, even in Giles's summary of
the fairy tale. The Gentlemen may reflect the way individuals can be oppressive without having to do any physical work. Rather, they seem to represent
pervasive, unspoken societal strictures that keep people from speaking out.
Through this, the episode is very much about suppression through silence.

Throughout "Hush," the heroes struggle with communication. As Karen

Eileen Overbey and Lahney Preston-Matto note in their discussion of speech acts in *Buffy*, the episode is "rich with language play and makes communication a subject: Giles and Olivia stumble through small talk; Willow complains that the Wiccan 'wanna-blessed-be's' are all talk...; Anya shocks Xander with her inability to distinguish between private and public conversations; and Buffy babbles at Riley" (74). Despite the number of otherworldly attacks and incidences that occur in Sunnydale, there is remarkably little news coverage shown throughout *Buffy*. In "Hush," however, we see a news broadcast attributing the town's loss of voices to a laryngitis outbreak caused by flu vaccinations, while other news articles announce the brutal murders committed by The Gentlemen. This may work as a larger critique of ineffective or inaccurate mass communication and our reliance on it. Meanwhile, Willow's Wicca group, in particular, represents the power and irony of verbal communication. The women proclaim themselves champions of female empowerment, calling each other "sisters" and referencing a woman-power shrine, while using language to silence and suppress other women. They balk at Willow's suggestion that the group try spells, saying that witch "stereotypes are not very empowering." When Tara, shy and stuttering, tries to say something in Willow's defense, one of the Wicca members silences everyone dramatically and asks her pointedly if she has a suggestion. Tara shakes her head and they continue with the meeting. Though the Wicca group preaches female empowerment and blessings, these women actually disempower the other women in the group. Ultimately, Tara and Willow (alone) are able to join their magic against The Gentlemen, in direct defiance of the Wicca group's objections, and their nonverbal witchcraft acts as a true means of empowerment outside of meaningless speech.

While communication is shown to be ineffective or actively harmful, speech is also Buffy's only weapon against The Gentlemen and their enforced silence. Though Riley and Buffy fight The Gentlemen and their footmen together, Buffy, the "brave princess," defeats the fairy tale monsters. Recognizing the box The Gentlemen use to steal voices from her dream, Buffy is able to nonverbally direct Riley to break the box, releasing the voices. Her voice returned, Buffy's screams kill The Gentlemen. "Hush," then, characterizes female speech as a powerful weapon against the patriarchal politeness and quiet, discreet suppression represented by The Gentlemen. This episode not only emphasizes female power through Willow and Tara's burgeoning relationship, "Hush" creates its own heroine-centric fairy tale, illustrating that narratives, a kind of communication, can be empowering for women. In this way, the fairy tale in "Hush" reflects what Whedon is doing throughout the series: it rewrites and subverts narrative tropes, eschewing the usual hero for a powerful heroine.

Thus, the show dismantles the patriarchal messages of fairy tales, instead showcasing the horrors of male control and criticizing the vilification of witches and women. Rather than a noble prince, a high-tech soldier, or a "Crew of Light," it offers an empowered, willful, and witty heroine who refuses to submit to male authority. While many have noted the very overt feminist messages of *Buffy*, no one has deconstructed the use of fairy tale elements as part of this. The series begins with an evil mother-witch, moves to critiquing the way "witches," or powerful women, have been persecuted, to finally using a witch to empower all potential slayers. At the end of the series, Willow uses magic to empower every "potential," as Buffy proclaims in "Chosen" (2003): "Every girl who could have the power, will have the power. Can stand up, will stand up. Slayers, every one of us. Make your choice. Are you ready to be strong?"

In *Buffy*, witches and women are heroes and goddesses. Not only does the series condemn the representation of powerful women as "bad girls," it offers an alternative, revised vision of womanhood meant to inspire not only the fictional potential slayers, but those watching the show as well.

Works Cited

Bacchilega, Christine. "Cracking the Mirror: Three Re-Visions of 'Snow White.'" *Boundary 2*, no. 15/16: (1988): 1–25.

Bishop, Kyle. "Technophobia and the Cyborg Menace: Buffy Summers as Neo-Human Avatar." *Journal of the Fantastic in the Arts* 19, no. 3 (2003): 349–362. Web. 28 Dec. 2015.

Dibdin, Emma, and GCG. "9 Reasons Buffy Summers Is TV'S Greatest Feminist." *Digital Spy*. 19 Dec. 2015. Web. 19 July 2018. http://www.digitalspy.com/tv/ustv/feature/a777065/9-reasons-buffy-summers-is-tvs-greatest-feminist/.

Gilbert, Sandra M., and Susan Gubar. *The Madwoman in the Attic: The Woman Writer and the Nineteenth-Century Literary Imagination*. Yale University Press, 2000.

Hagelin, Sarah. *Reel Vulnerability: Power, Pain, and Gender in Contemporary American Film and Television*. Rutgers University Press, 2013. Web. 30 May 2016.

Magee, Sara. "High School Is Hell: The TV Legacy of *Beverly Hills, 90210*, and *Buffy the Vampire Slayer*." *Journal of Popular Culture* 47, no. 4 (2014): 877–894. Web. 28 Dec. 2015.

Overbey, Karen Eileen, and Lahney Preston-Matto. "Staking in Tongues: Speech Act as Weapon in *Buffy*." *Fighting the Forces: What's at Stake in* Buffy the Vampire Slayer, edited by Rhonda V. Wilcox and David Lavery, pp. 195–204, Rowman & Littlefield, 2002.

Pender, Patrica. "'Kicking Ass Is Comfort Food': Buffy as Third Wave Feminist Icon." In *Third Wave Feminsim: A Critical Exploration*, edited by S. Gillis, G. Howie, and R. Munford, pp. 164–174, Palgrave Macmillan, 2004.

Ruddick, Nicholas. "'Not So Very Blue, After All': Resisting the Temptation to Correct Charles Perrault's 'Bluebeard.'" *Journal of the Fantastic in the Arts* 15, no. 4 (2004): 346–357. Web. 28 Dec. 2015.

Skwire, Sarah E. "Whose Side Are You On, Anyway? Children, Adults, and the Use of Fairy Tales in *Buffy*." In *Fighting the Forces: What's at Stake in* Buffy the Vampire Slayer, edited by Rhonda V. Wilcox and David Lavery, pp. 195–204, Rowman & Littlefield, 2002.

Snowden, Kim. "'What's in the Basket Little Girl?': Reading Buffy as Little Red Riding Hood." Buffy to Batgirl: Women and Gender in Science Fiction, Fantasy, and Comics Conference, Rutgers University, Camden, New Jersey, 2 May 2014.

Tatar, Maria. *The Hard Facts of the Grimms' Fairy Tales*. Princeton University Press, 1987.

Wee, Valerie. "Resurrecting and Updating the Teen Slasher: The Case of Scream." *Journal of Popular Film and Television* 34, no. 2 (2006): 50–61. *MLA International Bibliography*. Web. 27 Dec. 2015.

Williams, J.P. "Choosing Your Own Mother: Mother-Daughter Conflicts in *Buffy*." In *Fighting the Forces: What's at Stake in* Buffy the Vampire Slayer, edited by Rhonda V. Wilcox and David Lavery, pp. 61–72, Rowman & Littlefield, 2002.

Zipes, Jack. *Fairy Tales and the Art of Subversion: The Classical Genre for Children and the Process of Civilization.* New York: Wildman Press, 1983.

Selfish Girls

The Relationship Between Selfishness and Strength in the Divergent *and Tiffany Aching Series*

ALICE NUTTALL

No matter the age of the intended reader, or the era in which they were written, children's stories have often stressed the evils of one vice in particular: selfishness. In *Cinderella*, the wicked stepmother and the ugly sisters are characterized by their selfish behavior toward the heroine, who is expected to take on all the household chores in order to support their leisurely lifestyles. The selfishness of the first four ticket winners in Roald Dahl's *Charlie and the Chocolate Factory* serves as a foil to the wholesome kindness of the eponymous hero, who, as a result of his lack of selfishness, is the only child not to suffer an ironic punishment during his tour of the factory. Neil Gaiman's picture book *Mirrormask* revolves around the heroine Helena trying to fix the problems caused by the selfishness of her otherworldly double, who is destroying the worlds of light and shadow in order to steal Helena's life; similarly, his novel *Coraline* emphasizes the selfishness of the Other Mother, who is only able to love "like a dragon loves its hoard" (126).

Selfishness, as these examples imply, is often an identifying characteristic of a villain; selflessness is, therefore, a traditionally heroic quality. When the protagonist of a story is female, this selflessness is often closely linked to self-sacrifice. *The Hunger Games* by Suzanne Collins begins with Katniss Everdeen volunteering for the arena in order to save her sister, knowing that she is unlikely to survive the tournament. Similarly, in the *Buffy the Vampire Slayer* Season Five finale "The Gift," Buffy Summers sacrifices her own life in order to save that of her sister, Dawn. *The Giving Tree* features a female-coded tree who gives up her entire self to the boy she loves; one critic notes, "the boy uses the tree as a plaything, lives off her like a parasite, and then, when she's a shell of her former self and no longer serves any real purpose, he sits on her—which makes her happy?" (Holmes and Galchen). Self-sacrifice can also take a less fatal form, with female characters putting their own wants, wishes or interests aside for their husbands and families. For example, in the episode of the BBC's *Sherlock* entitled "His Last Vow," the viewer learns that Sherlock's mother sacrificed her career as a renowned mathematics professor to raise her two sons; likewise, in the *Harry Potter* series, Ginny Weasley left her Quidditch career with the Holyhead Harpies in order to raise her and Harry Potter's children, while Harry himself continued his work as an Auror ("J.K. Rowling Goes Beyond").

The message of these stories is clear: to be a good woman, one must always put others before oneself. Analysis of the concept of emotional labor, defined by Rose Hackman as "repeated, taxing, and under-acknowledged acts of gendered performance," suggests that this literary trend reflects Western society. In her article, Hackman describes the following behaviors as examples of emotional labor:

> In a work context, emotional labor refers to the expectation that a worker should *manipulate* either her actual feelings or the appearance of her feelings in order to satisfy the perceived requirements of her job. Emotional labor also covers the requirement that a worker should *modulate* her feelings in order to influence the positive experience of a client or colleague.

According to Hackman's research, emotional labor in a work environment is distinctly gendered:

> Boardroom members—male and female—may have to schmooze clients to the same extent ... but women may be expected, on top of this, to contribute to office harmony by remembering colleagues' birthdays, or making small chit-chat to staff. Male colleagues may do this too, but if they do it it will be noticed as a plus ("isn't he sweet and generous with his time?").

Those literary heroines who fail to perform emotional labor and display selfishness rather than selflessness are often punished. Katy of *What Katy Did* is paralyzed in an accident, her mobility only returning when she has performed a sufficient amount of emotional labor from her sickbed. *Mirrormask's* Helena atones for her own selfishness toward her mother by rebuilding the world that her doppelganger has broken, suggesting that only a great feat of heroism can make up for her initial failure to be a supportive daughter. However, the heroines of two prominent series, *Discworld's* Tiffany Aching and *Divergent's* Tris Prior, explore the relationship between selfishness, selflessness and heroism in a more nuanced way. For Tiffany and Tris, selfishness becomes a source of strength and an integral part of their roles as heroines, challenging both literary and social concepts of "good womanhood."

"*I am selfish. I am brave*": Tris' and Tiffany's Classification as Selfish

The *Divergent* series focuses on Tris, a girl in a dystopian future version of Chicago where society is arranged in factions—groups that promote specific values and condemn others. Tris was born a member of the charitable faction Abnegation, which champions selflessness and denounces selfishness. However, she is fascinated with the aggressive Dauntless, who promote bravery and reject cowardice. Before the Choosing Ceremony, an event where Tris, like the other teenagers of her year group, will "decide on a faction … decide the rest of my life … decide to stay with my family or abandon them" (Roth *Divergent* 2), she considers her own commitment to the faction of her birth, and how to determine whether she fits more completely in Abnegation or Dauntless: "It will require a great act of selflessness to choose Abnegation, or a great act of courage to choose Dauntless, and maybe just choosing one over the other will prove that I belong. Tomorrow, those two qualities will struggle within me, and only one can win" (37). At the ceremony, Tris wavers between these two decisions, particularly following her brother's decision to leave Abnegation for the intellectual faction Erudite: "I hear mutters that lift into outraged cries. I can barely think straight. My brother, my selfless brother, a faction transfer? My brother, born for Abnegation, *Erudite?*... I will be the child that stays; I have to do this for my parents. I have to" (46–7). However, she realizes that, despite the values that have been instilled in her as part of her upbringing, she cannot remain part of Abnegation, because "I am not selfless enough.... Sixteen years of trying and I am not enough" (43). Choosing Dauntless, she decides "I am selfish. I am brave" (47). Tris self-identifies as selfish, and, despite associating this trait with bravery, still feels guilt about her decision to transfer. This guilt is demonstrated through her thoughts immediately after her transfer, shown through the lens of her observations of her family:

> My father's eyes burn into mine with a look of accusation. At first, when I feel the heat behind my eyes, I think he's found a way to set me on fire, to punish me for what I've done, but no—I'm about to cry.
>
> …
>
> The easy smile [Caleb] wears is an act of betrayal. My stomach wrenches and I turn away. If it's so easy for him, maybe it should be easy for me, too [48–9].

Tris, drawing on her Abnegation background, is understandably conflicted about her own selfishness, initially viewing it as a negative quality.

In contrast to the way that Tris identifies herself as selfish, the *Discworld* series' trainee witch Tiffany Aching is first called selfish by an outsider. During a battle with the Queen of the Fairies in *The Wee Free Men*, the Queen mocks

Tiffany for her selfish attitude: "Selfishness. Mine, mine, mine. All a witch cares about is what's *hers*…. You thought you *owned* [your brother]?" (Pratchett *The Wee Free Men* 234). It is only later in the story that Tiffany accepts her selfishness as part of her:

> All witches are selfish, the Queen had said. But Tiffany's Third Thoughts said: Then turn selfishness into a weapon! Make all things yours! Make other lives and dreams and hopes yours! Protect them! Save them! Bring them into the sheepfold! Walk the gale for them! Keep away the wolf! My dreams! My brother! My family! My land! My world! How dare you try to take these things, because *they are mine!*
> I have a duty! [282].

Whereas Tris' selfishness was a source of guilt and uncertainty, Tiffany realizes that being selfish does not have to carry negative connotations. Instead, she finds that her selfishness is a source of strength and an integral part of her ability to protect herself and those she loves.

As these extracts indicate, selfishness for Tiffany and Tris is a more complex and nuanced quality than for characters in other series. Their positive selfishness is unusual, a fact that complements the representation of both girls as rather atypical heroines. They do not conform to traditional heroine archetypes, and their lack of conformity is reflected in their physical descriptions. Neither Tiffany nor Tris exhibit the traditional beauty standards associated with female protagonists. Tris, for example, describes herself as looking like a child: "In my reflection, I see a narrow face, wide, round eyes, and a long, thin nose—I still look like a little girl, though sometime in the last few months I turned sixteen" (Roth *Divergent* 2). Tris' description can be contrasted by the reader with the expected appearance of a heroine, presumably a beautiful adult woman with more conventionally attractive features. Tiffany has an even clearer image of a traditional heroine. She actively compares herself to the sorts of women she expects to have a role in adventure stories:

> Her mother called [her hair] chestnut, or sometimes auburn, but Tiffany knew it was brown, brown, brown, just like her eyes. Brown as earth. And did the book have any adventures for people who had brown eyes and brown hair? No, no, no … it was the blond people with blue eyes and the redheads with green eyes who got the stories. If you had brown hair you were probably just a servant or a woodcutter or something [Pratchett *The Wee Free Men* 38].

Tris and Tiffany's non-conformity to the beauty standards associated with female leads is linked to their non-conformity to typical standards of selflessness. They do not look the way heroines are expected to look, nor do they behave in the way heroines are expected to behave. Neither young woman focuses on making herself aesthetically pleasing for the society in which she lives; similarly, neither character starts out from a position of selflessness or self-sacrifice, as might be in line with traditional female gender roles.

These Things Are Mine: Tiffany's Relationships

One of the most important manifestations of the theme of selfishness as strength can be found in Tiffany and Tris' relationships with their families. From the beginning of *The Wee Free Men*, Tiffany's relationship with her younger brother Wentworth is presented as strained at best:

> "You think I don't like him because my parents make a fuss of him and spoil him, yes?"
>
> "Well, it did cross my mind," said Miss Tick… "I think it was the bit where you used him as bait for a slathering monster that gave me a hint."
>
> "He's just a nuisance!" said Tiffany. "He takes up my time and I'm always having to look after him and he always wants sweets" [Pratchett *The Wee Free Men* 42–3].

However, when Wentworth is kidnapped by the Queen of the Faeries, Tiffany's inherent selfishness means that the fact that she dislikes him is irrelevant. She ultimately chooses to rescue her brother, not because of love or out of sisterly instinct, but because he is "hers":

> "Why are you trying to take my boy away?"
>
> "He isn't yours! He's ours!" said Tiffany.
>
> "You never loved him. You have a heart like a little snowball. I can see it."
>
> Tiffany's forehead wrinkled. "Love?" she said. "What's that got to do with it? He's my *brother*!" [233–4].

Tiffany's attitude toward her family and friends is selfish, but in a way that is repeatedly presented as positive. Throughout the series, she defends and assists her loved ones and community; for example, in *Wintersmith*, she calls upon all of her magical energy to melt the snow and save her village's sheep, because she views the community as her charge:

> The lambs are dying under the dreadful snow. And I should have said no, I should have said I'm not that good [at magic] yet. But the lambs are dying under the dreadful snow!
>
> There will be other lambs, said her Second Thoughts.
>
> But these aren't those lambs, are they? These are the lambs that are dying, here and now.
>
> …
>
> "I'll come with—" her father began.
>
> "No! Watch the fire!" Tiffany shouted, too loud, frantic with fear. "You will do what I say!"
>
> I am not your daughter today! her mind screamed. I am your witch! *I* will protect *you*! [Pratchett *Wintersmith* 20–1].

Tiffany casts herself as the center of both her family and her community; this self-centering links with her inherent selfishness, leading her to not only defend herself and what is hers, but to use the people around her as tools in order to achieve these goals. In the early part of *The Wee Free Men*, Tiffany lures the monster Jenny Green-Teeth into a trap using Wentworth as bait. Miss Tick declares this decision indicative of Tiffany's "quick thinking." The fact that Miss Tick does not condemn Tiffany for using her brother to catch a monster is one of the first indications that Tiffany's selfishness makes her suited to being a witch. Far from being a character flaw—or perhaps in spite of it—Tiffany's selfishness is established as the trait that will make her powerful and successful in the world of magic.

Selfish Bravery: Tris's Relationships

Tris's relationship with her selfishness, and the way it intersects with her relationship with her family and community, is more complex than Tiffany's. While selfishness is a core aspect of Tris' character, as seen by her decision to join Dauntless, so, paradoxically, is selflessness. Throughout the series, Tris struggles with two aspects of her Divergent nature: the selfishness associated with her new faction, Dauntless, and the selflessness that she has learned from her birth faction, Abnegation.

Although *Divergent* tells us that the function of the Dauntless faction is to defend the city from the unspecified dangers of the outside world, Tris does not choose Dauntless because she wishes to protect the people she loves. Instead, her choice is a result of her fascination with the Dauntless children she has seen at school: "I pause by a window in the E Wing and wait for the Dauntless to arrive. I do this every morning. At exactly 7:25, the Dauntless prove their bravery by jumping from a moving train" (Roth *Divergent* 7). It is also a result of her frustration with Abnegation's focus on selflessness, which often seems to manifest as the obliteration of the self entirely:

> The reason for the simplicity [of Abnegation houses] isn't disdain for uniqueness, as the other factions have sometimes interpreted it. Everything—our houses, our clothes, our hairstyles—is meant to help us forget ourselves and to protect us from vanity, greed, and envy, which are just forms of selfishness. If we have little, and want for little, and we are all equal, we envy no one.
> I try to love it [7].

Tris's wish to be allowed to focus on herself as well as others—something that would, according to Abnegation's worldview, be considered selfish—is apparent from the beginning of the novel. *Divergent* opens with Tris thinking about the single mirror in her house and her quarterly haircuts, which are the only times that she is allowed to look at her own face. Tris compares her urge to "sneak a look at [her] reflection" to her mother's self-restraint: "I note how calm she looks and how focused she is. She is well-practiced in the art of losing herself. I can't say the same of myself" (7).

Tris's decision to join Dauntless comes from her desire to center herself in a way that she has not been allowed to in Abnegation. She is determined to know herself entirely and to understand her own fears and limitations, rather than be subsumed into Abnegation's "hive mind." However, Tris experiences guilt and regret as a result of her decision to be "selfish and brave":

> It will be all right here. I can look at my reflection whenever I want. I can befriend Christina, and cut my hair short, and let other people clean up their own messes.
> My hands shake and the tears come faster now, blurring my vision.
> It doesn't matter that the next time I see my parents, on Visiting Day, they will barely recognize me—if they come at all. It doesn't matter that I ache at even a split-second memory of their faces [73–4].

In order to be selfish, Tris has had to make a sacrifice that Tiffany has not. She has given up her old community and her family for a new and hostile environment, where she must either stay forever or leave and become factionless. Tris's selfishness carries more negative connotations than Tiffany's, but also, in spite of her expectations, leads to her reconciling with the selflessness that caused her difficulties as a member of Abnegation. By joining Dauntless and overcoming her fears, Tris is able to save both Abnegation and the wider city from Erudite's attempted coup. As the series continues, Tris focuses on combining her Abnegation selflessness with her Dauntless self-focus, using her bravery to help others and eventually sacrificing her own life to save those she loves. Tris's final moments portray her death both as a selfless act and as an example of selfishness, in that she is taking the peace she has finally earned:

> I smile and close my eyes.
> I feel a thread tugging me again, but this time I know that it isn't some sinister force dragging me toward death.
> This time I know it's my mother's hand, drawing me into her arms.
> And I go gladly into her embrace.
> ...
> Can I be forgiven for all I've done to get here?
> I want to be.
> I can.
> I believe it [Roth *Allegiant* 475–6].

The repetition of "I" in this section shows that Tris has continued to center herself, in a way that Abnegation would consider selfish, in the actions she takes to protect others. While Tris sacrifices herself to save her brother—a potentially selfless act—she also does so because, like Tiffany, she views her family, friends and community as hers to protect. Tris has only achieved the level of bravery necessary to die for those she loves by facing her own fears and limitations, which requires an inward focus that she could not have found in Abnegation.

Conclusion

The *Discworld* books that feature Tiffany Aching and the *Divergent* trilogy both portray young heroines who reject the pressures and limitations placed upon them by their respective societies. Instead, these girls focus on themselves and choose their own places in the world. Unlike traditionally selfless heroines, who often battle selfish villains, Tiffany and Tris are selfish, and their selfishness is portrayed as a desirable quality that enable them to perform heroic acts. Both girls are able turn their selfishness into a strength, using it as a positive force with which to help others. In doing so, they challenge traditional understandings of how to be a "good" woman and show young readers that selfishness does not necessarily harm others, but can, instead, be used as a means to understand and negotiate one's self.

WORKS CITED

Collins, Suzanne. *The Hunger Games*. Scholastic, 2008.
Coolidge, Susan. *What Katy Did*. Roberts Brothers, 1872.
Dahl, Roald. *Charlie and the Chocolate Factory*. Puffin Books, 1964.
Gaiman, Neil. *Coraline*. Bloomsbury, 2002.
_____. *MirrorMask*. HarperCollins, 2005.
"The Gift." *Buffy the Vampire Slayer: The Complete Fifth Season*, written and directed by Joss Whedon, Twentieth Century–Fox, 2003.
Hackman, Rose, "'Women Are Just Better at This Stuff': Is Emotional Labor Feminism's Next Frontier?" *The Guardian*, November 8, 2015, https://www.theguardian.com/world/2015/nov/08/women-gender-roles-sexism-emotional-labor-feminism.
"His Last Vow." *Sherlock*. Season 3, written by Steven Moffat, directed by Nick Hurran, BBC Home Entertainment, 2014.
Holmes, Anna, and Rivka Galchen, "*The Giving Tree:* Tender Story of Unconditional Love or Disturbing Tale of Selfishness?" *New York Times*, September 30, 2014, www.nytimes.com/2014/10/05/books/review/the-giving-tree-tender-story-of-unconditional-love-or-disturbing-tale-of-selfishness.html?_r=0. Accessed April 24 2016.
"J.K. Rowling Goes Beyond the Epilogue," Beyond Hogwarts, www.beyondhogwarts.com/harry-potter/articles/jk-rowling-goes-beyond-the-epilogue.html. Accessed April 24 2016.
Pratchett, Terry. *The Wee Free Men*. Random House, 2003.
_____. *Wintersmith*. Random House, 2006.
Roth, Veronica. *Allegiant*. HarperCollins, 2013
_____. *Divergent*. HarperCollins, 2011.

"Have good sex"

Empowerment Through Sexuality as Represented by the Character of Inara Serra in Joss Whedon's Firefly

PATRICIA ISABELLA SCHUMACHER

Joss Whedon's short-lived space Western *Firefly* portrays a diverse group of people and their attempts to live in a postwar futuristic world. Whedon himself describes the show as "about nine people looking into the blackness of space and seeing nine different things" (*Firefly* DVD Commentary). One of those unique perspectives belongs to Inara Serra, the tenant of one of the ship's shuttles and a licensed Companion. Her work as a prostitute, while notably different from contemporary sex workers, means that she encounters many prejudices and notions about the virtues and boundaries of female sexuality. As Beadling asks in her discussion of gender and feminism in *Firefly*, "Is [Inara] the typical hooker with a heart of gold who has it bad for the leading man? Or is she an empowered woman deploying her sexuality for monetary gain, yet doing so as a member of a dignified profession?" (Beadling 62).

Being a Companion within the fictional world created by Whedon might be respectable and of high standing, but it does not keep critics from questioning the character's empowerment. Some see her as restricted, powerless, and ultimately a fetish object for the male viewer to gaze at (cf. Lackey; Tresca; Amy-Chinn). Those interpretations of Inara neglect to account for the complexity of her character, which represents many ideas of third-wave feminism. She is presented throughout the series as active, powerful and in control, particularly during scenes in which she is sexualized. Her control is especially prevalent inside her shuttle, where most of her scenes take place, presenting her either during sex with her clients or in intimate situations with other

61

crew members. Those scenes show how Inara has carved out a space for herself and her feminism in the world created in *Firefly*, representing an identity for women rarely seen in popular culture. She is neither the damsel to be saved and rewarded to the hero for his deed, nor the warrior woman whose strength mostly forces her toward a celibate life, but a complex and sex-positive woman whose extreme femininity does not conflict with, but encourages, her empowerment.

Firefly is a mixture between a science fiction and Western TV series, created by Joss Whedon and released in 2002. The series ended due to an early cancellation after only fourteen episodes, and the story was concluded in a feature film called *Serenity* in 2005. *Firefly* is set in a futuristic world, which is deeply scarred from a war between the Alliance and the Independents. The main characters are a group of nine people living on board a spaceship of the classification *Firefly*, named *Serenity*. Captain Malcolm Reynolds and his first officer Zoe fought in the war on the losing side of the Independents and are therefore opposed to the current power structures. Zoe's husband Wash is the ship's pilot and *Serenity*'s mechanic is a young woman named Kaylee. Since the crew mainly earns their living by smuggling and petty thievery, the mercenary Jayne is also an important part of the crew. During the show's pilot episode, three more characters are added to the crew: a Shepherd named Book and the siblings Simon and River Tam, who are fugitives from the Alliance. The final crew member is the Companion Inara Serra, a prostitute, who lives and works in one of the ship's shuttles. While the majority of characters are in some conflict with the law, their criminal activities are in most cases ethically justifiable.

This essay analyzes scenes in the space of Inara's shuttle, most of which focus on her relationships to her clients. The first scene is her introduction to the audience during the pilot episode "Serenity," in which Inara is shown having sex with a young man. Afterward they have a brief conversation before he leaves. The next client's name is Fess and Inara meets with him in the episode "Jaynestown." Fess' father, the Magistrate, has decided that his twentysix-year old son has to lose his virginity. Inara is shown in bed with him, as well as in conversations afterward. In the episode "War Stories," Inara's client is an influential woman, introduced only as the Councilor. Inara massages her and they talk before having sex. This essay also discusses a scene in "Serenity," where Inara bathes herself with a sponge and is interrupted by Shepherd Book entering her shuttle. There is a short scene in the episode "The Train Job," where Inara brushes Kaylee's hair, while they talk about Inara's clients.

Firefly's creator Joss Whedon boasts a huge following of fans and academics alike, which has led to an array of essays and articles devoted to studying the so-called "Whedonverse." The Whedonverse contains all of Joss

Whedon's TV series, including *Buffy the Vampire Slayer, Angel, Dollhouse* and *Firefly*. While Whedonverse is an umbrella term for the different shows, "'verse" is routinely used to describe the world created within the TV series *Firefly*. "Serenity" is the name of the pilot episode for *Firefly*, the title of the feature film released in 2005, three years after the series' cancellation and the name given in-universe to the ship by Captain Malcolm Reynolds. As this essay only focuses on the TV series, "Serenity" is used to refer to the episode, while the use of *Serenity* refers to the ship. To describe the different kind of sex workers represented in *Firefly*, this text uses three distinct terms throughout the text. "Prostitute" or "sex worker" is used to refer to everyone who engages in sexual activities and receives payment for them, while "Companion" describes only characters in *Firefly* who were trained in the guild's academy. The term "whore" is used as well. While there certainly are negative connotations toward this word, it is commonly used in academic discussion about the different sex workers in *Firefly*, as well as in the show itself, to mark a distinction between registered Companions and prostitutes operating outside the guild laws.

Feminism has undergone several changes since the suffrage movement that marks its beginning. While the first wave was mainly concerned with winning women's right to vote, second-wave feminists focus on protruding into personal and professional realms previously dominated by men. Feminist critics of *Firefly* and critics of the character of Inara seem to be focused on more traditional second-wave feminism. While "many of the Firefly characters could be described as feminists in the second-wave sense" (Beadling 55), Inara does not seem to fit this standard. Nancy Holder holds the character's failure as a feminist to the fact that she "wears beautiful, sexy outfits" (151) and, contrary to Zoe and Kaylee, could not "have been cast as a male role" (Holder 151). In this line of argument, her femininity is therefore what keeps Inara from being a feminist; this viewpoint is not unusual within second-wave feminism but is no longer applicable by newer feminist theories (cf. Rowley 325). "Reclaiming stereotyped versions of femininity in the name of subverting and complicating them" (Beadling 60) is one ideal of third-wave feminism, as is "the rejection of norms" (Scholz 108), including those of sex, gender, sexuality, bodies and desires (cf. Scholz 108f). Third-wave feminists' focus on identity-formation, sexuality, and empowerment through popular culture (Karlyn 20f) separates them from the second wave, especially concerning their greater inclusion of issues affecting different races and sexualities (cf. Karlyn 18). Gender as shown in *Firefly* takes part in the "debates about feminism, postfeminism, and third-wave feminism. Whedon's work continues to provide not just 'good' or 'bad' images of women but ... complicated representations of women who fall into different categories of feminism" (Beadling 61f).

"That's the last time you get to call me 'whore'": Prostitution and Companions in the World of Firefly

Sexuality plays a big role in *Firefly*, especially in relation to the character of Inara. Female sexuality is inevitably linked to feminism and the role of patriarchy, as its "regulation … is deeply ingrained in our culture to hold the structures of patriarchy and heterosexuality in place" (Karlyn 23). Using their sexuality against women to silence them socially and to keep them from gaining agency is still achieved through shaming (cf. Caputi 95), while sexual morality is based within social norms and has no inherent value in terms of right and wrong (cf. Szabo 103). According to Porter, "*Firefly* shows an idealized world with regards to sex; even the most puritanical characters do not judge others for their sexual choices" (Porter 99), which embodies the spirit of third-wave feminism (cf. Karlyn 24). This sexual freedom explicitly includes the women on board the *Serenity*, who—with the exception of the teenage girl River—are portrayed as far more sexually active than their male counterparts and especially their captain (cf. Taylor 133).

Prostitution as a divergent form of sexuality comes with its own problematic. While "sexpositive feminists argue that women who choose to perform sex work—such as acting in pornography or engaging in prostitution—should have the right and ability to do so without shame or censure" (Burnett 119), others warn of the commodification of sex and its providers. In his discussion of "Images of Paraphilia in the Whedonverse," Don Tresca argues that Inara might seem empowered, but her prostitution reinforces "the tendency for men to treat the women as property, commodities whose only value is their material or sexual worth" (Tresca 168). Agreeing with him are the authors of "Selling Sex Sells: Representation of Prostitution and the Sex Industry in Sexualised Popular Culture as Symbolic Violence," who use the term "the sex of prostitution" to define heterosexual sex as inherently unequal in favoring men's desires (cf. Coy, Wakeling and Garner 443f). They also claim that sex work is based "on objectification and commodification of women, as well as on women's lack of subjectivity and suspension of the self to serve men's desires" (Coy, Wakeling and Garner 443). Neither of them see any responsibility on men for not treating women as property, but instead warn of normalized prostitution becoming a pattern for all relationships (cf. Coy, Wakeling and Garner 445). The authors' main problem with representations of prostitution seems to be that the shifting focus toward "notions of 'choice'" (Coy, Wakeling and Garner 445) might become more important than the harsh reality many sex workers face today. While this might accurately reflect real-life working conditions endured today, the depiction of prostitution in popular culture might be able to remove the stigma associated with the profession, which the authors themselves cite as one of the main causes for violence against sex workers (cf. Coy, Wakeling and Garner 443).

Prostitution within the *Firefly* 'verse is distinctly changed from prostitution in twenty first century America, through altered laws and attitudes within the society (cf. Aberdein 64). In *Firefly* a sex worker is "a respectable, legitimate businessperson" (Szabo 106) and receives the support and respect of the show's moral judgment. In "Still Flyin? Conventions, Reversals, and Musical Meaning in *Firefly*," Stanley C. Pelkey II explains how the common characteristics attributed to the prostitute in the Western are inverted by not only Inara, but also the whores in the episode "Heart of Gold." In contrast to Companions, their profession is not highly esteemed in the environment they occupy. Nevertheless, the show reverses conventions and presents them as keepers of morality, since "their community embodies the values—family, law, business, peace—of the good society in the classical Western" (Pelkey 360). Indeed, the Western narrative is changed by giving the position of "the true lawgiver, the legitimate businesswomen, and the genuine defender of family on the frontier" (Pelkey 357) to a prostitute. The sexual acts between the whores and other characters are portrayed just as positive as sex within committed relationships shown in *Firefly* (cf. Porter 99), the exception being sexual incidents in which the prostitute's choice is taken from her. In fact, "the commoditization of sexuality is no more remarked upon than any other act of commerce" (Porter 89), which contextualizes prostitution as an economic instead of moral choice. Autonomy is the most important attribute by which to morally judge prostitution in the 'verse (cf. Szabo 115).

The difference between prostitutes and Companions is emphasized throughout the series, with the latter being constructed in a succession to such traditions as geishas, courtesans and sacred prostitutes. Critics commonly assume that Inara's name is a modification of the ancient goddess Inanna, in whose temple sacred prostitutes worked (cf. Aberdein 67). Seeing Companions as "the holy whore" (Davidson 114), is surprisingly more prevalent than the superficial assumption that they represent Japanese geisha culture. Companions adhere to similar strict rules, are trained in a variety of cultural arts, and "worked not unlike geishas" ("Serenity: The Official Visual Companion 12–13" in Aberdein 64). Inara, who represents them in the series, shows, that her "bearing and training, and the way in which she conducts her business all fit into a well-established history of courtesan culture in China and South Asia, and many of the accoutrements surrounding her provide visual clues to connect us to that past" (Brown 21). The difference to geishas becomes especially apparent, when compared to the actual geisha-inspired figures throughout the series, such as a waitress in the episode "The Train Job" and a geisha doll in "Trash" (cf. Brown 19). The Companions' power as expressed in their high status and respectability stems from their autonomy, with emphasis on their ability to reject clients (cf. Aberdein 64; Porter 98). The positive portrayal of Companions impacts all involved parties, as the sex is "shown as positive for both the client and the provider" (Porter 98). Companions' empowered situation leads them to control their interactions with clients and therefore produces "the idealized situation for a prostitute" (Porter 99).

The respectability of their profession is shown through Inara's acceptance within the crew with the exception of Captain Malcolm Reynolds (cf. Porter 98). The main character Mal's opinion is seen by some critics as defining for the morality by which the show judges its characters. He constantly calls Inara a whore and diminishes her work, which can at first glance be seen as moral judgment. Since there is barely evidence toward his character's beliefs on sexuality, his disapproval of prostitution might have "nothing to do with sex, but rather with a dishonesty that he sees in it" (Szabo 109). His objection to prostitution seems also connected to its implications of human trafficking and non-consensual sex, as is shown in the episode "Our Mrs. Reynolds," when Jayne tries to trade Mal's temporary wife for a gun and is told: "She's not to be bought. Nor bartered, nor borrowed or lent. She's a human woman" (cf. Szabo 111). Since he is willing to protect the whores in "Heart of Gold," his objection "to Inara as a Companion could likely be attributed to his own feelings for her" (Porter 98). Mal's romantic feelings toward Inara as the reason for his comments about Companions seems the most common explanation. Goodfriend even goes so far as to state, that Mal "insulted [Inara] whenever possible, calling her names like 'whore' and implying she was common, in an ill-designed effort to make them more like equals" (98). This concurs with the assessment, that "higher-status individuals in the 'verse show Inara greater respect, whereas abuse is most likely to come from individuals of ambiguous status … or no status at all, such as Mal Reynolds" (Aberdein 70). The suggestion that his dislike of Companions originates from his status as the Western hero and therefore from an aversion toward the Asian (cf. Lively 189) seems unlikely.

Other characters who are presented as moral guides throughout the series are the mechanic Kaylee and the priest Book. Kaylee not only repeatedly asks Inara for tales of her admirers ("Serenity") but also describes her work as "glamorous romance" ("Jaynestown"). This mixture of openness and naivety defines her character, which "takes the sexual freedom of feminism and packages it into an innocent young woman without any obvious character contradictions" (Lively 185). Kaylee embodies the principles of third-wave feminism, regarding her liberal sexuality (cf. Beadling 60) and even considers engaging a male whore herself in "Heart of Gold" without "being embarrassed or ashamed of having sex with a prostitute" (Szabo 105). While Shepherd

Book seems initially shocked at the revelation that Inara is a Companion, just shortly thereafter they joke about him lecturing her "on the wickedness of [her] ways" ("Serenity"). By the end of the pilot episode, Book turns to Inara for moral guidance indicating that his first reaction was more likely a result of surprise than disapproval for her profession.

"A registered Companion on a Boat like this?" Civilization and Culture as the Other

Inara's first mention in the pilot episode of *Firefly* is Mal talking about her being the only one making "an honest living" ("Serenity") on the ship. This theme of her lending Serenity "a certain respectability" ("Out of Gas") is repeated throughout the series. In an inversion of a traditional Western cliché, the prostitute is the character most closely linked with notions of culture and civilization in the bunch of outlaw heroes (cf. Lively 185; cf. Goodfriend 96). Her Companion training and her mastery of cultural arts designate her as the representation of "the civilized society" (Lively 191). This reading is further supported by the change in music used whenever Inara is on screen. According to Pelkey "music that could be broadly described as classical ... represents 'civilization' generally and Inara in particular" (Pelkey 335). This music often deviates from the Western tradition and is influenced by Asian sounds and instruments, which matches Inara's Asian inspired clothes, the interior decoration of her shuttle, as well as her use of Chinese phrases, in which she is the only character to refer to Buddha instead of God (Sullivan in: Amy-Chinn 185).

Firefly boasts a variety of Asian elements, such as language, visual clues and musical styles, but the culmination of all those features can be found in the vicinity of Inara and her shuttle (cf. Brown 19). There is certainly exoticism presented in this, but the ethnic elements used are also profoundly connected to issues of class (cf. Jencson 386). A closer look at the characters' costumes in relation to their social standing shows this connection. Mal, Zoe and Jayne all wear clothes reminiscent of military styles, with varying degrees of leather incorporated in their outfits through belts, shoes and coats. This marks them clearly as the warriors and fighters of the group. Mal's coat is an important piece of costuming, as it defines him as a "Browncoat" and therefore someone, who fought on the losing side of the Unification War. The coat, according to *Firefly*'s leather artist Jonathan A. Logan, gives "a very masculine presence to the person who wears it" (*Firefly: A Celebration* 90). It is rugged, worn-down and unlined, clearly "not the coat of a rich man or core-planet dandy" (*Firefly: A Celebration* 90). Mal was supposed to look "American" and ended up influenced by Cowboys and Star Wars' Han Solo (cf. *Firefly: A Celebration* 296). The three warrior characters are closely connected to the American Western in their appearance and are also the characters that partake in the most criminal and violent behavior throughout the series, therefore being the farthest removed from the notion of culture and civilization. The characters of Book, Kaylee, and Wash occupy a middle ground, with their clothes integrating different styles and material. The third group consists of Inara, Simon and River. Their clothes are made from richly textured Asian inspired fabrics and utilize styles that are stereotypically Asian, such as kimono patterns. They are also more intricately tailored and seem expensive. The Tam siblings come from an upper-class family and possess a high degree of education, which—similar to Inara—would under different circumstances assure them an elevated social standing.

Through those visual clues, as well as the musical choices, Inara, River, and Simon are grouped together as the representatives of civilization. Pelkey emphasizes that "musical moments that masquerade as classical Chinese music" (Pelkey 349) are connected to the trio and he concludes that "this opposition of the piano and classical music generally (the Tams, Inara) to fiddle (Mal/Serenity) can be mapped onto the civilization-frontier dichotomy" (Pelkey 349). This binary opposition can also be seen in presenting Serenity's crew in contrast with an "Other," which includes "villains who lack moral compasses, sex workers, and exotic cultures" (Hung 407). This simultaneous connection to civilization and exoticism joins the two otherwise conflicting concepts together. This is especially important as the Asian elements also serve to construct an "Other," which while still tied to the concept of Orientalism, seems to be deconstructed within *Firefly*.

The bathing scene during "Serenity" intensifies the construction of Inara's identity as an exoticized prostitute, when "the camera frames a view we have seen before: the nude back of the Ottoman/Maghrebi harem woman in French 19th century Orientalist painting" (Brown 22). Inara's nude back is toward the camera with some lose fabric barely covering her bottom, and her head slightly tilted to the side so a faint outline of her face is visible. This iconography is used by the painting "The Valpincon Bather" by Jean-Auguste-Dominique Ingres, which was presumably a model for his later painting "The Turkish Bath" (Brown note 25). Both paintings clearly combine the female nude with the exotic setting of the Orient. The success of the image can also be seen in its influence on artists such as Man Ray. The similarities between the photograph "Violin d'Ingres." and Inara's framing are unmistakable.

Through her connection to the tradition of Asian courtesans and the Asian elements, Inara herself is constructed as Other. She is presented as "sexually exotic" (Pelkey 333), the use of orientalizing visual and musical cues "plays up the mysterious sexuality attainable" (Brown 22), and the assumed male gaze objectifies her not only as woman, but also as Other (cf. Smelik 364). Whedon's construction of active female sexuality as Other seems familiar, as "in Buffy, prostitutes are quite often presented as vampires and, in the case of the series Angel, as demons" (Porter 87). In her discussion of sexuality in *Buffy, the Vampire Slayer,* Smith repeatedly suggests the binary opposition between sexual repression and sexual liberation and links them to "the social and anti-social, humanity and animality, culture and nature" (Smith 18). While the character of Buffy is able to at least temporarily transcend these concepts, this is only possible through "her position as Other" (Smith 29). Kendra Leonard calls Inara "the classic feminine Other" (Leonard 185) and Dee Amy-Chinn also notes that Inara is presented as "the Racialized 'Other'" (Amy-Chinn 184). In these readings of Inara, the larger context of the Other within *Firefly* is seldom taken into consideration.

The position of the Other is not easily defined in *Firefly*, as the story is told by a group of outlaws operating decisively outside of the social center. By changing the focus to the "narrative from the periphery [*Firefly*] offers new ways of thinking the Other, as it calls the audience to relate to those on the margin" (Brown 16). The Othering of Inara cannot be read as a simple repetition of the previously used Orientalism (cf. Hung 414). Those concepts "are replaced by new constructions (Independents by Reavers) and the old Others (Asian language, dress, behavior) are often incorporated into the Self in complex ways" (Brown 25). Brown identifies this "as a metaphor for contemporary postmodern/postcolonial nomadic identity" (Brown 16), which seems to align perfectly with the aims of third-wave feminism. In its rejection of normative identities, "third wave feminism tries to turn the problem of norms back on itself, destroying all the limiting standards that put some people in the center while some are on the margins" (Scholz 108f).

"All of them wish you were in their bed": Inverting the Male Gaze in the Bathing Scene in "Serenity"

Reading Inara and her sexual actions as pornographic robs the character of her power by changing her actions from active to passive. When the presumably male viewership gains pleasure from her sexuality, she is turned into a sexual object and therefore is safe for patriarchal society to consume. Critics of sex-positive feminism argue that even when women feel empowered through their sexuality, the male gaze turns them into an object (cf. Burnett 120), while pornography in general is presented as a disempowering place for women in patriarchy (cf. Caputi 19). This view ignores the possibility of a female gaze and denies "that pornography can (and should) be enjoyed by women, rather than condemned as an exclusively male entertainment genre and tool of patriarchal oppression" (Burnett 119). Still, pornographic images, as described in Jane Caputi's "Goddesses and Monsters," rely on the representation of inequality, in which masculinity is defined as powerful and femininity as weak and dominated. Inara clearly defies those categories by being the controlling element, rather than being the controlled during her sexual encounters, while leaving her femininity unquestioned.

The most prominent example of a scene seemingly constructed exclusively for the male gaze is the scene in "Serenity" when Inara bathes herself with a sponge. The sound played during her bathing is "gentle guitar music" (Pelkey 335) and invokes the Othering mentioned earlier. At the same time, the camera uses close-ups, in which her body parts are presented as separate, sexualized fragments, instead of showing a whole individual. The focus on her body reveals details in "a kind of proximity not possible in reality" (Greco 245). The camera lingers on her washing herself, which clearly changes the meaning from a utilitarian to an eroticized act. While the script for this episode empathizes that this is "the only type of bathing you'll find on this ship" (*Firefly: A Celebration* 40), this information is not available for the viewer. In later instances, Inara's body might be shown sexualized but throughout the series never in this same intensity, as she becomes a character well known to the viewer, which destroys the distance necessary for the gazes' voyeurism (Smelik 356).

This scene not only constructs Inara in the male gaze, but does so with full intent to illustrate the problems and possibilities of the male gaze. The traditional definition of the male gaze strips the objectified female of any power to further the narrative (cf. Lively 193), yet Inara remains a complex character, who throughout the series proofs her worth to the crew's actions (and therefore the story's plot) time and time again. The question of who the spectator is in this performed sexuality is what distinguishes it from other incarnations. The only male character who views Inara in this situation, is Shepherd Book. Yet when he enters, after Inara actively invites him in, he immediately averts his eyes, marking him as passive, even unwilling to participate in the act of looking. He clearly seems more uncomfortable with her nudity than she is, and the script goes so far as to imply she expresses her "defiance" (*Firefly: A Celebration* 40) through her naked body. Furthermore, his profession as a priest designates Book as a character who appears somewhat nonsexual. Of all crew members aboard Serenity, he seems the least likely to relish in viewing a sexualized act. Assuming the television audience as the true intended audience allows a subversion of the male gaze. Smelik describes that the direct contact between the spectator and the fetishized woman allows her to "deliberately uses her body as spectacle, manipulating the men within the film narrative for her own ends" (Smelik 363). Inara is in a position of power, opposite the series audience (cf. Greco 246), since she is the active participant in this sexual act. This concurs with third-wave feminist, who "have complicated the older feminist critique of the male gaze as a weapon to put women in their place, and instead exploit the spotlight as a source of power and energy" (Karlyn 25).

"Have you got time to do my hair?" Femininity and Female Friendship Between Inara and Kaylee in "The Train Job"

Inara presents a female character unapologetic for her femininity, transcending earlier stereotypes of the impossibility of the simultaneous existence of femininity and feminism (cf. Rowley 325). While Holder criticizes the fact that in *Firefly* "women can and do still accrue power through sexual attractiveness" (Holder 148), she does confirm that Inara's achievements are tied to her presentation of femininity. Criticizing beauty and femininity, especially achieved through artificial means, is common throughout feminist criticism, using the argument, that "to seek the societal idea of beauty is to conform to the limits men want to place upon women" (Brace 117). Others focus on how this critique instead of empowering women, creates a new set of standards. Instead of deconstructing old structures of gender identity, new categories are formed determining the right way to be female (cf. Lenzhofer 50). Idealizing "certain expressions of gender" would only "produce new forms of hierarchy and exclusion" (Butler viii).

As discussed earlier, Inara's costumes support her strong connection to Asian traditions. They are also often free flowing, relying more on draping than actual hard seams or construction. Her dress during "Serenity" is almost indistinguishable from any piece of fabric used to adorn her shuttle, displaying similar intricate ornamentation and being designed without any fastening, but by being thrown over her shoulder, therefore depending solely on the draping. Her clothing's similarity to the fabrics draped to decorate her shuttle empathizes the way in which Inara's shuttle represents an extension of her personality. While her dress from "Serenity" is certainly an exaggeration of those features, at least some of the elements can be found in all her dresses and the softness achieved by omitting any technical construction or visible seams is concurrent with the traditional analogy of a soft femininity and a hard masculinity.

The clothes Inara wears also represent her sexuality, as they are often low cut and revealing. While clearly being sexualized, her clothes remain tasteful and appropriate for a woman of her social status. According to *Firefly*'s costume designer Shawna Trpcic, the general inspiration for Inara's clothing was taken from lingerie (cf. *Firefly: A Celebration* 320). This confirms that within *Firefly* "sex is not something to be outlawed or looked down upon, and beauty not a trait to be taken lightly" (Taylor 132). Supporting femininity and a women's right to "adorn herself *for herself* and not merely to attain fulfillment via the male gaze" (Brace 121), is another ideal of third-wave feminists, arguing that limiting personal expression is oppressive whether it comes from the patriarchy or feminism. The ambition is "reclaiming the right not only to the term 'girl' but to 'girly pleasures'" (Karlyn 25). This part of third-wave feminism can be found in the scene between Inara and Kaylee during "The Train Job," where Inara is brushing Kaylee's hair and talking about beautifying her, therefore engaging in an essential "girly pleasure." Kaylee's connection to this school of feminism has been demonstrated before with her representing "female sexuality openly, playfully, and boldly" (Beadling 60). Tamy Burnett explains in "Anya as Feminist Model of Positive Female Sexuality," that within *Buffy, The Vampire Slayer* the character Anya represents "woman's sexual desires, in both word and deed" (Burnett 134). *Firefly* splits those representations with Inara being sexually active, while Kaylee is the most outspoken crew member with regard to her sexuality. She is the one who tells Inara to "Have good sex" in "Jaynestown," calls Mal "Captain Tightpants" in "Shindig," and reacts after entering the brothel in "Heart of Gold" by exclaiming, "Look, they got boy whores! Isn't that thoughtful?" She embodies all the "traits formerly viewed as demeaning by both feminists and misogynists: prettiness, brattiness, and sexual flamboyance" (Karlyn 25). Her focus on the classical "girly" issue of outward beauty can be found in her exchange with Wash in "Heart of Gold," in which she demands, "Wash, tell me I'm pretty."

The scene in which Inara is brushing Kaylee's hair during "The Train Job" is set inside Inara's shuttle and accompanied by the Asian music associated with the sexual Inara. Mal even suggests that Kaylee has become a client of Inara's (cf. Pelkey 333), but this reading seems rather circumstantial to me. While Kaylee seems to enjoy herself, the conversation focuses on the women's respective potential lovers. The interaction between the two seems to reinforce the friendship, which is shown frequently between the two women. It allows Kaylee to leave her role as mechanic outside the shuttle and enjoy being pampered. Interestingly, this scene is also when Inara explains, that she values personality over outward appearances, supporting that beauty is not necessary for—but also not contradicting to—being a good person. Kaylee's dirty and grease-stained face stands in contrast to her "lovely hair," which shows the "combination of 'feminist' and 'feminine' elements" (Rowley 320), which is displayed through the female characters in *Firefly*. The reaffirmation of their female friendship also fits with aims of third-wave feminism (cf. Karlyn 3). All of this is disrupted, when Mal, representing the masculine opposition to Inara, enters the shuttle and says, "You're holding my mechanic in thrall." This reduces Kaylee to her previously established role and implies that it is contradictory to this feminine kind of enjoyment.

"Aren't I supposed to be a man now?" Deconstruction of Gender in "Jaynestown"

The question of how gender is constructed in the *Firefly* 'verse is approached directly in the character of Inara's client Fess Higgins during the episode "Jaynestown." The encounter between him and Inara is orchestrated by his father the Magistrate so that Fess can "make a man" of himself, because, as his father puts it, "he ain't yet a man." In opposition to this, Magistrate Higgins calls Inara "the lady" and "young lady," thereby emphasizing her femaleness. Initially, Fess adopts a similar attitude and seems somewhat disappointed about the lack of change after his loss of virginity. He asks Inara, "Aren't I supposed to be a man now?" She answers him with, "A man's just a boy who's old enough to ask that question. Our time together is a ritual, a symbol." This focus on gender as symbolic instead of naturalized is coherent third-wave feminism reinterpretation of identities such as male and female (cf. Karlyn 21). Judith Butler goes so far as to state, that "there is no gender identity behind the expressions of gender; that identity is performatively constituted by the very 'expressions' that are said to be its results" (Butler 34).

In *Gender Trouble*, Butler argues that "the reconceptualization of identity as an effect, that is, as produced or generated opens up possibilities of agency that are insidiously foreclosed by positions that take identity categories as foundational and fixed" (Butler 201). This matches the concept of "fluid cate - gories of gender" (Karlyn 24), which allows "young women [to] freely engage in masculinity ... in order to 'take up' the sense of power our culture still identifies with boys and men" (Karlyn 22). This possibility of the reversal and change of gender is especially interesting when linked to the concepts of pornography and the male gaze. In those views, masculinity is always identified with the active and femininity with the passive (cf. Smelik 357). Caputi even goes so far as to state that "in the pornographic view, male potency veritably requires female impotence, and whenever there is a truly sovereign woman…, there is a weak and castrated man" (Caputi 115). Since Inara clearly initiates the sex and is shown as controlling the interaction between her and her client (cf. Porter 97), he becomes passive, while she remains active, temporarily switching the assigned gender roles. One might even argue that a reversal of "the controlling power of the male characters" (Smelik 353) and "the objectified representation of the female character" (Smelik 353) is taking place. This is based on Fess being the objectified virgin with whom Inara is having sex, in a scene presented from her point of view. Not coincidentally this is taking place on a planet mostly defined by mud, and therefore on "the edge of civilization, a place where gender constructions are fluid" (Lively 185).

In the episode "War Stories," Inara and the female Councilor mention in their conversation that "one cannot always be one's self in the company of men," which Rowley interprets as the constant need for women to perform their femininity (cf. 323f). This suits the question of artifice in a Companion's profession as prostitution is "inextricably linked to deceit" (Aberdein 75). In her discussion of "The Rhetoric of Seduction in Firefly" Cynthea Masson states that Inara uses almost constant rhetorical artifice to satisfy her customers' needs. While Davidson and Holder agree on Inara being able to "shed pretenses and … revel in the splendor of shared intimacy" (Davidson 125) with the Councilor, I agree with Masson, that "companion seduction rhetoric reveals merely the semblance of true feelings" (30). Inara simply changes her performance without abandoning it. Still, the performativity of gender cannot be seen as comparable to Inara's performance of enjoyment with her clients. As Butler states, "the performance is effected with the strategic aim of maintaining gender within its binary frame—an aim that cannot be attributed to a subject, but, rather, must be understood to found and consolidate the subject" (191).

Throughout "Jaynestown," though, gender can be seen as symbolic for empowerment and while "the Companion … presents her client with what they both know to be a performance, … he can derive not merely physical gratification but genuine aesthetic, intellectual, and emotional insight" (Aberdein 75). While the sexual act does not change Fess, his understanding of power relation and gender changes, allowing him to defy his father at the end of the episode. When he does, he says, "You wanted to make a man of me, Dad. I guess it worked." This fluidity of gender is only possible within Inara's shuttle. While gender constructions in the larger *Firefly* universe are presented as ambiguous and their inherent status is questioned, the show "leaves more deeply entrenched gendered norms intact, unexamined and thus naturalised" (Rowley 324).

"No power in the 'verse can stop me": Power Relations Between Inara and Her Clients in *"Serenity"* and *"Jaynestown"*

Prostitutes in *Firefly*, as long as they are Companions, are shown as in control and powerful during the scenes of their sexual activity (cf. Porter 97). They are in "charge of their sexuality" (Ginn 36) and therefore hold power, even if some critics still challenge this power based on what they perceive to be "contexts that are rife with questionable ethics" (Greco 246). According to Tresca, the power-relation between a prostitute and her client always remains complex, as it "is based on the illusion of control. The economics of the situation would suggest the client is in the power position.... However ... the prostitute is actually the one who controls the power, not the client" (Tresca 166). Other critics cannot stress the position of power Inara is in enough, stating "make no mistake, her social class grants her an inordinate amount of power" (Lively 191) and that, when "she flexes her power, the audience is well aware that a line has been crossed" (Lively 191). The source of her power is not only her sexual attractiveness (cf. Holder 148), but also her autonomy (cf. Porter 98), as well as her rhetorical skills (cf. Masson 30).

Inara's articulate and skillful conversations set her apart from the more Western characters in *Firefly* and are also one source of her control. Companions are trained to "use their rhetorical skills to maintain a degree of control within the power struggles of this final frontier" (Masson 19). This control is acknowledged within the series by Mal, when he is afraid that Inara might manipulate him and accuses her of using her "feminine wiles: "Your Companion training, your some-might-say uncanny ability to make a man sweaty and/or compliant" ("Trash"). His fear of her rhetoric skills supports the assumption of power inside her words (cf. Masson 27). Indeed, when Inara engages in conversation with her clients, her rhetoric notably changes, and she often relies on the use of stock phrases and sentiments, borrowed from small talk to avoid having meaningful conversations (cf. Masson 20).

When Magistrate Higgins insists on accompanying his son Fess inside Inara's shuttle during "Jaynestown," she first politely and then very assertively banishes him from her shuttle. She places a hand on his arm and guides him firmly toward the exit, interrupting his sentence, while insisting, "Mr. Higgins, you're not allowed here." She then employs the same patronizing tone that he uses on his son, telling him, "Now, why don't you go on and let us begin our work?" Later Inara effectively ends the conversation, using the phrase, "Goodnight, Mr. Higgins." While she relies on stock phrases and clichés, her tone clearly shows her in control of the situation, while the Magistrate is out of his depth. Masson observes that "she uses her rhetorical skill to maintain power within the verbal exchange" (21). She does this to such an extent that the Magistrate's rhetoric falters from asserting his power over women, when explaining that Fess, in contrast to him, "can't find a willin' woman himself" to incomplete sentences, such as "Well, I'm—" (cf. Masson 21).

When Fess is embarrassed by his status as a virgin, he mimics what can be identified as the Magistrate's attitude, saying, "We have to bring you here." Inara's response is, "As far as bringing me here, Companions choose the people they're to be with very carefully." This exchange shows how Inara's rhetoric abilities let her maintain her active position without using aggression. When Fess suggests that she was passively brought to him, Inara interrupts him to emphasize that she chose to come after they asked her. She therefore highlights the active role she played in setting up the encounter, and thus shifts the power back to herself. In reading the same exchange, Masson focuses on Inara's disempowering of the Magistrate; she changes Fess' "My father's right again" to "Your father isn't right," therefore "bonding with him on the level of diction" (cf. Masson 21). Masson then states that Inara's insistence on the Companions' choice of their clients is used to "flatter[s] Fess by implying that he is more attractive as a sexual partner than his father" (22).

Her empowering of at least some of the clients she is with confirms her position of power in opposition to them. Only the fact that she is in complete control and seen as ultimately empowered and respectable by her clients allows her to act this way. Her first client during "Serenity" is enthralled by her, asking her to stay and revering her superior knowledge when hearing about a place he as "a young man from an influential family" (Aberdein 65) has never been to himself. The script goes even further, in him talking about his cousin hoping to become a Companion, but being barred from it due to her insufficient grades (cf. *Firefly: A Celebration* 30). The fact that his family seems to wish for his cousin to become a Companion leads only to the conclusion that he has the highest regard for Inara and her profession. His subordination is represented through his body language when talking to Inara after their sexual intercourse. He repeatedly looks down away from her face or directly into his cup, while she is openly looking at his face, answering his questions. When he proposes that she could stay with him, the question is formulated indirectly, asking, "Do you really have to leave?" While his passive phrasing and body language indicates his high esteem for Inara and her autonomy, his follow up explanation indicates that he does not have any agency himself, as he explains, "I, my father is very influential, we could … I could arrange for you to be with…" Contrary to Inara, he relies on his family for influence and power and without it he is quite literally stripped naked. There is a perceivable change in his behavior after he is dressed. He still appears nervous and insecure about what to say, but he is considerably more confident in his position, backed by a patriarchal society. He goes so far as to accuse Inara of her clock being "rigged to speed up." The accusation seems not to be serious as he immediately leaves and Inara appears to be more annoyed than offended (cf. Goodfriend 96).

The viewer does not know what happens to him after his engagement with Inara, but one might imagine that she has made an impact on him. His power solely results from patriarchy and his families' stand in society, while Inara, even as "a lowly whore" ("Serenity"), remains in complete control of their encounter. Inara's ability to navigate between civilization and the frontier gives her "an inordinate amount of power both personally and socially" (Lively 191). This influence of empowerment is much more distinct in "Jaynestown," where her functions outside of sexual pleasure are shown when "she empowers Fess and aids his development into a confident, independent adult" (Szabo 107). She does this by "disempowering the father" (Masson 21), who "continues to assert his domineering parental control over Fess even in private matters" (Masson 21). Her ability to do so by interrupting, defying and finally throwing him out of her shuttle, confirms the immense agency she herself possesses. These interactions in which Inara clearly represents the active and powerful part, while the men are presented as passive and powerless, reverses established narrative structures (cf. Smelik 353). Traditionally, "Action, agency, movement, change belong to the male hero, and action—even violent action—is not only sanctioned for him but serves as a means of proving his courage and strength" (Karlyn 43). Neither Fess, nor the client in "Serenity," seem especially violent. In fact, Inara's expulsion of the Magistrate from her shuttle uses more physical force than Fess' final defiance of his father, when he "sent an override to Port Control" ("Jaynestown") to aid Serenity's flight. This construction of Inara's clients as nonviolent also contradicts the concept of penetrative sex as violent and masculine dominated (cf. Caputi 90). In all sexual acts involving Inara, she is the one who "holds the power in these relationships and always has the choice to reject the client or walk away at any time" (Porter 98). During those scenes, *Firefly* reconstructs the roles of females as "active participants in cutting a place for themselves on the frontier" (Lively 196), while using rhetorics to "maintain power over their lovers" (Masson 30).

"You can't take the sky from me": Inara's Freedom and Restrictions

Firefly's overarching theme is the quest for freedom, as every single one of the main characters is in some way running away from restrictions and imprisonment (some more literally than others). The heroes have "fought for the Independents" ("Out of Gas") and the presence of the law-abiding Alliance is generally presented as a threat. The series' theme song embodies the significance of individual liberty, therefore, freedom is the ultimate motivation within *Firefly*, and Inara's prostitution is no exception to this. Her profession is judged on her independence (cf. Szabo 115) and after she comes aboard Serenity for the first time, she demands that "there are a few things I would require from you [Captain Reynolds]. The foremost being complete autonomy" ("Out of Gas"). Her clothing choices also point toward this theme, as "fashion freedom often equates to personal freedom in the Whedonverse" (Brace 123). The most notable sign of her freedom, in contrast to most traditional portrayals of prostitutes, would be the fact that she chooses her own clients. When Kaylee asks Inara if she ever "had to service a really hideous client," she replies with insistence that "a Companion chooses her own clients; that's guild law" ("The Train Job"). This control is what separates "good" from "bad" sex in *Firefly*, as "sex is not necessarily about commitment and love. It is about choice" (Porter 99). Those choices present Inara as an empowered prostitute (cf. Tresca 166) and are not even restricted by her financial needs. When Inara explains in "The Train Job" that she does not choose according to physical attractiveness, Mal implies that her selection is purely based on monetary value. Actually, "Inara's choice of client is often made for personal, not purely commercial, reasons" (Aberdein 68), and in several instances she trades in favors to benefit the other crew members on board Serenity (cf. Aberdein 68).

The guild law, which enables her to choose her own clients, is often cited by critics to show the alleged artifice of her freedom. Mercedes Lackey has written that "her freedom is as thin as the piece of paper her license is printed on" (69), and this license is the only distinction between Inara and one of the whores (cf. Lackey 69). In her article "*Serenity* and Bobby McGee," Lackey writes about Inara being in a cage and "tightly corseted by those restrictions" (69), with her only option being self-sacrifice (cf. Lackey 72f). This insistence on Inara's need to reject the restrictions laid upon her by the guild seems unnecessary, as "other than the voluntary choice to obey Guild law, Inara enjoys complete autonomy" (Szabo 115).

The only restriction on Inara shown during the series is her physical exam in "Ariel" to renew her license, which she has to undergo once a year. While she certainly does not seem ecstatic about the hospital stay, Inara also presents no indication that she is somehow opposed to this mandatory health check. Therefore, this seems something she chooses to do, rather than something she is forced to. Still, Lackey's point of view is supported by Rabb and Richardson, who cite her and then add, that "Mal has, in actual fact, already cautioned Inara that following Alliance rules may buy her a nice life, but these same rules simultaneously make her a slave" (144f). What Mal is actually reacting to in "Shindig" is Atherton's proposal that Inara might become his personal Companion. Mal does warn her "you think following rules will buy you a nice life, even if the rules make you a slave" and immediately follows it pleading "Don't take his offer." His objections are therefore against her ingratiating herself further in this society, since "remaining a Companion as she is means freedom, but becoming Atherton's personal Companion would be the end of her freedom" (Szabo 110).

Critics fail to see—just as Atherton—the value Inara places on her established freedom, where "offering to make her his 'private property' was asking her to accept less privilege than she already possessed, not gifting her with more" (Davidson 119). This reasoning is backed by another conversation between Inara and Mal in "Shindig," in which he questions her continuing association with Atherton, after Mal has—in his view—proven Atherton's low opinion of Inara. She rebukes Mal, insisting "Because it's my decision. Not yours." She hereby establishes that her choices will not be taken away by either of them. This might lead to further problems, as a romantic connection between Mal and Inara is displayed throughout the series. Inara seems unable to accept this "old-fashioned chivalric love" (Jencson 391). Contrary to Lackey, Tresca and Amy-Chinn, who believe that Inara becoming involved with Mal would violate guild laws and lead to the loss of Inara's Companion license, there is no textual proof to support this.

"She done somethin' to it": Defying the Heteronormative in "War Stories" and Inara's Shuttle as a Post-Patriarchal Space

The shuttle inhabited by Inara is used as an expansion of her personality. The visit of a female Councilor as a regular client of Inara's occurs in the episode "War Stories," marking Inara as the only *Firefly* character not compliant with a heteronormative sexuality. While Tresca claims that "normative sexuality is not an option" (146) in the Whedonverse, the majority of all characters in *Firefly* present at least the desire for normative heterosexual relationships. Even Inara is not exempt from this, as she is portrayed to "desire for a love-based, heterosexual, monogamous relationship with Mal" (Amy-Chinn 181). This does not negate the fact that she voluntarily decides to also choose women as her sexual partners and is using the same techniques of seduction she applies to her male clients (cf. Masson 23). While most of her clients are men, the portrayed interactions are treated almost equally, showing

Inara and the clients in bed together, at least partially undressed, with the difference being that the scene between Inara and the Councilor also includes a drawn-out kiss. While this is seen by some critics as pandering to the alleged male audience, others consider it in fact positive (cf. Ginn 37f) and some go so far as to believe in the genuineness of the emotions portrayed (cf. Davidson 125; Holder 149). When the Councilor tells Inara that "there's no need for the show," Inara pretends to discontinue the performing aspect of her work, but behaves as she did with her male clients, relying on a mixture of "flattery and emotional bonding" (Masson 23) to fulfill their needs. This allows "her 'once again' to perform rather than purely be 'cast in the role of whore as social worker'" (Masson 23).

Still, Inara and the Councilor's encounter is clearly coded as deviating from the norms outside Inara's shuttle. The other crew members are surprised (but not opposed) to Inara's client being a woman. The discussion between the Councilor and Inara implies that they are required to participate in a performance in spaces inhabited by men. While Inara's statement has to be seen in the context of providing a service to her client, the Councilor appears for all intents and purposes as a lesbian. After Inara expresses, "One cannot always be one's self in the company of men," she emphatically answers, "Never, actually." This makes it even more surprising that the script includes a scene at her house, where Inara, to her surprise, encounters the Councilor's husband and son. They are unaware of the sexual relationship their wife and mother has with another woman. While this scene did not become part of the show, it would have furthered the already implied suggestion that while it is possible and even accepted to depart from the norms of patriarchal society on board *Serenity* and especially inside Inara's shuttle, this is not true for the rest of the 'verse.

Inara's shuttle is presented to the viewer as Other much as Inara herself is. It always has a certain oriental sound to it (cf. Hung 413) and is "the hub of all Asian elements within the show" (Brown 19). The shuttle's interior evokes the image of a Middle Eastern harem (cf. Brown 19) and features Asian textiles, calligraphy, objects used for the Companions' tea ceremony, alongside "sculptures of Krishna and Radha, the youthful South Asian god and his consort, indicating connections between the physical love between a man and woman and the relation between god and devotee" (Brown 21). This connection to the spiritual is emphasized by Inara herself, when she calls the shuttle "a consecrated Place of Union" in "Jaynestown" (cf. Aberdein 67), and "it is no accident that at the end of the episode 'Serenity' the Shepherd comes to Inara's shuttle where she offers both counseling and healing, and bestows a form of blessing" (Amy-Chinn 180). The meaning and presentation of her home clearly separates Inara from the rest of Serenity and the 'verse, with the shuttle even being described as "womblike" by Davidson (cf. 124).

The world of *Firefly* consists not of one homogeneous society but is composed of many different worlds, with some closer to the norms and beliefs of traditional patriarchy than others. The 'verse is presented with some parts "still dominated by patriarchal values ... and others as feminist" (Rowley 322), which seems to highlight the process of feminism instead of showing a finished result. *Firefly* therefore constructs a world "where sexism, racism and bigotry are distractions made by a few instead of institutional problems affecting the many" (Lively 196). The shuttle is a place that Inara has created to exist in post-patriarchal space, where she and others do not need to conform to gender roles and to behavior the outside world expects from them. Similar to the larger world outside, this contrast is demonstrated by her repeating defense against intruders. When Inara first rents the shuttle from Mal in "Out of Gas," she insists that "no crew member, including yourself, would be allowed entrance without my express invitation," a rule, which Mal is determined to test repeatedly. Inara reacts by expelling Mal from her shuttle, while reminding him of her previously established rule (e.g., "The Train Job") or the fact, that he may own the shuttle, but has no rights to it, as long as she rents it ("Serenity"). Other intruders include the Magistrate Higgins, whom she banishes, and her first client in "Serenity" after he got dressed, who quickly leaves of his own accord. The intruders are shown as not only intellectually disagreeing with the space Inara presents, but also visually, with their clothes contrasting to the shuttle's interior and their framing almost always including the exits.

Conclusion

Prostitutes in *Firefly* possess an impressive amount of power. Companions especially are shown to be in control of themselves and their surroundings. This power is not held by them despite their role as sex workers, but because of their expression of sexuality. The high social status of a Companion is hardly achieved by anyone else in the show, and Inara is presented as being able to empower others as well as herself. She embodies the concepts of third-wave feminism, which can be found throughout the series *Firefly*. Through her work as a prostitute, she portrays female sexuality. She is continuously linked to Asian culture and history, which connects her to exoticism. She is also the embodiment of civilization, due to her being the character with the highest education—except for the doctor—on board Serenity. She therefore represents the construction of an Other taken to the extreme. While the Other is already destabilized in the larger context of *Firefly* by protagonists who occupy the margins of their society, Inara is able to invert the concept by refusing to let herself be objectified, insisting on behaving actively, and offering her point of view as a character. Thereby she also transcends the imagined gender binary of male/female, active/passive and subject/object. Her deconstruction of other familiar concepts, such as heteronormativity, the male gaze and gender, all take place within her shuttle, marking it as a space outside of the patriarchy still prevalent in the *Firefly* 'verse. While Inara is generally free and enjoys as much liberty as the other characters in *Firefly*, they are still expected to behave according to societal expectations and patriarchal norms. Her shuttle is the one place where those norms do not exist and where gender, sexuality and the identities based thereupon are presented as fluid, rather than static. Ultimately, she is able to control her own life by using her femininity, her sexuality, and the freedom those afford her to her advantage, and by carving out a space in which a complex and sex-positive woman, such as herself, can exist.

Works Cited

Aberdein, Andrew. "The Companion and Socrates: Is Inara a Hetaera?" In *Investigating Firefly and Serenity: Science Fiction on the Frontier*, edited by Rhonda V. Wilcox and Tanya Cochran, pp. 63–75, I.B. Tauris, 2008.

Amy-Chinn, Dee. "'Tis Pity She's a Whore: Postfeminist Prostitution in Joss Whedon's Firefly?" *Feminist Media Studies* 6, no. 2 (2006): 175–189. Web. 20 July 2013.

"Ariel." *Firefly*. Dir. Joss Whedon. Twentieth Century–Fox, 2002. DVD.

Beadling, Laura L. "The Threat of the 'Good Wife': Feminism, Postfeminism, and Third-Wave Feminism in Firefly." In *Investigating Firefly and Serenity: Science Fiction on the Frontier*, edited by Rhonda V. Wilcox and Tanya Cochran, pp. 53–62, I.B. Tauris, 2008.

Brace, Patricia. "Fashioning Feminism: Whedon, Women, and Wardrobe." In *The Philosophy of Joss Whedon*, edited by Dean A. Kowalski, pp. 117–32, University Press of Kentucky, 2011.

Brown, Rebecca M. "Orientalism in Firefly and Serenity." *Slayage: The Journal of The Whedon Studies Association* 7, no. 1 (2008). Web. 22 July 2013.

Burnett, Tamy. "Anya as Feminist Model of Positive Female Sexuality." In *Sexual Rhetoric in the Works of Joss Whedon*, edited by Erin Waggoner, pp. 117–45, McFarland, 2010. EPUB file.

Butler, Judith. *Gender Trouble: Feminism and the Subversion of Identity*. Routledge, 1990.

Caputi, Jane. *Goddesses and Monsters: Women, Myth, Power, and Popular Culture*. University of Wisconsin Press, 2004.

Coy, Maddy, Josephine Wakeling, and Maria Garner. "Selling Sex Sells: Representations of Prostitution and the Sex Industry in Sexualised Popular Culture as Symbolic Violence." *Women's Studies International Forum* 34, no. 5 (2011): 441–48. Web. 22 July 2013.

Christopher, Renny. "Little Miss Tough Chick of the Universe: Farscape's Inverted Sexual Dynamics." In *Action Chicks: New Images of Tough Women in Popular Culture*, edited by Sherrie A. Inness, pp. 257–81, Palgrave Macmillian, 2004.

Davidson, Joy. "Whores and Goddesses: The Archetypal Domain of Inara Serra." In *Finding Serenity: Anti-Heroes, Lost Shepherds and Space Hookers in Joss Whedon's Firefly*, edited by Jane Espenson, pp. 113–29, BenBella Books, 2004.

Espenson, Jane, ed. *Finding Serenity: Anti-Heroes, Lost Shepherds and Space Hookers in Joss Whedon's Firefly*. BenBella Books, 2004.

Ginn, Sherry. *Power and Control in the Television Worlds of Joss Whedon*. McFarland, 2012.

Goodfriend, Wind. "Terror Management Aboard Serenity." In *The Psychology of Joss Whedon*, edited by Joy Davidson, pp. 91–104, BenBella Books, 2007.

Greco, Nicholas. "The Companion as a Doll: The Female Enigma in *Firefly* and *Dollhouse*."

In *Sexual Rhetoric in the Works of Joss Whedon,* edited by Erin Waggoner, pp. 239–47, McFarland, 2010. EPUB file.

"Heart of Gold." *Firefly.* Dir. Joss Whedon. Twentieth Century–Fox, 2002. DVD.

Holder, Nancy. "I Want Your Sex: Gender and Power in Joss Whedon's Dystopian Future World." In *Finding Serenity: Anti-Heroes, Lost Shepherds and Space Hookers in Joss Whedon's* Firefly, edited by Jane Espenson, pp. 139–53, BenBella Books, 2004.

Hung, Eric. "The Meaning of 'World Music' in *Firefly.*" In *Buffy, Ballads, and Bad Guys Who Sing: Music in the Worlds of Joss Whedon,* edited by Kendra Preston Leonard, pp. 402–31, Scarecrow, 2011. EPUB file.

"Jaynestown." *Firefly.* Dir. Joss Whedon. Twentieth Century–Fox, 2002. DVD.

Jencson, Linda. "'My Rifle's as Bright as My Sweetheart's Eyes': Joss Whedon's Firefly and the Songs of the Clancy Brothers." In *Buffy, Ballads, and Bad Guys Who Sing: Music in the Worlds of Joss Whedon,* edited by Kendra Preston Leonard, pp. 384–401, Scarecrow, 2011. EPUB file.

Karlyn, Kathleen Rowe. "Scream, Popular Culture, and Feminism's Third Wave: 'I'm Not My Mother.'" *Genders Journal* 38 (2003). n. pag. Web. 22 July 2013.

Kowalski, Dean A., and S. Evan Kreider, eds. *The Philosophy of Joss Whedon.* University Press of Kentucky, 2011.

Lackey, Mercedes. "Serenity and Bobby Mcgee: Freedom and the Illusion of Freedom in Joss Whedon's Firefly." In *Finding Serenity: Anti-Heroes, Lost Shepherds and Space Hookers in Joss Whedon's* Firefly, edited by Jane Espenson, pp. 63–73, BenBella Books, 2004.

Lenzhofer, Karin. *Chicks Rule!: Die Schönen Neuen Heldinnen in US-Amerikanischen Fernsehserien.* Transcript, 2006.

Leonard, Kendra Preston, ed. *Buffy, Ballads, and Bad Guys Who Sing: Music in the Worlds of Joss Whedon.* Scarecrow, 2011. EPUB file.

Lively, Robert L. "Remapping the Feminine in Joss Whedon's *Firefly.*" In *Channeling the Future: Essays on Science Fiction and Fantasy Television,* edited by Lincoln Geraghty, 183–97, Scarecrow, 2009.

Masson, Cynthea. "'But She Was Naked! And All Articulate!': The Rhetoric of Seduction in *Firefly.*" Wilcox, pp. 19–30.

"Our Mrs. Reynolds." *Firefly.* Dir. Joss Whedon. Twentieth Century–Fox, 2002. DVD.

"Out of Gas." *Firefly.* Dir. Joss Whedon. Twentieth Century–Fox, 2002. DVD.

Pelkey, Stanley C., II. "Still Flyin'?: Conventions, Reversals, and Musical Meaning in *Firefly.*" In *Buffy, Ballads, and Bad Guys Who Sing: Music in the Worlds of Joss Whedon,* edited by Kendra Preston Leonard, pp. 329–83, Scarecrow Press, 2011. EPUB file.

Porter, Heather M. "'They Teach You That in Whore Academy?': A Quantitative Examination of Sex and Sex Workers in Joss Whedon's *Firefly* and *Dollhouse.*" In *The Sex Is Out of This World: Essays on the Carnal Side of Science Fiction,* edited by Sherry Ginn and Michael G. Cornelius, pp. 86–101, McFarland, 2012. EPUB file.

Rabb, Douglas J., and J. Michael Richardson. *The Existential Joss Whedon.* McFarland, 2007.

Rowley, Christina. "Firefly/Serenity: Gendered Space and Gendered Bodies." *The British Journal of Politics & International Relations* 9.2 (2007): 318–25. Web.

Scholz, Sally J. *Feminism: A Beginner's Guide.* New York: Oneworld Publications, 2010.

"Serenity." *Firefly.* Dir. Joss Whedon. Twentieth Century–Fox, 2002. DVD.

"Shindig." *Firefly.* Dir. Joss Whedon. Twentieth Century–Fox, 2002. DVD.

Smelik, Anneke. "Feminist Film Theory." In *The Cinema Book,* edited by Pam Cook and Mieke Bernink, pp. 353–65, British Film Institute, 1999. Web. 22 July 2013.

Smith, Madeleine. "Sex, Society and the Slayer." In *Television, Sex and Society: Analyzing Contemporary Representations,* edited by Basil Glynn, James Aston and Beth Johnson, 17–32. New York: Continuum International Publishing Group, 2012.

Szabo, Tait. "Companions, Dolls, and Whores: Joss Whedon on Sex and Prostitution." In *The Philosophy of Joss Whedon,* edited by Dean A. Kowalski, pp. 103–16, University Press of Kentucky, 2011.

Taylor, Robert B. "The Captain May Wear the Tight Pants, but It's the Gals Who Make Serenity Soar." In *Finding Serenity: Anti-Heroes, Lost Shepherds and Space Hookers in Joss Whedon's* Firefly, edited by Jane Espenson, pp. 131–37, BenBella Books, 2004.

"The Train Job." *Firefly*. Dir. Joss Whedon. Twentieth Century–Fox, 2002. DVD.

Tresca, Don. "Images of Paraphilia in the Whedonverse." In *Sexual Rhetoric in the Works of Joss Whedon*, edited by Erin Waggoner, pp. 146–72, McFarland, 2010. EPUB file.

Waggoner, Erin B., ed. *Sexual Rhetoric in the Works of Joss Whedon: New Essays*. McFarland, 2010. EPUB file.

"War Stories." *Firefly*. Dir. Joss Whedon. Twentieth Century–Fox, 2002. DVD.

Whedon, Joss. *Firefly: A Celebration*. London: Titan Books, 2012.

Wilcox, Rhonda V., and Tanya R. Cochram, ed. *Investigating Firefly and Serenity: Science Fiction on the Frontier*. I.B. Tauris, 2008.

Girl Power and Depression in *Buffy the Vampire Slayer*

SHYLA SALTZMAN

"Postfeminist" is a term that describes a popular iteration of female empowerment: the belief that the feminist movement has done its job and can be laid to rest because women have fully gained their equality and rights. Jeffrey A. Brown's *Dangerous Curves: Action Heroines, Gender, Fetishism, and Popular Culture* explains that "this younger generation of feminism is differentiated by embracing popular culture and focusing on individual choice, consumerism, sexual freedom, cultural diversity, personal empowerment, and an ironic sensibility" (Brown 147). Brown's text cites shows like *Sex and the City*, *Charmed*, and *The Powerpuff Girls* as examples of media that propagate postfeminist ideals. At one time, these shows were cheerfully summed up as representing "Girl Power." In Girl Power media, girls can do absolutely anything; they can attain prestigious careers and be athletes or intellectuals, while they also shop, make themselves gorgeous, have great sex, and prove themselves to be exceptional mothers, students, daughters, and/or wives. Popular media is at the forefront of the postfeminist campaign. Audience members are inundated with female protagonists on television and in film who have Girl Power. These women can do it all; they are fashionable and successful, attract gorgeous men, and can save the world in the meantime if the genre calls for it.

There is a downside to Girl Power, however. Angela McRobbie, in "Postfeminsism and Popular Culture: Bridget Jones and the New Gender Regime," explains that because equality has been "achieved" and girls are allowed to do whatever they like, "the new female subject is, despite her freedom, called upon to be silent, to withhold critique in order to count as a modern, sophisticated girl" (36). Feminism is, at best, old fashioned and, at worst, viewed as misguided and/or negative. Girls are supposed to be happy with everything

85

now that equality has been achieved, to the point where one unfortunate trend in postfeminism is that trauma and oppression are read as merely "empowering" instead of unjust hardships.

Among discussions of feminist and postfeminist heroines, common TV series such as *Xena: Warrior Princess, Charlie's Angels,* and *Buffy the Vampire Slayer* are referenced frequently. *Buffy* is arguably one of the most enduring of these shows and has certainly inspired a disproportional share of academic interest. David Lavery's foreword to *Buffy Goes Dark: Essays on the Final Two Seasons of* Buffy the Vampire Slayer *on Television* begins:

> At "Staking A Claim: Exploring the Global Reach of Buffy" at the University of South Australia, we experienced firsthand to what extent Joss Whedon's creation had become a world-wide, multi-hemispheric phenomenon (and this was back in the day before books in Italian on Buffy and a conference—"Buffy Hereafter: From the Whedonverse to the Whedonesque"—in Istanbul!) [Lavery 1].

Buffy the Vampire Slayer's heroine is a combination of glamour and strength in the form of a bubbly, blonde, middle class girl who is also the Slayer. Because she is the Slayer, Buffy is gifted with super strength and a mythical duty to fight and protect humans from demons.

The usually seamless combination of Buffy's teen-star beauty with super-human strength breaks down alarmingly in the sixth season of the series, wherein Buffy becomes severely depressed and wishes she were dead. This period of her narrative is troubling, but also innovative and fascinating. Why is it important to have the postfeminist heroine suffer in this way? How is her depression a powerful reflection on her role, on the paradoxical job of being the "normal" girl who can do everything? Buffy's depression makes the viewer question what these modern narratives so rarely question: what are the consequences of postfeminist toughness? *Buffy the Vampire Slayer* not only dares to challenge the surety that the action heroine is an inherently progressive figure, but also provides a self-destructive solution for the damage done by postfeminism.

Buffy is a shining example of the postfeminist heroine because she can repeatedly save the world while still going to school, shopping, dating, and clubbing with friends. One very illustrative plot appears in an episode toward the end of Season Three titled "The Prom." The supernatural drama of this episode is centered on a classmate named Tucker who unleashes a pack of hellhounds to slaughter all of the students at the prom (he is bitter because he did not get a date). Buffy assures her friends that she will take care of the monsters and that they should go to the dance and not worry. Once the prom begins, Buffy is seen chasing the pack of hellhounds through the woods. Using her crossbow and a dagger, she kills all but one who makes it into the school. She throws herself on top of it and snaps its neck after a brief struggle, inches away from a slightly alarmed student in a tuxedo. She drags the bodies of the dead hounds away from the school, piles them up in the woods, picks up a duffle bag, and soon after arrives at the dance in a stunning pink Pamela Dennis gown. To top off the image of the postfeminist hero who can wrestle with demons and still look fabulous, Buffy is also quite popular that night; the students have made up an award just for her. The announcer says, "We're proud to say that the class of '99 has the lowest mortality rate of any class in Sunnydale history!" thanks to Buffy's heroism ("The Prom"). She is presented with a golden umbrella that says, "Class Protector." Then, miraculously, her boyfriend and epic true love strides in just in time for a slow dance to The Sundays' cover of "Wild Horses." An extraordinarily perfect night, this prom night establishes Buffy as the model heroine whose prowess extends from fierceness to glamour.

The Consequences of Buffy's Girl Power

Buffy is supposedly the ideal balance of tough and girly. *Buffy*'s creator, Joss Whedon, says she is supposed to represent the helpless female victim who is always chased down and murdered in horror movies: "I saw so many horror movies where there was that blonde girl who would always get herself killed. ... The idea of Buffy came from just the very simple thought of a beautiful blonde girl walks into an alley, a monster attacks her, and she's not only ready for him—she trounces him" (Season 1 DVD featurette, "Joss Whedon on 'Welcome to the Hellmouth' and 'The Harvest'"). On many occasions, Buffy exaggerates her appearance as bubbly and weak while fleeing from a demon or vampire, only to whip around and attack with a smile. She is just a "normal girl," but underneath that she is the Slayer (and underneath *that*, she is a normal girl). At the end of Season Five, while Buffy and her friends are once again brainstorming ways to save the world, she steps out into a back alley to slay a vampire who is trying to kill a random pedestrian. After Buffy kills it, the man she saves is staring after her, incredulous:

> MALE VICTIM: How'd you do that?
> BUFFY: It's what I do.
> MALE VICTIM: But you're ... just a girl.
> BUFFY: That's what I keep saying ["The Gift"].

This exchange is surprising because the expected response is some retort or challenge about the notion that a girl cannot be a superhero. But Buffy is not responding to sexism. When she says, "That's what I keep saying," Buffy is not hearing the sexism of "you're just a *girl*," but the loneliness of "you're just *a* girl." She is just one person, never allowed to rest, always called on to do

the impossible. Within Buffy is a depiction of the price of postfeminist toughness, which proves that heroism can be ironically disempowering.

In *Tough Girls: Women Warriors and Wonder Women in Popular Culture*,
Sherrie A. Inness discusses the trajectory of female heroes in film and television. The challenge for writers often seems to be the cultural expectation
that men, not women, are strong and active. Their dilemma revolves around
how to make female toughness palatable to a male audience: "Her toughness
and more masculine image suggests that a greater variety of gender roles are
open to women; at the same time, however, her toughness is often mitigated
by her femininity, which American culture commonly associates with weak-
ness" (Inness 5). The threat of the tough girl must be more feminine, more
sexualized, in order to reassure the audience that she is still in some sense
an object. This feminizing tactic can also serve to imply that women's natural
state is to not be tough: "Tough women can offer women new role models,
but their toughness may also bind women more tightly to traditional feminine
roles—especially when the tough woman is portrayed as a pretender to male
power and authority, and someone who is not tough enough to escape being
punished by society for her gender-bending behaviors" (Inness 5).

Buffy raises and confronts the trend Inness points out of the tough-girl
-as-pretender. In Season Three's "Helpless," as Buffy nears her eighteenth
birthday, she learns that there is a special ritual, a "test" she must pass, orchestrated by the Watcher's Council. The Watcher's Council is an organization of
(mostly) British men who oversee the Slayer and appoint a Watcher to her.
The Watcher trains the Slayer for combat and teaches her about demons,
vampires, and the Slayer's responsibility to the world. Buffy's watcher, Rupert
Giles, must prepare her for the test. Preparing her means slowly draining her
of her powers temporarily and without her knowledge, so that the Council
can arrange for her to confront a vampire with nothing but her wit and normal human strength. That the Council arrives with the intent of suspending
Buffy's powers implies that it is their power to give or take away as they
choose. She has to prove, by killing a vampire without super strength, that
she *deserves* the power. When Giles expresses some concern for her, the head
of the Council confidently reassures him, "Once this is all over, your Buffy
will be stronger for it" ("Helpless").

Being without her strength renders Buffy vulnerable in a way she has
never been since she became the Slayer: not just vulnerable to violent attack,
but also to sexual harassment. Buffy first discovers that she is losing her powers during a fight with a vampire. He straddles her and turns her wooden
stake around, attempting to push it into her chest. "Let me know if I'm not
doing this right," he says, smirking ("Helpless"). It is an obvious sexual joke,
made more disturbing by the fact that Buffy's first experience of "helplessness"
involves a metaphor for sexual assault. This particular vulnerability further

suggests that Buffy is only a pretender to male power: "Tough men do not face the kind of sexual threat that tough women face constantly ... no matter how tough she might appear on the surface, she still can be subjected to the ultimate indignity of rape" (Inness 71). Not only does Buffy have to endure catcalls on her walk home at night, but the vampire she has been assigned to kill was formerly a psychopath who "murdered and tortured more than a dozen women before he was committed to an asylum for the criminally insane" ("Helpless"). That the council would deliberately place her, powerless, in an arena with a man who preys on women, is telling. Buffy eventually alienates the council, and she and her Watcher Giles operate on their own terms until the Council returns to Sunnydale in a last effort to put Buffy in her place.

In Season Five's "Checkpoint," a large group of Council members, mostly men, arrive at Giles' store, fully equipped with crisp British accents, tweed jackets, and briefcases—in many ways a parody of patriarchal authority. In this season Buffy's foe is an evil goddess, Glory, who is out to find and kill Buffy's younger sister, Dawn. The Council possesses top-secret files on Glory's origin and weaknesses, but refuses to share them until Buffy has passed a formal "review," to prove that she is worthy and can be trusted with vital information. The Council earnestly tries to remind Buffy that she is using borrowed power: "The Council fights evil; the Slayer is the instrument by which we fight. The Council remains, the Slayers change. Been that way from the beginning" ("Checkpoint"). One thing to note here is the word "change." The implication is that the Slayer's job is only temporary, and therefore she can never truly be as knowledgeable or respectable as the Council. But the reason Slayers have such a high turnover rate is that they are eventually murdered violently by a demon. So "change" is a convenient, diplomatic euphemism for "die." The Council decrees that not only must she meet their standards in combat, not only must they approve of her friends, but she is also forbidden to "resist [their] recommendations" ("Checkpoint"). When Buffy still seems mutinous, the Council leader, Quentin Travers, threatens to have Giles deported. Once the stakes are clear, Travers condescendingly warns, "Perhaps you're used to idle threats ... but you're dealing with grownups now" ("Checkpoint"). There is a great deal of residual bitterness on both sides from Buffy's eighteenth birthday and her later refusal to acknowledge the Council's authority. They are back to prove that she is "an instrument" at best, and at worst, just a girl, in need of "grownup" discipline and boundaries.

But *Buffy* allows its hero to have the last word. By the end of the episode, Buffy has an inspiring revelation: "I've had a lot of people talking at me the last few days. Everyone just lining up to tell me how unimportant I am. And I finally figured out why. Power. I have it. They don't. This bothers them"

("Checkpoint"). The Council came in intending to punish Buffy for denying their authority—for her "gender-bending behavior," as Inness puts it. Instead, Buffy informs the Council that there will be no review, because she has had a realization: "You guys didn't come all the way from England to determine whether or not I was good enough to be let back in. You came to beg me to let you back in. To give your jobs, your lives, some semblance of meaning" ("Checkpoint"). Buffy defies the absurdly patriarchal Council by pointing out they are nothing without her. *Buffy* sets up this notion of men coming to take their power back from women who need to learn their place, or as Travers says, "the relative status of the players in our little game," only to prove that these men are the true pretenders to female power ("Checkpoint").

How Much Is Too Much?

In "Fool for Love," Buffy barely survives a fight with an unremarkable vampire one night, during a routine cemetery patrol. The realization that she can be bested by a single, "ordinary" vampire makes Buffy newly aware of her mortality, of the fact that every Slayer eventually loses a battle, and she wants to learn more about those final battles so she can safeguard herself against past Slayers' mistakes: "I realize that every Slayer comes with an expiration mark on the package; but I want mine to be a long time from now. Like a Cheeto" ("Fool for Love"). In order to learn more, she pays a visit to Spike, a vampire who is known to have killed two Slayers in the past. In a series of flashbacks, Spike narrates these two battles to explain to Buffy how he bested the Slayers. This is where *Buffy* forcefully and successfully troubles postfeminism. The show takes pains to demonstrate that Buffy is in fact a postfeminist Slayer.

Spike's memories provide a truncated evolution of the Slayer. The first Slayer he killed was in China, during the Boxer Rebellion. She is grim and determined while Spike is grinning and laughing, enjoying a natural high from the fight. The Chinese Slayer is "all business," as Spike puts it, the prefeminist Slayer who follows the rules and fights with a strict discipline. She only speaks once, when she knows she has lost. The subtitles read, "Tell my mother I'm sorry," to which Spike responds, "Sorry, love—I don't speak Chinese," before letting her fall to the floor ("Fool for Love"). We are not given an explanation of the Slayer's message, but one reading is that she is apologizing for losing the fight, for failing to do her duty to rid the world of evil. "The first one was all business," Spike narrates, "the second—well, she had a touch of *your* style" ("Fool for Love"), signaling the dawn of a new era and a new kind of Slayer. Spike's memory reveals his fight with the second Slayer he killed, in a New York subway train in 1977. This Slayer, a single mother named Nikki Woods, is not at all like the Chinese Slayer. During the fight, Spike describes her as "cunning, resourceful, and ... hot" ("Fool for Love"). Nikki is clearly a 70s black feminist, with natural hair and a fierce attitude. Unlike the martial arts of the 1900s Slayer, Nikki is not bound by a formal fighting style. She kicks Spike in the groin, and some of her moves involve swinging around the poles in the aisle. She is dressed in street clothes, with a long leather jacket reminiscent of Samuel L. Jackson in *Shaft*. In fact, Nikki's style is such an inspiration to Spike that he steals her jacket after he kills her, which becomes his trademark look.

That Spike says Nikki had a "touch" of Buffy's style indicates that Buffy is the new and improved version of what came before. Buffy has perfected the modernized "resourcefulness" that Spike respected in Nikki. Buffy is known to slay vampires with wooden unicorns and signposts. She banters and flirts with her foes, proving that she is sexually appealing in addition to being a fierce fighter. Enemies often comment on Buffy's surprising well-roundedness. Spike, for example, when he first tries to kill Buffy in Season Two's "School Hard," is quite frustrated with Buffy's support system: "A Slayer with family and friends," he sighs, "that sure as Hell wasn't in the brochure" ("School Hard"). Buffy is unique because of her ties to her mother and sister as well as a close network of friends and fellow evil-fighters who have grown with her over the years. This was almost true about Nikki as well—but she prioritizes slaying over her son. Her mantra is "The mission comes first" ("Lies My Parents Told Me"). Buffy is unique because the Slayer is supposed to be alone, isolated and secretive, but she defies those expectations and somewhat balances her life. But, according to Spike, the aspiration for a multifaceted life is still a dangerous burden, and Buffy's social ties also present profound dilemmas.

Once present Spike reveals the secret he has learned about Slayers while past Spike is killing Nikki, it becomes clear that the Slayer has a history of wishing for release from her constant and extraordinary pressures: "Death is on your heels, baby, and sooner or later it's going to catch up with you. And part of you wants it. Not only to stop the fear and uncertainty, but because you're just a little bit in love with it. Death is your art ... part of you is desperate to know, what's it like? Where does it lead you? ... Every Slayer has a death wish. Even you" ("Fool for Love"). Buffy is fairly good at juggling her responsibilities until the end of Season Five, when her life begins to fall apart, therein illuminating the trap of the postfeminist narrative. First, in "The Body," her mother dies unexpectedly from complications of her surgery. Then the foes pile on: evil goddess Glory and a separate army of knights set on killing Dawn before Glory can get to her. Glory has horribly injured a member of Buffy's inner circle, who becomes a constant source of worry and grief. "It just keeps coming," Buffy says hopelessly, "Glory, Riley, Tara ... Mom"

("Spiral"). The episode is aptly titled "Spiral," because this is the time when the plot spirals out of Buffy's control. In one scene, Buffy is sword-fighting on top of the team's RV, killing knights (complete with chain mail and horses) until Giles is impaled by a spear while driving and the RV flips over. This literal spiraling is particularly ominous because the show has prompted viewers to wonder: how much heroic responsibility is too much? What happens if Buffy gets to that point? Season Five asks these questions, informed by Spike's troubling secret about the Slayer's death wish.

The end of Season Five makes it clear that death and rest is on Buffy's mind. While on the run, after some of her friends have been maimed, Dawn has been abducted by Glory, and she herself is still mourning the recent loss of her mother, Buffy falls into a catatonic stupor. The episode then reveals her secret fantasy of killing Dawn just so this endless chase will be over. Eventually, killing Dawn in order to stop Glory's destruction of the world becomes a very pragmatic plan. Buffy is forced to consider it, and she refuses even though she might be aiding in bringing about the apocalypse. The Buffy we see at the start of the Season Five finale is not the typical "Girl Power" Buffy who develops strategies or gathers weapons while spouting witty lines and joking with the gang. This time she is exhausted and disillusioned: "I sacrificed Angel [her first boyfriend] to save the world. I loved him so much. But I knew what was right. I don't have that anymore. I don't understand. I don't know how to live in this world if these are the choices. If everything just gets stripped away. I don't see the point. I just wish… I just wish my mom was here" ("The Gift"). In the end, Buffy's suicide is the perfect solution—she realizes that her body and Dawn's are interchangeable, that her own death is just as effective in saving the world as her sister's. The narrative also hints that this is the right answer because the spirit of the first Slayer once gave her a cryptic message: "Death is your gift" ("The Gift").

Jes Battis, in *Blood Relations: Chosen Families in Buffy the Vampire Slayer*, describes Buffy's self-sacrifice as "visibly selfish," because "[s]he is not acting in line with the Slayer's philosophy—indeed, she is acting precisely against it" (Battis 75). Battis is not truly condemning Buffy—he goes on to discuss how Buffy always breaks the rules, and how the characters' "selfishness" in caring more for each other than the world is ultimately what saves the world every season. Still, the notion of Buffy killing herself (instead of Dawn) being selfish is worth addressing. Buffy sacrifices herself because she cannot bear to lose Dawn—but I also believe she is ready to die. The "selfishness" Battis points out is not only selfishness in preserving her sister, who "represents everything that Buffy has lost—her freedom, her innocence, her childish wonder, her fear of the supernatural, her chance for a normal life and most acutely, her connection with Joyce" (Battis 76), but also the selfishness of wanting to quit. But what if this were an understandable decision? What if

Buffy deserves to quit? The first Slayer says, "Death is your gift." The immediate understanding is that death is her gift to the world, because Buffy saves it by ending her life. But what if it also means that death is a gift *to* Buffy? She protects her sister one last time before finally resting. She looks past Dawn, beyond the ledge they are standing on, and the sun is rising. She runs and leaps from the edge, the music swells, and her friends cry, but they are all safe. Buffy's body looks peaceful. Her tombstone reads, "She Saved the World a Lot"—a fitting line for a protagonist who has reasonably done enough.

To be clear, this is not to say that death is a reward; rather, it is a release. Sara Crosby in "The Cruelest Season: Female Heroes Snapped into Sacrificial Heroines" points out that Buffy's suicide was actually part of a concerning phenomenon on prime time television that Spring (2001); Crosby observed (through simultaneously airing seasons of *Dark Angel*, *Xena: Warrior Princess*, and *Buffy*) that "in one brief, bloody Spring, American television orchestrated the suicides of almost its entire cast of tough, heroic female leads" (Crosby 153). She explores possible readings of the self-sacrifices and pushes back against one notion that this is the ultimate act against the patriarchy, a way for the female protagonists to escape from and outstrip the men who once controlled them. Crosby says this reading fails because the female heroes' "guilt, abject self-hatred, and regressive sacrifice to the needs of a patriarchal community undercut the rhetorical posture of feminist transcendence" (Crosby 154). Guilt and self-hatred are prominent themes at the end of Season Five, because Buffy is tormented by her inability to beat Glory and her secret desire to let Glory win. The Slayer is supposed to live and die in service to the world. The self-sacrifice is practically part of the job description, so Buffy's death should not be read as progressive. However, Buffy's death is significant in that she is able to experience having, at last, finished saving the world: "The phallic authority, which *Buffy's* male heroes wield with aplomb, wears heavily on Buffy, wears her out; so when in 2001 she finds herself faced with the sacrificial moment (her life or her sister's and the world's), she releases her friends and embraces her death with relief" (Crosby 164).

Post-Death Postfeminism

When Buffy comes back to life the following fall, things are wrong from the beginning. Female heroes are "conventionally beautiful, glamorous, and sexualized" (Brown 7) and Buffy is usually no exception. But Buffy's resurrection in "Bargaining" is anything but beautiful. The ritual involved is horrific, and includes slaughtering a fawn and vomiting a giant snake (all orchestrated by Buffy's best friend, Willow). When we first see Buffy, she is still buried—a rotted corpse in a coffin. She is unrecognizable and grotesque, with wisps of hair stuck to a leathery skull. When the magic touches the body the rotten limbs gradually fill out, her eyes grow back in a rush, and the last image before the credits is of her buried alive, confused and unable to breathe.

Aside from the trauma of clawing out of her own grave, Buffy's sister and friends cannot quite understand why she is not "herself." She behaves oddly, woodenly; she rarely smiles. Willow's rationale is that while Buffy was dead, she was trapped and tormented in a Hellish dimension, which is why they had to rescue her, and why she is having trouble adjusting. Tired of the pressure to be full of cheer and gratitude and prove she is not insane or somewhat zombie-like, Buffy delivers a toneless speech to appease them all: "You brought me back. I was in... I was in Hell. I can't think too much about what it was like, but it felt like the world abandoned me there, and then suddenly you guys did what you did.... And the world came rushing back. Thank you" ("After Life"). Everyone is happy to hear this; they shuffle into a group hug. Ironically, the happy news would be that Buffy spent her afterlife writhing in Hell, and the horrifying truth, which she reveals moments later to Spike, is that she lied about her misery: "I was happy.... And I was warm. And I was loved. And I was finished. Complete.... I think I was in Heaven. And now I'm not. I was torn out of there; pulled out by my friends. Everything here is hard, and bright, and violent.... This is Hell—just getting through the next moment, and the one after that, knowing what I've lost" ("After Life"). Not only was Buffy happy being dead, but she resents her friends for bringing her back. Brown warns us that the new female action hero, in control of her desires, is still underdeveloped: "the close association of these heroines with Girl Power rhetoric means that what exactly she knows 'she wants' needs to be better understood" (Brown 149). But the tension in Season Six is about what Buffy is *not allowed* to want. She is not supposed to desire death—that is not a heroic desire, not a postfeminist desire, not one that her friends (so desperate to know that she suffered in Hell) are willing to hear. Once the secret is out, Xander (Buffy's other best friend), articulates this confusion with his signature sense of humor: "maybe we were [selfish]. I just feel weird feeling bad that my friend's not dead—it's too mind-boggling. So I've decided to simplify the whole thing: Me like Buffy. Buffy's alive, so me glad" ("Tabula Rosa").

There is also a metatextual discussion happening: the question is not only is it right to bring Buffy back, but is it right to bring *Buffy* back? The finale of Season Five, when Buffy dies, was almost the series finale. The creators were not sure that *Buffy* would be taken up by another network after it was dropped by the WB network. Joss Whedon says of this episode, "I wanted to kill Buffy at the end of season five. I think originally I had thought about the idea of ending the series then, and I wanted to make that day truly different and sum up the whole series. That's why 'The Gift' begins with a very generic vampire killing" (Season 5 DVD featurette). To some extent, the audience is as responsible for bringing Buffy back as are her friends. Our protagonist, then, has *two* inconceivable desires: not wanting to be alive again and not wanting the show to continue on.

Buffy's depression is often cast as an obstacle that Buffy needs to move past. In "Normal Again," Buffy experiences magic-induced hallucinations wherein she is a normal girl who has been in an insane asylum for the past five years because she thinks she kills monsters in a fictional town. This is a tragic episode because Buffy's deepest wish to be done with living her Slayer life is made tantalizingly real, and she is shown a world where her mother is alive, a world she does not have to save again and again. In *Buffy and the Heroine's Journey: Vampire Slayer as Feminine Chosen One*, Valerie Estelle Frankel takes the common depression-as-obstacle route to illustrate what is at stake in this episode: "In that other world she has no responsibilities, no awful job or house payments, no Dawn.... This infantilism is a sign of immaturity, a final temptation Buffy must leave behind" (Frankel 167). What Frankel does not mention is the haunting note that "Normal Again" ends on: an ambiguity that destabilizes which world is the "real" one and thereby calls into question what the show and the audience are asking of Buffy by returning her to Sunnydale. Deepening Buffy's anguish at being brought back from a place of peace "infantile" is problematic. From the moment she returns, she is forced to be the Slayer. She comes out of her coffin to find the neighborhood in utter chaos: demons are ransacking the houses and stores, and her gang of evil-fighting friends has become completely inept at fighting them off. Still in shock, Buffy has to kill or chase away the demons. In following episodes, she is told that she is in debt, that she needs to pay for the house, that Dawn needs to be looked after, that maybe she should go back to school, and that she needs a loan and a job. Buffy, Willow, and Willow's girlfriend Tara live together, and yet all of the responsibility falls solely on Buffy's shoulders. Why should Buffy, the recently dead girl, save and take care of everyone?

In some respects, Buffy's life is daunting and unreasonable, and this is made clear when she transfers this ominous weight to Dawn. Crosby has a useful insight into Buffy's death scene, in which she gives Dawn a last loving message and tells Dawn to carry on in her footsteps: "In actuality, Buffy's final exhortation tells Dawn that she should live not for herself but for someone else, dooming her to the sacrificial heroine cycle. Buffy wills her younger sister a 'strong' and 'brave' heritage of misery and self-abnegation cloaked in a life-affirming statement" (Crosby 164). Buffy hints at the crushing responsibility she is finally free of in her last words to Dawn: "You have to take care of them now.... The hardest thing in this world is to live in it. Be brave" ("The Gift"). With this in mind, one can just as easily argue that Buffy's resurrection and her resultant depression point to her *friends'* infantilism. Everyone wants Buffy to "move on," but that is just it—she did. She was dead. Buffy's depression is striking because it is so unnatural in a postfeminist protagonist. That Buffy, a typically blonde, beautiful, bubbly girl action hero is tormented for an entire season by a desire to be dead again is unusually troubling. Considering the repetitive horrors of Buffy's life as a Slayer, why *should* she want to come back? Postfeminism decrees that women can do it all. As *Buffy* demonstrates, however, doing "it all" will drive them insane. In "Mass Magazine Cover Girls: Some Reflections on Postfeminist Girls and Postfeminsm's Daughters," Sarah Projansky points out that "postfeminism is by definition contradictory, simultaneously feminist and antifeminist, liberating and repressive, productive and obstructive of progressive social change" (Projansky 68). Buffy is being silenced by this postfeminist attitude: she cannot complain because wanting to be dead is unacceptable. A female protagonist who does not have a voice, who is not *allowed* to be miserable, is not truly feminist or progressive.

Death Is Still a Gift

Buffy does eventually emerge from her depression. She literally crawls out of a grave at the end of Season Six, with Dawn at her side, at the beginning of a new day. The scene seems to suggest that Buffy no longer has qualms about being the postfeminist Slayer and protagonist. Rather than accepting her postfeminist burden, however, Buffy ultimately seeks to end the "heritage of misery and self-abnegation" that comes with being the female hero (Crosby 164). Season Seven's "Get It Done" reveals that the legacy of the Slayer is deeply troubling and shows Buffy refusing to meet impossible expectations. In this season, not only is Buffy looking after her friends, but also a swarm of young women from around the world, "potential Slayers" who are being targeted by an evil force who wants to end the Slayer line. Finally, after the struggle of Seasons Five and Six, Buffy has had enough of everyone's dead weight: "I've been carrying you, all of you, too far, too long. Ride's over.... Be as scared as you like, just be useful while you're at it" ("Get It Done"). The misery of Season Six is constructive: being forced back into the world by friends who would not let her go pushes Buffy to demand that everyone else take initiative. She forces them to handle powerful magic and demon-fighting while she goes into a portal to learn the truth about the first Slayer.

The Slayer has such a bleak origin that it forcefully calls into question whether there should by a Slayer at all: "First there was the earth.... Then there came the demons. After demons there came men. Men found a girl, they took the girl to fight the demon—all demons. They chained her to the earth" ("Get It Done"). A girl is shown with a chain around her neck that connects to the ground, backing away in terror from a monster while a group of men jeer and shake their staffs from a safe distance. When Buffy enters the portal, she comes to truly understand the legend: the men who became the Watchers made the first Slayer by chaining her to the ground and injecting her with demonic energy. What ensues is something like a mythical-rape attempt until Buffy puts a stop to it. The demonic energy, an amorphous black substance, forces its way into her ears, eyes and mouth, and twists around her legs. "It must become one with you," the first Watchers say ("Get It Done"). Buffy rejects the power they are offering: "You think I came all this way to get knocked up by some demon dust? … you're just men. Just the men who did this. To her. Whoever that girl was before she was the first Slayer…. You violated that girl. Made her kill for you because you're weak, you're pathetic, and you obviously have nothing to show me" ("Get It Done"). The Slayer's history is ghastly exploitation. The Slayer is forced to live a short life of violence and loneliness and pain, to fight endless battles because the men are afraid to. The first Watchers took a powerless girl and forced power into her, yet still expected her to submit to their will. She is normally required to work alone, to stay a secret, to be subjected to cruel and life-threatening tests orchestrated by the Watcher's Council. With extreme unease, in this episode the show and the audience slowly approach the question: what is *Buffy the Vampire Slayer* really about?

Buffy herself redeems the concept of the Slayer. She is done with the repetitiveness of being called again and again to do it all. She ultimately breaks the most important rule at the end of the series: the Slayer is supposed to be alone. Only one girl can have the power, one girl who is checked not only by the Watcher's Council, but by her short lifespan. In the series finale "Chosen," Buffy shares her strength with every potential Slayer in the world, which means hundreds and possibly thousands of women and girls now have the power she has. "In every generation one Slayer is born," Buffy orates, "because a bunch of men who died thousands of years ago made up that rule…. I say we change the rule. I say my power should be *our* power" ("Chosen"). Buffy not only ends the haunting, oppressive legacy of the Slayer, but also the series in its current form. She destroys the expectation of the one girl who must do everything. "You're not the one and only Chosen anymore," someone points out, "you just gotta live like a person. How does that feel?" ("Chosen"). Buffy merely smiles; she is glad to be in some ways at an end and in some ways at a beginning. Buffy's death, resurrection, and depression should not be dismissed as a metaphor for the challenges of growing up. Her desire to die jolts her viewers out of complacency with the depiction of a female protagonist who is relentlessly cheerful and can-do despite all of the hardships and abuses she must endure, as someone who is clearly free of patriarchy and so blessed with the legacy of feminism that she can easily achieve the superhuman.

"The Slayer" has ended—and it is about time.

WORKS CITED

Battis, Jes. *Blood Relations: Chosen Families in Buffy, the Vampire Slayer and Angel*. McFarland, 2005.

Brown, Jeffrey A. *Dangerous Curves: Action Heroines, Gender, Fetishism, and Popular Culture*. University Press of Mississippi, 2011.

Buffy the Vampire Slayer: The Complete First Season, created by Joss Whedon, Twentieth Century–Fox Home Entertainment, 2001.

Buffy the Vampire Slayer: The Complete Second Season, created by Joss Whedon, Twentieth Century–Fox Home Entertainment, 2002.

Buffy, the Vampire Slayer: The Complete Third Season, created by Joss Whedon, Twentieth Century–Fox Home Entertainment, 2003.

Buffy, the Vampire Slayer: The Complete Fourth Season, created by Joss Whedon, Twentieth Century–Fox, 2003.

Buffy the Vampire Slayer: The Complete Fifth Season, created by Joss Whedon, Twentieth Century–Fox, 2003.

Buffy the Vampire Slayer: The Complete Sixth Season, created by Joss Whedon, Twentieth Century–Fox, 2003.

Buffy the Vampire Slayer: The Complete Seventh Season, created by Joss Whedon, Twentieth Century–Fox, 2004.

Crosby, Sara. "The Cruelest Season: Female Heroes Snapped into Sacrificial Heroines." *Action Chicks: New Images of Tough Women in Popular Culture*. Edited by Sherrie A. Inness, Palgrave Macmillan, 2004, pp. 153–180.

Frankel, Valerie Estelle. *Buffy and the Heroine's Journey: Vampire Slayer as Feminine Chosen One*. McFarland, 2012.

Inness, Sherrie A. *Tough Girls: Women Warriors and Wonder Women in Popular Culture*. University of Pennsylvania Press, 1999.

Lavery, David. Foreword. *Buffy Goes Dark: Essays on the Final Two Seasons of* Buffy the Vampire Slayer *On Television*. Edited by Lynne Y. Edwards, Elizabeth L. Rambo and James B. South. McFarland, 2009.

McRobbie, Angela. "Postfeminism and Popular Culture: Bridget Jones and the New Gender Regime." *Interrogating Postfeminism: Gender and the Politics of Popular Culture*. Edited by Yvonne Tasker and Diane Negra. Duke University Press, 2007, pp. 27–39.

II.

Evolving Femininity

Girl Rebooted

Transforming Doctor Who's Sarah Jane Smith from Sidekick to Hero

SHEILA SANDAPEN

Introduction

The BBC television show *Doctor Who* has been around for more than 50 years, and the Time Lord who travels through time and space is both a fixture in popular culture and the basis of a highly successful franchise. The series spawned countless novelizations, radio plays, multiple animated series and comic books. In the 1980s, a spinoff called *K-9 and Company* was proposed. *K-9 and Company,* which ultimately failed to launch, would have featured two former companions of the Doctor: Sarah Jane Smith, played by Elisabeth Sladen, and the robot dog K-9. The first successful *Doctor Who* spinoff was the show *Torchwood,* which was produced between 2006 and 2011. Not to be deterred, Elisabeth Sladen attempted her second spinoff and fared much better with *The Sarah Jane Adventures,* which aired from 2007 to 2011. In some ways, with its emphasis on connecting to children, *The Sarah Jane Adventures* was more closely linked to the original spirit of the *Doctor Who* series, but in other ways the show broke new ground by providing viewers with a strong female heroine for the *Doctor Who* universe.

What Came Before

First broadcast in 1963 on the BBC, the science fiction television show *Doctor Who* started out as a half-hour show aimed squarely at children. It was originally shown in black and white, converting to color in 1970. Adventures with the First Doctor (William Hartnell) had several historical overtones such as the 1965 serial, a multi-episode self-contained story arc, in which the Doctor and his companions land in Rome during Nero's reign and must learn how to live in the ancient city. The First Doctor, an irascible old man, was introduced when travelling with a young woman named Susan who called him "Grandfather." Eventually he took on human companions Ian and Barbara, teachers from Susan's school. The Doctor may have been old, but he was not mortal and did not experience death in the same way as humans. Instead, the character regenerated into another form that had a distinct voice, face and personality (i.e., another actor) but still retained the memories of the previous Doctor(s).

Although the Doctor changed his face and each of his companions left him, the show was still at heart a child's show. By the 1970s, however, there were some television critics who questioned whether *Doctor Who* truly was children's programming. In a 2014 article that appeared in the *Telegraph*, Michael Hogan asked whether *Doctor Who* had become too frightening. He reminds us:

> In the Seventies, Mary Whitehouse was wailing her familiar cry, 'Won't someone please think of the children?' The mid–Eighties Colin Baker [who played the sixth Doctor] period was criticised for being too violent. Such storms in teacups have happened at regular intervals in Who's 51-year history. Almost as often, it's been said the show's not scary enough and become too cute, cuddly and toy-driven.

Hogan goes on to note that children like being scared when it is in a safe environment, i.e., hiding behind the couch in the safety of their own living rooms. Furthermore, as Hogan explains, Philip Hinchcliffe, who produced the show between 1974 and 1977, was renowned for "being darkly Gothic and creating downright terrifying episodes" and was clearly an influence on the show's current creators. One of the things to note about the series from 1963 through 1989 is that the show didn't have a very large budget and the special effects were, by today's standard, subpar at best. Perhaps this is why the show was considered to be more of a child's show.

Doctor Who went off the air in 1989 during the run of the Seventh Doctor. In 1996, American broadcasting studios Universal Pictures and 20th century Fox Television attempted to resurrect the show by producing a film featuring the Eighth Doctor, played by Paul McGann. That attempt was unsuccessful. Sixteen years later, *Doctor Who* was given new life when the show was re-booted in 2005. The "new" *Doctor Who* was re-imagined as an hour-long series starring Christopher Eccleston as the Ninth Doctor. The Ninth Doctor in the new Season One is portrayed as a dark, tortured soul who is brought back from his darkness by his female (human) companion, who ultimately falls in love with him. His successor, the Tenth Doctor, played by David Tennant, also has romantic woes. The one-hour standalone episodes of the new series are filled with special effects and are no longer touted as a children's show, although certainly children still watch, mainly because the show's plots are very complex and the action is geared more to adults. The four- to six-part multiple stories that made up the "serials" or story arcs of classic *Doctor Who* are no longer. These serials were usually standalone stories that featured the characters in unrelated adventures. Now, story arcs can take up the whole season, which can lead to loose threads and sloppy connections. The show has gone from being good fun to being dramatic, brooding, dark and sometimes just a bit overcomplicated.

Despite the increased complexity, the "new" Doctor is now written by adults who were and are fans of the original, and thus they continue some of the established tropes of old. As before, the Doctor doesn't die but regenerates into a new version of himself portrayed by a different actor. As of 2017, there are twelve Doctors in total, including Paul McGann, whose status was unclear until he returned to the new series for "The Night of the Doctor," a webcast mini-episode in 2013. "The Night of the Doctor" also introduced the War Doctor (John Hurt), who is not numbered because he was a regeneration of the Doctor who didn't use the title "Doctor." Explains Steven Moffat, the current showrunner for *Doctor Who,*

> I've been really, really quite careful about the numbering of the Doctors…. He's very specific, the John Hurt Doctor, that he doesn't take the name of the Doctor. He doesn't call himself that. He's the same Time Lord, the same being as the Doctors either side of him, but he's the one who says, 'I'm not the Doctor.' So the Eleventh Doctor is still the Eleventh Doctor, the Tenth Doctor is still the Tenth… ["Steven Moffat Clears Up Confusion"].

Thus, Matt Smith, who succeeds David Tennant, is considered the Eleventh Doctor, and Peter Capaldi is the Twelfth. Jodie Whittaker, who currently portrays the first female Doctor, is the Thirteenth.

Something About Sarah Jane

Sarah Jane Smith is consistently voted as one of the most popular of the Doctor's companions. As portrayed by Sladen, Sarah Jane Smith has the further honor of being one of the longest non-continuous companions in the *Doctor Who* universe. She is surpassed in that only by Jo Grant (Katy Manning), who left the show in 1971 and guest appeared on *The Sarah Jane Adventures* in 2010. Other characters from *Doctor Who* have similarly long tenures. For example, the Master, a fellow Time Lord and "arch nemesis" of the Doctor was first introduced in 1971 and most recently appeared as Missy (having

changed gender) on *Doctor Who* in 2016. The Brigadier first appeared alongside the Second Doctor in 1968, and in 2014 he, in Cyberman form, helped
the Doctor avert a crisis on earth. While Sarah Jane is not the only long-
running character on *Doctor Who*, she is the only one who gets her own
show. Thirty years after Sarah Jane stopped travelling with the Doctor, she
returned to his universe and was ultimately awarded her own series, which
was marketed as a *Doctor Who* spinoff aimed at children. In *The Language of
Doctor Who,* Jason Barr and Camille D.G. Mustachio remind us that "Sarah
Jane Smith (Elisabeth Sladen) bridges the divide between classic and new
Who by her established relationship with the Doctor in two iterations, The
Third Doctor (Jon Pertwee) and Fourth Doctor (Tom Baker), before reuniting
with him as the Tenth Doctor (David Tennant)" (ix). She then trod new
ground when she continued her work without the Doctor in *The Sarah Jane
Adventures*. The idea of the show being aimed at children tends to make it
underappreciated by adult *Doctor Who* fans and academics, but the show
consistently earned high ratings while it aired ("The Sarah Jane Adventures
Ratings").

Those who did watch the show began to realize it had carved its own
niche within the *Doctor Who* universe. One blogger comments on the impact
of *The Sarah Jane Adventures*:

> While I knew I was going to enjoy the Sarah Jane Adventures when I first saw the
> pilot, I had no idea the profound impact it would have on me. [...] While Sarah Jane
> Adventures may be a kid's show, by no means is it child's play. It tackles heavy issues
> such as absentee parents, racism, divorce and does so without talking down to chil-
> dren. It's also one of the most progressive television shows on the air. The lead char-
> acter is a fleshed-out extraordinary heroine with a diverse cast where the POCs
> actually outnumber the white cast members 4–2. And the POCs have prominent
> leading roles and did I mention the show was a hit! [Drupkins].

This blogger has it exactly right: Sarah Jane Smith, Luke and Maria are white,
but Clyde and Rani are people of color. When compared to *Doctor Who*, *The
Sarah Jane Adventures* more accurately reflects the demographics of London
and the experiences of the children watching the show. Sarah Jane's world is
a lot more colorful than the universe The Doctor typically inhabits, although
Doctor Who does have storylines in which alien races, such as the Ood, sym-
bolize minorities. For these reasons and more, the show was a success and
in 2010 received the Royal Television Society award for Best Children's Drama.

The Sarah Jane Adventures found an audience of people who enjoyed
the show for what it was. A sampling of viewer responses on Amazon.com
USA show that for every viewer like S. Jones, who in 2008 dismissed the
show ("As an adult viewer, there is much here to make you cringe. Occasionally, the series will throw you a bone, but for the most part, it's a hyperactive
little affair"), there were scores of other reviewers who loved the show for its

entertainment value and even, like the reviewer Kimberley, applauded the fact that the main character was a middle aged woman: "something not seen in science fiction." This latter comment reinforces Damien Walters' comment, "There's a huge audience of people who love science fiction, but do not see themselves reflected in white male faces that dominate it today." J. Rosenberg, another Amazon reviewer, even noted on the second season of *Sarah Jane Adventures* "the writing and acting on all levels has reached a level of smooth confidence in collaboration that's a wonder to behold in a half-hour kids' show." The same reviewer continued with praise for both the series and its star:

> It's great to see the show developing its own internal mythology, a scrappy subset of the larger Doctor Who universe. Lis Sladen must thank her lucky stars and Russell Davies every day for the opportunity of this great later-career resurgence. It has given her a chance to demonstrate that she's a stronger, more deeply-felt actress than she was in the '70s; she takes what these talented writers and co-stars toss her and consistently hits it out of the park....

The Sarah Jane Adventures hasn't reached cult status to the same degree as *Doctor Who* and *Torchwood*, but it is a good show. Most academic studies, however, tend to bypass the show or focus on Sarah Jane as a middle-aged character. By and large, these existing studies fail to appreciate how the character has come into her own, moving beyond a former companion who is "waiting" for the Doctor to return and becoming a bona fide heroine.

As previously documented, *The Sarah Jane Adventures* is the second spin off of *Doctor Who* that Elisabeth Sladen was involved in. The show resumes some thirty years after Sarah stopped being a companion, although not very long after she meets up with the Doctor again (as played by David Tennant) in the 2006 episode "School Reunion." In *The Sarah Jane Adventures*, Sarah Jane is a freelance journalist who lives in a large house on Bannerman Road in London. Both her profession and her location, not to mention her past experience traveling with the Doctor, make her more than equipped to identify and deal with potential alien threats. She lives in a large house, drives a limited-edition car (the Retro Nissan Figaro in emerald green) and answers to no one. Apparently, the aunt who raised her left her some money. At its core, the show is about how Sara Jane befriends some of the teenagers on her block and how together they fight aliens.

In the first episode, "Invasion of the Bane," Sarah Jane and her teenage neighbor Maria come to realize that the Bane are marketing a soft drink that is preparing the Earth's population for invasion, as well as collecting human DNA. They team up to save the world. In the process, Sarah Jane discovers an abandoned boy that the Bane have created, the "Archetype," who is an amalgamation of the DNA collected. Sarah Jane adopts him and names him Luke. Luke is a human child, highly intelligent, and "evolved." Thus, in the first episode, Sarah Jane goes from being a person who kept away from her neighbors to a friend and mother.

Without a doubt, the Sarah Jane Smith who appears in the show was, as viewers noted, very different from her earlier incarnation. In some ways, Sarah Jane's transformation echoes the very real transformation that any person goes through as they age, from callow youth to some kind of maturity in middle age. However, there are other factors that have shaped how Sarah Jane is written: our concept of what it means to be a hero and the long-term effects of feminism.

The Girl Who Asked Questions

London. England. The 1970s. The memory of the British Empire on which the sun never set is still a living, viable one. In 1973, Sarah Jane Smith enters the *Doctor Who* universe. She is a journalist who, while investigating a case concerning a missing scientist, encounters the Third Doctor (Jon Pertwee) and finds him suspicious. She ends up stowing away on the Doctor's star ship (aka TARDIS), where she finds herself in the 13th century. It is the start of a beautiful friendship.

Initially, Sarah Jane Smith is determined to prove her journalist training: she asks questions and has the ability to hear the answers and learn from them. Further, she demonstrates an ability to wrap her mind around some the concepts to which the Doctor exposes her, as evidenced by this exchange between her and the Third Doctor in the second episode of the Season 11 serial called "Planet of the Spiders":

> SARAH JANE: You know, this is barmy. Here we are calmly discussing happiness, planets with blue moons, giant spiders, magic crystals as if I was talking about … umm … pussycats, fish and chips and the Liverpool docks.
> DOCTOR WHO: Well, they're just as real.
> SARAH JANE: Oh, I know. That's what gets me.

What is fascinating about Sarah Jane as written in this episode, is that she is undeniably a "new woman"—she works as a journalist, a job that was traditionally a man's, and exudes confidence and competence, but she is not strident, nor does she seem unfeminine. She is the ideal companion, autonomous but not managing. She is open to new possibilities—i.e., new worlds and alien species—in the same ways British society seemed opened to the idea of feminism, which must have struck some as an equally barmy idea. This Sarah Jane is very human and stands in for us the viewer, she asks the questions that help us, the viewer, connect to the story. We relate because we can relate to Sarah Jane, and we accept her voyages as being within the realm of possibility. Thirty years after she debuted the character, *The Telegraph* praised

Sladen, an actress trained in theater, for developing Sarah Jane as "an independent-minded journalist, giv[ing] the two-dimensional role a hint of depth" (Hogan). However, Hannah Hamad points out that Sarah Jane's brand of feminism was sometimes "nominal" ("A Tear"). Perhaps both have it right. Sarah Jane was a feminist, but the show limited her role so she became nominal. However, with the passage of time, the character was able to show how she had moved forward and what her brand of feminism looked like.

The sense that viewers get of this early incarnation of Sarah Jane is that she has a voice and is unafraid of speaking up—indeed, she is paid to ask questions. She stands in for the viewers, to some extent, when she questions the Doctor and his intentions. However, this side of Sarah Jane is muted as the show progresses. When the Third Doctor regenerates, Sarah Jane remains with the Fourth Doctor (now the actor Tom Baker), but it is evident that her character is rewritten to be a little less forward-thinking and perhaps not on par intellectually with the "new" Doctor. This is clearly established in the Fourth Doctor's and Sarah Jane's first adventure together in the Season 12 serial "The Ark in Space." In Episode 1 of "The Ark in Space," the Fourth Doctor takes Sarah Jane and Harry Sullivan (played by Ian Marter) along. When they arrive at their destination, the Doctor notes, "Yes, almost certainly we're inside some kind of artificial satellite. Now, isn't that interesting?" which is typical of *his* wonder at the universe, to which Sarah Jane replies, "Not very." The Doctor, as usual, is intrigued by the puzzle; Sarah Jane is more concerned with the fact there is limited oxygen. She, unlike the Doctor, needs oxygen to survive, but she is here characterized as a creature that fails to appreciate the larger picture, which is a contradiction of her original personality. This characterization sets the tone for rest of the series, which places a premium on more "action" in the plots.

In a later interview, Elisabeth Sladen recalled of her character, "Sarah had to be able to stick up for herself. She was pretty forceful, especially at first, and then we allowed her to soften and adapt more to the circumstances she was living in. Sarah was not only feminist, she was feminine—a rather happy, forthright girl with a lot of intelligence, and plenty of courage" ("Elisabeth Sladen 1980's"). This "softening" of Sarah Jane seemed to involve her becoming a damsel in distress in which she screamed. A lot. It is also reflective of 1970s British society, which continued to advertise jobs by gender, made no bones about the fact that females were paid less than men, and for which the concept of "sexual harassment" was not yet part of the lexicon. Conversely, this is also the era in which Oxford University opened five of its all male colleges to women, Gloria Steinem published *MS* magazine in the U.S., and her British counterparts Rosie Boycott and Marsha Rowe published *Spare Rib* in the U.K. Could the plucky Sarah Jane be experiencing a backlash against pushy women who seemed to be cropping up everywhere?

It is perhaps significant that the vocal Sarah Jane, who is not afraid to ask searching questions, loses her voice in "The Ark in Space." She tries to talk to the Doctor, but he tells her to wait a minute. She then, childishly, makes a face at him. She spends part of the serial either unconscious or in a state of suspended animation. When she is awake, Sarah Jane seems to be one step behind Harry and the Doctor. In Episode 2, for example, the Doctor realizes the larvae of an alien species named the Wirm has hatched and exclaims, "It's escaped! We're too late." Sarah Jane, bewildered, responds, "What's escaped?" It is a question that goes unanswered. The transformation is complete; Sarah Jane has been regaled to sidekick, and not a very smart one at that. The Sarah Jane who was on par with the Third Doctor is clearly absent. In another interview on her iconic character, Sladen disclosed that she felt "very excluded" in the changeover between Doctors because Tom Baker (the Fourth Doctor) and Ian Marter (Harry Sullivan) got along so well and the viewer can pick up on this. While Sarah Jane Smith might still be the conduit between the alien Doctor and the viewer, her role is less crucial and sets up a trope of how women have typically been portrayed in science fiction: pretty, but not necessary.

Sarah Jane, Feminism and Society

The allure of science fiction is that we can imagine and re-imagine worlds that offer countless possibilities. These boundless possibilities, however, are limited by our collective imagination. In *Doctor Who*, Sarah Jane, an initially powerful woman, descends into a slightly hysterical woman who needs reassurance from the authority figure. This transformation, while disturbing, is not particularly surprising and is in keeping with cultural critics such as Seo-Young Chu, who have noted that the nature of science fiction is less about exploring an alternative past or a possible future than it is about an investigation of the viewers' or readers' present conditions. In 1974, Sarah Jane Smith was a threat. If she was capable of asking questions and obtaining answers, then why did she need the Doctor (a man)? Increasingly dissatisfied with the limits of her role, Sladen later commented, "Sarah Jane used to be a bit of a cardboard cut-out. Each week it used to be, 'Yes Doctor, no Doctor,' and you had to flesh your character out in your mind—because if you didn't, no one else would" ("Dr. Who's 'Cut Out' Girl"). Perhaps this de-evolution in her character had to do with poor writing or a lack of imagination. More generously, one could argue in the early Sarah Jane we see a character that suddenly finds herself encountering out-of-this-world villains and locales, and, echoing the viewers' fears, she cries out and seeks assurance from the Doctor. Maybe this accounts for why Sarah Jane Smith consistently places high in the polls for favorite companion: she is the one the audience can identify with the most.

By 1976, Sladen was ready to move on. Years after the fact, Sladen mused about her departure from the show:

> Originally I'd planned one year. That became two, then three. I got a great deal of satisfaction from making Sarah Jane what she was. Even so, there were boundaries that couldn't be crossed and I felt I'd really done my best, had my day, and should hand over to somebody else. I felt regret, of course, but I was happy that it was I who took the initiative, and not somebody giving me a quiet push—in fact, they asked me how I should go out and I said make it quiet, not over-dramatic ["Elisabeth Sladen 1980's"].

In 1976, when Sladen was asked about how she was going to leave, she showed some of the same spirit that made Sarah Jane so popular: "I hope it will be imaginative. I hope they don't just marry me off, unless they marry me off to a monster which would be a call for something different" (Elisabeth Sladen 1976"). Sladen's fear that she would be married off is valid. The first companion to the Doctor, Susan, played by Carole Ann Ford, was married off to a freedom fighter on an earth that had been almost destroyed by the Daleks. Sarah Jane's immediate predecessor Jo Grant (played by Katy Manning) traveled with the Third Doctor, Jon Pertwee, before meeting and marrying Professor Clifford Jones (played by Stewart Bevan). The companion after Sarah, Leela (played by Louise Jameson) also exits the show by meeting a man. In her final adventure with the Doctor, Leela travels to his home planet of Gallifrey and meets Andred, with whom she decides to stay. The trend of marrying off companions and giving them a happy ending continues into the rebooted series; companions Rose Tyler, Martha Jones, Donna Noble, and Amy Pond are all shown in romantic relationships after (and often as a result of) ending their travels with the Doctor.

Sarah Jane Takes Action

Thirty years after her first appearance as a companion, Sarah Jane returns in the rebooted *Doctor Who* episode "School Reunion" and encounters the Tenth Doctor (played by David Tennant). She is introduced to him as John Smith; he knows her instantly but she doesn't recognize him. Later, when she uncovers the mystery, this exchange occurs:

> SARAH JANE: It's you. Doctor. Oh my God, it's you, isn't it? You've regenerated....
>   What are you doing here?
> THE DOCTOR: Well, UFO sightings, school gets record results. I couldn't resist.
>   What about you?
> SARAH JANE: Same.
> They laugh.

"School Reunion" is the first time we discover on screen what has happened to a companion, and it is gratifying to know that the screaming, ineffectual Sarah Jane has grown into an inquiring and powerful person who, like the Doctor, seeks the answers to intriguing questions. While there have been plenty of audio plays, graphic novels, and a few retrospective episodes that provide continuation of stories for the companions, the 2005 episode "School Reunion" was the first to revisit a companion on screen within a *Doctor Who* storyline. Sladen recalls how she came on board:

> I got there and they [lead writer Russell T. Davies and producer Phil Collinson] started to talk about the character and what they thought about the character and where she would actually be now, so many years later. A scene had already been written and all of a sudden I realised this would be an episode where I'd have an integral part so we ordered more wine, became a very rowdy table, and I said, "Yes, ok" [Barber].

While the appearance of Sarah Jane and K-9, her metal dog, was a nod to connections between the "original" and the "new" Doctors, it is clear there is some subtext to Sarah Jane's appearance. On one level, it is a sop to longtime fans of the show and a reconnection between the old and the new, but it also allows for fresh drama in the *Doctor Who* universe. Ross P. Garner characterizes the format of the *Doctor Who* and later *Sarah Jane Adventures* as science fiction, adventure and soap drama (164, 169). He stresses the binary element at the heart of the relationships between the Doctor and his companions; he is an alien, they are human. Sarah Jane is indeed human, and this is more evident than ever in "School Reunion." Sarah Jane is visibly older than the actor playing the new incarnation of the Doctor, but she has aged in other, more important ways as well. Her character appears to be centered and secure in her place in the universe and no longer needs the Doctor to tell her what to do. She might have waited for the Doctor to return for her, but ultimately she moved on. She established her career and supported herself. While we don't know much about what Sarah Jane Smith has been doing since she separated from the Doctor, we do know she is not retiring in either disposition or life. She is a working journalist who has used the knowledge she has of other worlds and potential alien threats to fight back, and she is not waiting for anyone to rescue her. She is clearly one of the good guys.

At the end of "School Reunion," the Doctor asks Sarah Jane to travel with him and his current companion, and she turns him down. She is not interested in retreading old paths. She has worked to establish a life and career and is no longer interested in being a sidekick. Despite not continuing on as a companion, Sarah Jane's resurrection was so popular and so full of storytelling possibilities that she was given her own show a year later: *The Sarah Jane Adventures* (2007–2011). Her character continues on from "School Reunion." She is still a journalist and seems to have been spending her time watching and interacting with aliens. In the pilot for the *Sarah Jane Adventures* "Invasion of the Bane (2007)," we are introduced to a Sarah Jane Smith who is more willing to speak to aliens than to her neighbors. Seemingly self-sufficient, she drives a sporty but modest green car and owns a nice house on Bannerman road in a residential neighborhood. Other neighbors note Sarah Jane's oddness, but no one talks directly to her, and some refer to her as the "mad woman." The perky *young* Sarah Jane Smith is gone. Left in her place is a middle- aged woman who has no partner or children (or even cats) and who seems rude (mainly because she doesn't smile) and distracted.

When the new neighbor Maria and her father introduce themselves, Sarah Jane's response is "I hope you're not going to make too much noise. It's just I work from home and I don't like to be disturbed"—and then she immediately apologizes before driving off. As it turns out, she and her neighbor Maria are heading to the same place: an alien factory mass-producing a drink that allows them to control the humans. Sarah Jane Smith is suspicious, while Maria, who doesn't like the drink, is just going for a day trip with a new friend. Once in the factory, Sarah Jane Smith is brought to Mrs. Wormwood, whom she suspects is up to no good. Mrs. Wormwood seeks to misdirect Sarah Jane Smith's questions and accusations by attacking her personally:

> MRS. WORMWOOD: Go ahead and print your story, by all means. But consider your career. Are you going to expose this as some kind of alien plot? You'll be considered insane.
> SARAH JANE: I don't care what people think of me. Never have. I just want to find the truth.
> MRS. WORMWOOD: But at such a cost. I take it, Miss Smith, that you're single?
> SARAH JANE: Yes, I am.
> MRS. WORMWOOD: No children?
> SARAH JANE: No.
> MRS. WORMWOOD: Such a wasted life.

This interchange is reflective of the cultural shift in perceptions of what a woman can be and her ascribed roles in the last thirty years. She can't have it all, but she has the right to chose. However, if what she wants is against the norm, she will be judged. Here Mrs. Wormwood, who is an alien, is the one that is espousing these "reactionary" views. The alien might look human but her understanding of society is not a nuanced as a true native, and her pronouncement on Sarah Jane's singlehood sounds like it belongs to another time. The subtext in this statement is that the woman making the choice to live alone is not beyond the norm; it is the people who are judging her. In order to make Sarah Jane more palatable to viewers, she must lose her "old lady" status and be converted from abandoned sidekick and perennial spinster status to hero, something the series does admirably as Sarah Jane is shown coming out of her reclusive shell and understanding that her sidekicks (first

Maria, then Luke, Clyde, Rani and Sky) can help her be a more effective fighter against alien threats.

Sarah Jane's age is at the heart of Hannah Hamad's article on celebrity, culture and aging. Hamad highlights how Sladen, who had aged gracefully, was marketed in photos and promotional materials ("Sell by Date"). While all these are pertinent points, Sarah Jane Smith is remarkable not because of her age or continuing good looks, but because she has a mission, and she is consistently pursuing it. Ross P. Garner points out that the binary relationship between the Doctor, who is alien and has the ability to travel off world, and Sarah Jane, who is human and earth bound, has a twist that is visible in the show (166). Sarah Jane now has access to alien technology, so while she is physically earthbound her understanding isn't. She has a super computer called "Mr. Smith" hidden in her attic, and K-9, the robot dog, is a gift from the Doctor. K-9 traveled with the Doctor after Sarah Jane left the show, but the two were brought together in the failed pilot of the 1981 spin off, *K-9 and Company*. The Doctor also gives Sarah Jane a sonic lipstick that, like his sonic screwdriver, can jam signals, cut out electricity, open/close doors, disable cars and disrupt invisibility cloaking devices on space ships. Yet these gifts are not to signal his permission; instead, they are intended to aid her in the work she is already engaging in. Through these gifts, the Doctor acknowledges that Sarah Jane has graduated to hero status while he was gone.

Like many heroes, Sarah Jane has to make sacrifices for the greater good. In the episode "The Temptation of Sarah Jane Smith," which aired in the second season, viewers learn that Sarah Jane is an orphan and her parents seemingly abandoned her when she was a baby only to die in an automobile accident. Sarah Jane is given the opportunity to time travel and is able to both meet her parents and see herself as baby. She comes to understand how much her parents cared for her. She saves her parents from death only to realize that she has changed the future (her present) and plunged her world into a chaotic dystopia. Sarah Jane ultimately discovers that her parents' death was a fixed point in time and that she had been tricked into changing her past. Sarah Jane is faced with a difficult choice: save her parents and change her past or let them die. Like a true hero, she makes personal sacrifices and is willing to put the rest of humanity before her own needs. Sarah Jane willingly sacrifices her happiness and desires for the greater good, she allows her parents to die but keeping the knowledge that she was not unwanted. She doesn't only do it once. This trope appears again in the episode "The Wedding of Sarah Jane," in which Sarah Jane meets a man she loves (and who loves her back) but she gives him up because if she doesn't the world as she knows it will end. By emulating the male hero pattern of sacrifice for the sake of others, Sarah Jane demonstrates once again that she has come into her own as a protector of the earth and is nobody's sidekick.

Sarah Jane follows the heroic pattern of hiding her true work/identity from casual observers in order to protect them. In her "normal" life, she is a journalist—an occupation that worked for Superman, after all. She has willingly missed opportunities to reach out to connect to people because the path of the hero is typically a lonely one. This trope of the hero has been slowly changing, and superheroes increasingly have sidekicks and support systems which become part of their strength. While Sarah Jane initially seems to be a lonely hero who fights behind the scenes without the glory (à la Bruce Wayne), she and her viewers come to realize her strength comes from her friends. She has Mr. Smith, an adopted son, K-9, and friends. Her life has made her a better superhero because she has experienced love and life and understands for what she is fighting. When Sarah Jane lets Maria and Luke join her on her adventures, she does so while realizing the following: "I can handle life on my own. But after today I don't want to." As the feminist movement has moved from the first wave to the third wave and beyond, Sarah Jane Smith has found a television viewership that is more accepting of the choices she has made: she is a single mother, provider, protector, and a woman who is self-sufficient but still pretty. She is, in essence, the frightened child who has grown up to take her rightful place in the world as a woman who is equal to even the great Doctor.

Conclusion

By 2009, *The Sarah Jane Adventures* had become an established part of the *Doctor Who* canon. When questioned how long she would play the role, Sladen said, "I'm never going to stay until there's no more life in it. It's still got to be fresh and it's still got to be good" (Wilkes). Sadly, Sladen died of cancer in 2011, while filming was suspended due to her illness. In the final episode of the series, Sarah Jane Smith has the following monologue: "I've seen amazing things out there in space, but strange things can happen wherever you are. I have learned that life on Earth can be an adventure too. In all the universe, I never expected to find a family." While the family Sarah Jane Smith refers to is obviously the one she is accorded by the writers of the show, she might as well have been talking about the family of viewers in the *Doctor Who* universe who have come to love her character.

After the show ended, many viewers commented on what Sarah Jane Smith represented and how the character captured viewers' ambivalence to feminism and children. Hannah Hamad commented, "I thought *SJA* was extraordinary for its discursive centralization of a sixty-something single woman with agency and amiability. I shall miss her" ("A Tear"). James Delingpole commended the show for being "truly remarkable" and further expressed his delight that the show was a throwback to an age you thought had vanished years ago, in which it wasn't thought embarrassing for polite, well-scrubbed children to enjoy perilous adventures with a middle-class, educated white woman of a certain age, unconstrained by health and safety, eco-consciousness, or any manner of socio-political worthiness, and where the idea of a happy ending is to return safely to your cosy bourgeois suburb just in time for tea.

No matter the peril or which alien they faced, the children of *The Sarah Jane Adventures* ended up at their homes in time for homework and tea. No one questioned Sarah Jane's motives or thought it odd that she spent so much time with teenagers. The storytelling in *The Sarah Jane Adventures* in some ways is a direct descendent of the stories told by such writers as E. Nesbit, Enid Blyton, and Edward Eager, in which children had nice homes and loving parents but weren't micromanaged. *The Sarah Jane Adventures* also has ties to another type of storytelling: the superhero tale. In recent years, women have been coming out of the shadows and taking front stage as heroes and not sidekicks or love interests to the hero. Women are now increasingly being portrayed as heroes who fight for what is right and just and who have friends, and love interests, and families. Slowly science fiction is allowing its female heroes to gain substance and agency. Some recent high-profile women who are heroes in their own right include Skye aka Daisy Johnson on *Marvel's Agents of S.H.I.E.L.D.*, Supergirl on the show of the same name, Katniss from *The Hunger Games* book and film trilogies, and General Leia (who was promoted from princess) in the *Star Wars* movies. A generation of girls and boys are watching and paying attention and reimagining what their realities could be like: a reality in which men and women both get to be heroes, get to make choices suited for them, and get to simply be.

WORKS CITED

Barber, Martin. "*Doctor Who*: Elisabeth Sladen Talks." *BBC.com*, April 19 2006, www.bbc.co.uk/norfolk/content/articles/2006/04/19/film_doctor_who_lis_sladen_interview_feature.shtml.
Barr, Jason, and Camille D.G. Mustachio. "Introduction: 'It Looks Like You Need a Doctor.'" *The Language of Doctor Who*. Edited by Jason Barr and Camille D.G. Mustachio, Rowman & Littlefield, 2014.
Chu, Seo-Young. *Do Metaphors Dream of Literal Sleep? A Science-Fictional Theory of Representation*. Harvard University Press, 2010.
Delingpole, James. "Farewell, Sarah Jane." *The Spectator*, May 7, 2011, www.spectator.co.uk/2011/05/farewell-sarah-jane. Accessed April 2016.
Doctor Who: Planet of the Spiders. Written by Robert Sloman. 1973. London: BBC Home Entertainment, 2011.
Doctor Who: School Reunion. Written by Toby Whithouse. 2006. London: BBC Home Entertainment, 2009.
Doctor Who: The Ark in Space. Written by Robert Holmes. 1975. London: BBC Home Entertainment, 2002.
"Dr. Who's 'Cut Out' Girl Back." *Daily Mirror*, April 18, 2006, www.mirror.co.uk/3am/celebrity-news/exclusive-dr-whos-cut-out-girl-621265.

Drupkins. "Character Study: Sarah Jane Smith." *GeeksOut*, April 20, 2015, http://geeksout. org/blogs/drupkins/character-study-sarah-jane-smith.

"Elisabeth Sladen (1976)." *Dr Who Interviews*, August 7, 2009, www.drwhointerviews. wordpress.com/2009/08/07/elisabeth-sladen-1976.

"Elisabeth Sladen (1980's)." *Dr Who Interviews*, November 20, 2009, www.drwhointerviews. wordpress.com/2009/11/20/elisabeth-sladen-1980s.

"Elisabeth Sladen (2002)." *Dr Who Interviews*, September 13, 2009, www.drwhointerviews. wordpress.com/2009/09/13/elisabeth-sladen-2002.

Garner, Ross P. "'Don't You Forget About Me': Intertextuality and Generic Anchoring." *Impossible Worlds, Impossible Things: Cultural Perspectives on Doctor Who, Torchwood and the Sarah Jane Adventures.* Edited by Melissa Beattie et al., pp. 161–181. Cambridge Scholars, 2010.

Hamad, Hannah. "'I'm Not Past My Sell by Date Yet!': Sarah Jane's Adventures in Postfeminist Rejuvenation and the Later-Life Celebrity of Elisabeth Sladen." *Women, Celebrity and Cultures of Ageing: Freeze Frame.* Edited by Deborah Jermyn and Su Holmes, pp. 162–177. Palgrave, 2014.

_____. "A Tear for Sarah Jane a Feminist ACA-Obit." *Flow*, May 2011, www.flowjournal.org/2011/05/a-tear-for-sarah-jane/#identifier_7_9077.

Hogan, Michael. "Has *Doctor Who* Become Too Frightening?" *Telegraph*, October 4, 2014, www.telegraph.co.uk/culture/tvandradio/doctor-who/11138261/Has-Doctor-Who-become-too-frightening.html.

The Sarah Jane Adventures. "Invasion of the Bane." Written by Russell T Davies and Gareth Roberts. 2007. London: BBC Home Entertainment, 2008.

The Sarah Jane Adventures. "The Wedding of Sarah Jane Smith Part I & II." Written by Russell T. Davies and Gareth Roberts. 2007. London: BBC Home Entertainment, 2009.

"The Sarah Jane Adventures Ratings." *The Doctor Who Site*, November 20, 2009, http://news. thedoctorwhosite.co.uk/the-sarah-jane-adventures-ratings.

"Steven Moffat Clears Up Confusion Around the Number of John Hurt's Doctor." *Radio Times*. November 15, 2013, www.radiotimes.com/news/2013-11-15/doctor-who-steven-moffat-clears-up-confusion-around-the-number-of-john-hurts-doctor.

Walters, Damien. "Science Fiction's Invisible Women." *The Guardian*, August 8, 2013, www. theguardian.com/books/booksblog/2013/aug/08/science-fiction-invisible-women-recognition-status.

Wilkes, Neil. "Elisabeth Sladen ('Sarah Jane Adventures')." *Digital Spy*, September 28, 2009, www.digitalspy.com/tv/sarah-jane-adventures/interviews/a176657/elisabeth-sladen-sarah-jane-adventures/#~pp3ddHlSrpnxsi.

The Evolution of Lois Lane

Reflections on Women in Society

SANDRA ECKARD

Each generation has several female models that stand out as highly visible representatives of that generation. World War II had Rosie the Riveter, a cultural icon of the late 1930s and early 1940s that represented women's power and the first strands of modern feminism. In the 1960s, there was Gidget, and the 1970s brought about the *Mary Tyler Moore Show* and other iconic pop culture characters that are still recognized today, such as *Charlie's Angels*. However, while these pop icons are all still recognizable as a monumental part of our pop culture history, these images of women are each linked solely to one generation; they are frozen as part of that particular time period alone. Lois Lane, however, has been around since 1938, and as times have changed, she has morphed into different incarnations of herself. Through the years, Lois has changed in her appearance both in comics and on screens large and small, representing changes in the roles that women could have in society as well as beliefs they could hold. Lois Lane has a unique role, then, as a mirror to the evolution of women and their changing roles in society.

The Origin of Lois Lane

When she appears in the first *Action Comics #1* in 1938, Lois is, surprisingly, a career girl. She is not a damsel in distress, but rather a "firecracker right from the start" ("Part I") Lois is at her desk, typing, when Clark Kent interrupts her to ask for a date. She doesn't respond with a happy-to-be-asked "yes." Instead, she states, "I suppose I will give you a break … for a change" (Siegel and Shuster "Superman: Champion of the Oppressed" 14 panel 6). It is clear that she is not overly concerned with finding a husband—and more interesting, perhaps, is that she is completely not interested in Clark as a potential suitor. She makes it clear later that she has her own mind and is independent. She is not willing to accept just any man's attention. While on a date, another man attempts to force her to dance and right in the middle of the dance floor she slaps him for his insolent behavior (Siegel and Shuster "Superman: Champion of the Oppressed" 15 panel 3).

Throughout the rest of the 1930s, the comics usually depict Lois as determined to get a quality story to report for *The Daily Planet*. She often accompanies Clark to dangerous war spots, as in "War in San Monte," and desperately tries to uncover Superman imposters in "The Man Who Sold Superman." Lois's work assignments reflect her independent image. In the early issues of the comics, and through the forties, she often tackles crime assignments rather than just features or human-interest stories, as might have been expected of a female reporter at the time. In the first issue, Lois tellingly displays frustration over covering what might seem like a feminine story, stating, "I've been scribbling 'sob stories' all day long!" (Siegel and Shuster "Superman: Champion of the Oppressed" 14 panel 7). Rather than being invested in her coworker, Lois usually ignores Clark or uses him to get closer to Superman; her main mission is to investigate crime and learn more about the marvel of Superman. These early issues also help cement what Fleisher describes as the set up for a traditional Superman story with three parts: Clark feigns fear, then secretly shows up as Superman; Lois tries to capture the story by herself, sometimes dangerously; and last, Clark mysteriously scoops her by writing the story first (Fleisher 441–415).

While Clark remains a competitor for Lois and her career goals, she manages to avoid being a damsel-in-distress with adventures like "Lois Lane, Girl Reporter: The Foiled Frame Up," from *Superman #34* in 1945. In this story, Lois is the central character, and Superman does not appear at all. Lois investigates a mobster who wants to set up *The Daily Planet* editor Perry White, and she covers the story all on her own. She is conscious of her surroundings, figuring out early on that the criminal wants her to record something untrue; she also uses items at her disposal, such as a bucket of soapy water and a fake gun, to get away from the men chasing her. At the police station, she turns over the men to the police, and all of the men involved are flabbergasted that she got criminals to cooperate by using a candy gun. In the end, Lois is proud of her solo adventure, exclaiming, "I guess this should prove I don't need Superman to help me all the time, Chief!" (Ellsworth 59, panel 6). Crime stories and those that revolve around Lois as a reporter provide female readers with a role model. Siegel and Shuster's original vision for Lois was to construct a heroine worthy of standing next to the Man of Steel. As a result, although the majority of the comics center on Superman's exploits,

Lois is never portrayed as silly or flighty. She is equal to Clark as a reporter, illustrating that women could prosper in the workforce after the war.

During the 1940s and 1950s, Lois's curiosity about Superman's secret identity starts to become more central to her storyline. In addition to being competitive with Clark Kent over stories, she begins to have suspicions about Superman's identity in 1942. In "Man or Superman?" Lois compares Clark and Superman. One thought bubble shows timid, shy Clark, while the second paints the portrait of strong, heroic Superman. She senses there is more to this than what she can prove, but in the end, she does not get any further with her investigation. She is relieved at the end, just happy to make it out of the dangerous situation alive: "Both Clark and I will die—and all because I was silly enough to suspect him of being Superman!" (Ellsworth 59, panel 7). Lois appears to have lost interest, then, in uncovering Superman's secret identity; she even seems to believe her assumptions were wrong and silly. Interestingly, this issue sets up what might be the most successful—or repetitive—pattern for a *Superman* story. Lois is suspicious and tries to get Clark to admit he is Superman, but ultimately Superman manages to save Lois from a dangerous situation without revealing his identity (Siegel and Shuster "Man or Superman?" 11 panel 6).

This early version of Lois Lane is a woman that the period created—and, perhaps more importantly—could relate to. Women were permeating the work force, and the war had presented even more opportunities for women with both factory jobs and careers. However, the fact that Lois did always need saving—and couldn't figure out Clark's identity—is in stark contrast to her portrayal of an assertive career woman who was often the only female in the *Daily Planet* workplace. In other words, this Lois was strong when the stories needed her to be strong. This contrast reflected the mixed feelings of the audience at the time for women's place in society as "Lois Lane was a powerful symbol, one whose ambition would have to be kept in check if the status quo was to be preserved" (Siegel and Shuster, "Man or Superman?"). In short, she was a mirror for the women in this tumultuous period, women who were struggling to be independent yet still confined by the standards of the time.

Lois Lane on the Screen

If the comics provided a forum for Lois to be viewed as powerful, independent, and possibly even equal to Superman, the silver screen and television screen versions of Lois reinforced a different image—a housewife or mother, such as June Cleaver on *Leave It to Beaver*. The sixteen-week serial simply titled *Superman* premiered in 1948 and was shown before feature films. The serial starts out with Lois as a non-traditional career woman much like the character from the comic strips. Rather than being portrayed as a background character, she is clearly both central to the story and committed to her career, and the first entry "establishes Lois's confidence and willpower and her ability to dominate over her male colleagues" (Williams 4). However, as the series progresses, Lois's character gradually assumes the role of damsel in distress— or even petty competitor. For example, in "Superman's Dilemma," she "allows Clark to use her car to chase a lead and then immediately reports the car as stolen to get him arrested and out of her way" because she wants the scoop first (Tresca 13). However, scenarios such as these lead to a near- inevitable conclusion: Lois gets herself into situations where she needs Superman's help to escape. As Tresca concludes, "The message is clear: the only way for a woman to get ahead in a man's profession is through trickery, but such trickery will always lead to failure" (13).

When *The Adventures of Superman* began on television in 1952, once again Lois Lane resembled the character from the comics: a tough cookie whose primary focus was being a hard-hitting journalist. However, because of the formula of television and the short time frame, Lois was often used as the means to showcase Superman's heroism: she would be in danger, and Superman would rescue her. Many viewers saw her as a plot device "rather than a fully realized character" (Tresca 13). Despite this, in the first season Lois always does her best, and she is determined to be as active as possible; however, her character changed as a result of the break between Seasons One and Two, as well as because the series obtained a new producer. This new producer, Whitney Ellsworth, focused on a child audience, making the show "lighter and more comical" (Tresca 16). This changed Lois's character the most. In many of these new episodes, such as "Money to Burn" or "The Big Forget," Lois is presented as "completely inadequate" (Tresca 17) as the stories rely on the formula of Lois finding herself in trouble—usually due to her own recklessness—and Superman needing to save her. Lois's lack of independence and thoughtlessness is also illustrated in her inability to recognize that Clark and Superman are the same person. For example, in one episode, titled "The Secret of Superman," an evil scientist becomes obsessed with figuring out Superman's identity. He tricks Lois into drinking some coffee laced with a truth serum, leaving her vulnerable. Still drugged when Superman arrives to save her, Lois mumbles, "You are Clark Kent" ("The Secret of Superman"). Of course, she does not remember the truth once the drug wears off, resetting the show back to the original dynamic by the end of the episode. In order to become what the audience would enjoy, the show runners "softened Lois's character, transforming her from a hardened, fearless big-city front-page journalist to a bland love interest" (Tresca 17). She remained a passive plot device for the rest of the show's run through 1958, waiting, figuratively and literally, for someone to rescue her.

Lois's character benefited from the women's rights movement in the 1960s and 1970s. On the silver screen, she got a much-needed overhaul in 1978 with *Superman: The Movie*, which returned her character to her independent career girl roots. When this incarnation of Lois first appears onscreen, she is—like in the early comics—working on a story. Furiously typing, she wants to deliver this latest story to her editor. When Jimmy Olsen, a young photographer, asks her why she gets all the great stories, she confidently replies, "A good reporter doesn't get great stories; a good reporter makes them great" (*Superman: The Movie*). Lois barely acknowledges Clark's new presence at *The Daily Planet* and manages to alternate between being annoyed by him and unaware of his existence. The first real exchange between Clark and Lois comes when they are held up at gunpoint by a robber when leaving work. Rather than giving her purse to the gunman as Clark suggests, she allows it to drop on the ground, offering her a chance to kick him. Her plan, though brave, backfires, and Clark has to catch the bullet aimed at Lois. Clark covers up his help with "Golly, I guess I must have fainted" (*Superman: The Movie*). While the audience finds this interplay comical, Lois's reaction is to believe firmly that Clark is incompetent. Although this initial exchange might imply that Lois once again needs Superman to save her, Lois's presentation here is of a spunky reporter and independent woman, mirroring what occurred in the comics. In 1977, "The Great Superman Locked-Door Puzzle" presents a Lois similar to the version in *Superman: The Movie*. First, she spends more time with Clark than with Superman, and second, she has more on her mind than simply following Superman's exploits or finagling him into marriage. When Lois was reframed as a more multi-dimensional woman, she became a mirror of the women of the time who were eager to be independent and pursue a career: "In effect, the flighty, immature character from the 1950s and 1960s was gone" (Williams 104).

In *Superman II*, this pattern continues as Lois focuses on being a better, more serious reporter. She is offended that editor Perry White has sent her and Clark on an undercover assignment investigating how Niagara Falls tourist spots might be swindling newlyweds. Perry White, this film establishes, thinks that Lois is a better reporter than Clark, and her powers of deduction become the focal point of the plot when she considers that Clark might just be Superman. Like the "good reporter that she is, she sets out to prove it" (Tresca 20). This version of Lois Lane, then, is not just Superman's girlfriend, so even when she really does *become* his girlfriend, her character is more robust than in past incarnations, revealing a well-rounded, relatable woman who embodies the many roles and desires of the women of the time.

Lois Is in on the Secret

For almost forty years, "an essential element of all Superman comics was maintaining the status quo" (Siegel and Shuster, *Lois Lane*, 292). The formula—still holding true in *Superman II*—was that, in the end, the story was about Clark and his dual identity, with Lois getting into trouble trying to figure out who Superman really was. Despite some stories outside of the main continuity, this formula held true until the late 1980s. The 1980s brought about a modern age of comics, focusing on character development. As part of a wide-scale reboot of DC Comics as a whole, Lois Lane became an even stronger reflection of the modern, intelligent woman. In 1986's *Action Comics #662*, "Secrets in the Night," Lois—without the standard plot device of being drugged or undergoing a memory wipe—learns Clark Kent's secret. Surprise is written on her face, and she can only reply with a whisper of his name (Stern 184 panel 7). In the documentary *Look, Up in the Sky!*, Mike Carlin, the Senior Group Editor at DC Comics, revealed that the decision to allow Clark to reveal his secret was prompted by the writers "being a little tired of Lois not figuring it out. It was starting to make her look a little stupid. And you can't be a top reporter and be stupid." As a result, Lois's image and role progressed in the 1990s comics. Lois and Clark moved from co-workers and friends to a romantic couple, and many times their tales focused on how both of them could help maintain his secret.

This trend continued with *Lois & Clark: The New Adventures of Superman*, a modern television take on the Superman myth, launched in 1993 by Warner Brothers. The first clue that this show would be slightly different than other versions is that Lois's name appears in the title before either Clark *or* Superman. This show, much like the 1950s *Adventures of Superman*, was intended for a family audience, but it also functioned as much more of a romance. In the show, Lois is drawn to both Clark and Superman. Despite traditional plot formulas such as the villain of the week and Lois getting into trouble that only Superman can help her get out of, this show was different: it was deliberately written as a postmodern romance. Clark, played by Dean Cain, was compelling, interesting, and pretty much a hunky reporter who happens to wear glasses. He is attractive to Lois, and after a season of working together and flirting, they become involved as a couple.

Lois & Clark: The New Adventures of Superman invites its viewers to root for Clark as much as for Superman, if not more. If there is a third wheel in his relationship with Lois, it might just be, surprisingly, Superman. Superman is only present in a few scenes per episode, sometimes to save the day with a heroic act, sometimes to be mere eye-candy. In "Woman on Top," Matthew Freeman argues that the series reverses Laura Mulvey's classic concept of male gaze theory, that women are present to be looked-at by the men.

Both Superman and Clark are there for Lois—and the female viewers—to gaze upon. As Freeman concludes, Clark is the more equally drawn and supported character, while Superman "is constructed less as a character in *Lois & Clark* and more as the object of female desire" (195). Lois's journey and Lois's vision take top priority, and it is clear early on that Lois spends more time worrying about Clark's whereabouts than Superman's—often expressing frustration at his mysterious absences or abrupt departures, a feeling that would resonate with busy working women trying to juggle multiple tasks.

The Season Two finale "And the Answer Is…" showcases that Lois's preoccupation is with Clark rather than Superman, an explicit departure from the comics. The episode begins with Clark, who is picking Lois up for a breakfast date, waiting in the living room while she finishes getting ready. This scene plays like a bit of homage to a similar scene in *Superman: The Movie* (1978), where Clark waits for Lois to get a sweater—and debates telling Lois his double identity. Clark decides to reveal his secret to Lois, beginning his speech with an acknowledgment of her frustration about his frequent absences: "You know you are always complaining that I seem to run off every time we start talking about something important? It has nothing to do with my fear of intimacy or falling in love or anything like that. I think I should just tell you this as simply and as honestly as I can. Lois, I'm Super—." At that moment, however, his declaration of his dual identity is interrupted comically by a ringing telephone, thus ending the conversation mid-reveal.

Lois's frustration with Clark is evident, and she confronts him later at work. As Clark tries again to explain, and perhaps tell Lois his secret, she angrily interrupts him: "Don't! I cannot listen to one more stupid story about your barber or your doctor or how you suddenly have to return a book to the library. What you owe me is some respect. I am so tired of the excuses, Clark. How can we have a relationship if you're not going to be honest with me?" ("And the Answer Is…"). This conversation shows that the Lois of the 1990s is not just concerned with who is behind the glasses; she is concerned with being treated fairly by her partner, super or not. At one point, she says, "I thought you were the last honest man. I thought you were … Clark Kent. Who *are* you?" ("And the Answer Is…"). Interestingly, this set-up reveals more about Lois than Clark. This modern woman wants to uncover more about the man she loves: Clark, not Superman. This Lois wants to see behind the walls that Clark has built, not to learn about Superman, but rather about Clark himself. In every previous incarnation, Clark has been a friend, a co-worker, a rival, and a sounding board. Now, the modern Lois sees him as her love interest. This reinvention shows that Clark is truly the man *within* the costume; he is the one who is the primary character, not Superman. *Lois & Clark* "goes the furthest to humanize the character than any other Superman adaptation and does so by challenging the notion of what we've come to expect from Superman—the idea that Clark is the disguise and Superman is the 'real' person" (Esposito). The characters Lois and Clark are the main characters who grow and learn, and Superman is simply the disguise Clark uses to do good in the world.

By the end of the episode, viewers expect that Clark will tell Lois his secret. Instead, he proposes marriage. This surprising plot development leads to one more twist. Lois takes a breath and replies, "Who's asking? Clark or Superman?" ("We Have a Lot to Talk About"). This updated version of Lois Lane is independent, and her character had to grow to reflect the intelligent and observation skills that the audience would assume an intelligent reporter would have. Instead of having to be told that Clark is Superman, this one utterance reveals not just that she knows that Clark is Superman, but perhaps more importantly, she has known for a while. This Lois, unlike those before her, had been able to figure it out on her own, making her even more relatable to the viewers.

New Constructions of Lois

The 1990s Lois Lane, popular with both men and women for her smarts, attitude, and image, led to the next television version: *Smallville,* which premiered in 2001, four years after the cancellation of *Lois and Clark: The New Adventures of Superman.* This time, though, Lois was not envisioned as one-half of a romantic duo. This WB show envisioned a teenager with superpowers as a metaphor for the adolescent experience—not fitting in, feeling different, and discovering inner strength. In the beginning, the show centered on high school teen Clark Kent, who dealt with football, girls, and friends. Lois was not even introduced until Season Four's "Crusade." Although audiences were familiar with Lois and her romantic ties to Superman, the twist here is that Superman did not yet exist and Clark was still just Clark Kent. Audiences had quite a while to enjoy Clark and Lois as separate characters, each with their own issues, adventures, and love interests.

In many episodes, Lois focuses on her career, sister, or cousin Chloe, who just so happens to be Clark's best friend. Much of the humor comes from the fact that Chloe knows Clark's secret, and her loyalty to hiding the truth often puts her at odds with Lois. Some of Lois and Clark's adventures are completely separate, converging only when their interests bumped up against each other, such as with the episode "Combat." Lois is desperate to find a story that would move her up the ladder from tabloids to a reputable paper, and she uses a piece of paper that Chloe has thrown in the trash as a lead. Clark, meanwhile, is following this story for a different reason, and the pair bump into each other at an underground boxing ring. Adventures like these allowed Lois to develop fully as a character with many layers—career ambitions, loyalty to family, independent personality—all the while allowing the audience to grow with her.

Season Six's "Crimson" shows a glimpse of the chemistry between Lois and Clark. It almost plays as an inside joke because the two—both heartbroken over recent breakups—are set up by Jimmy Olsen. While at a party, Lois tries on red lipstick laced with kryptonite; this lipstick removes her inhibitions, and she falls "in love" with Clark on the spot. Once she kisses him, the red kryptonite releases his inhibitions, and he not only kisses her back, but he also shares his powers with her, whisking her off for a romantic fling. This episode follows the traditional formula where Lois forgets what happens afterward, but it sets up a bit of a tease for the audience. The audience is in on the joke, as they know that these two will eventually fall in love. Even though Lois does have the traditional memory loss, both characters grow because of their experience; the audience members now know that Lois does have a vulnerable side that she keeps hidden and are encouraged to hope that she just might have feelings beyond friendship for Clark ("Crimson").

Smallville's Lois became a fan favorite, perhaps because viewers were given time to get to know her. In "Five Reasons Why Erica Durance Is the Best Lois Lane Ever," the author listed all the reasons why fans can relate to this version of Lois, ranging from her looks to her intelligence to her believability in a fight (Ramos). Developing her as a character over time paid off. With each adventure, the audience could see her growth: "She had her own struggles to deal with, like finding her place and purpose in the world, and deciding how best to do what she believed was right, which gave her depth that we often don't get to see from Lois Lane" (Ramos). Karen Hirmer argues in "*Smallville's* Lois Lane: From New Woman to Female Hero" that Durance's Lois is more than just an updated version of a traditional female character. She is a modernization, a new construction of a female character that is "appealing and compelling to a young female audience" (254).

This re-envisioning of Lois Lane continued in the 2013 film *Man of Steel.* In contrast to other versions of Lois Lane, the most recent silver screen Lois, played by Amy Adams, is not first presented to audiences in an office setting or even as a teenager. Instead, she emerges from a helicopter, surrounded by military and other official personnel. After some chitchat with the officers, Lois sets up her stance quite firmly, "Look—let's get one thing straight, guys, okay? The only reason I'm here is because we're on Canadian soil, and an appellate court overruled your injunction to keep me away. So, if we're done measuring dicks, can you show me what you found?" This scene is one of the strongest openings for a female character, let alone for Lois Lane. This Lois is an active, seasoned investigator who travels to find the best story, and audiences are aware, right away, that she is not intimidated by men or by adverse circumstances. This new construction of Lois is interesting in that her whole storyline in the film is figuring out where the mysterious man who might have special powers originated. This version of Clark Kent has less of the red-and-blue suit than other versions. Instead of a dual identity, he has more of a secret identity, which Lois ambitiously traces from story to story back to Clark Kent and his hometown. This reveals yet another update to Lois Lane—instead of having to be told Clark's secret (as in the comics) or having to figure it out after multiple frustrating disappearances (as in *Lois & Clark*), this time, Lois is able to figure it out from the beginning. As a result, she is the only one throughout *Man of Steel* who knows who Superman, the mysterious savior of Metropolis, truly is.

The Lois Lane in *Man of Steel* signified a renewed interest in *The Daily Planet*'s intrepid reporter. In 2014, DC Comics released a stand-alone Lois-centered comic called "Nostalgia," a special issue of *Superman: Lois Lane*. In this story, Lois traces a mystery involving her sister Lucy, drugs, and a potential alien invasion. Superman appears only in one panel, and largely the story centers on Lois and Lucy. As the title suggests, this comic brings together a current story with Lois's memories of the past. Lois feels guilty that she raised Lucy after their mother died: "When I think of mom today, there is no complete picture ... the scent of bread, and cinnamon, and meat, cooking. That is the kind of mother that Lucy should have had. But when our mother died, Lucy had to make due with me" (2014 panel 7). By the end of the story, Lois realizes that family is more important than any story, and she and Lucy have repaired the distance between them. Although a single issue, this stand-alone comic allowed a glimpse into Lois's younger years and her personal life., reflecting a greater demand for stories about Lois that emphasize her experiences, even wholly separate from Superman.

In 2015, DC Comics created *Superman: Lois and Clark* and cast Lois in yet another role: mother. The comic's title harkens back to the 1990s, when the duo was a couple, and indeed this comic focuses on an alternate reality in which Lois and Clark are married and have a child. Superman, Lois, and their baby Jon have escaped Earth and have assumed aliases on a different Earth so that they can keep their son safe. In the first issue, Lois's growth is revealed through Clark's thoughts as he looks at a bookshelf filled with the work that Lois has done anonymously over the nine years that they have been in hiding: "What Lois has done with her books.... She's an amazing agent of change" ("Arrival" Part 1, 15 panel 4). As writer Dan Jergens asserts, "This is not the same life they enjoyed while working at *The Daily Planet*.... Clark and Lois's most notable priority is keeping Jon safe" (4). Although Lois has not given up on writing or on being a force of positive change, she has clearly developed new priorities. Instead of being merely a career girl or Superman's sometime-girlfriend, Lois has become a wife and protective mother.

The most recent, and most interesting, construction of Lois blends the concept of *Smallville* with the idea of a stand-alone story like "Nostalgia." In 2015, *Fallout*, a young adult novel that caters to teen female readers, was released. The novel stands in stark contrast to most other depictions of Lois by completely omitting Superman: "For her entire 76-year existence, Lois Lane has been stuck with Superman, to the point where even her long-running solo comic book series was titled *Superman's Girlfriend Lois Lane*" (McMillan). Instead of focusing on Superman, this young adult novel centers on teen Lois's journey, as she has just moved to the suburbs with her family. She gets her first job at *The Daily Scoop*, an extension of *The Daily Planet* for high school journalists, and she deals with fitting in at a new school, making friends, and dealing with her younger sister Lucy. She determined to blend in on her first day at her new school: "Fit in. Don't make waves," she repeats to herself (Bond 5). However, even her first moments in the hallway near the entrance reveal her true nature, as she stands up for a girl who is trying to report being bullied (Bond 7). After finishing her story and saving the day, Lois has grown in her confidence and has found a home with *The Daily Scoop*. Her thoughts reveal her satisfaction: "I knew what I was doing. I had a place where I belonged. Finally" (Bond 299). This construction of Lois Lane, then, helps fill in the backstory for how she became the grown-up Lois that audiences already know. The book centers on a female protagonist, and this approach allows a multi-dimensional character to emerge. Girls of all ages can now see Lois Lane as a role model and vicarious heroine worthy of value and respect.

Reflections and Conclusions

A critical analysis of the evolution of Lois Lane allows audiences to see just how unique a heroine she is. The character of Lois Lane has been around for over 76 years now, and each construction of her character reflects each generation's view of women—whether actual, perceived, or desired. While each version has a similar theme, the fact that she has been reinvented as many times as Superman is amazing in and of itself. Most iconic images of women, while memorable and instantly recognizable, seem frozen in time, representing one particular generation. Lois, however, has changed in both appearance and construction. Each new creator shifts pieces of her around and adds new layers to develop her character in some new way, appealing to that current generation more precisely. While most versions of Lois Lane have been "hits," there have also been a few "misses." During the era of the homemaker of the fifties, Lois became the single girl focused solely on getting married: "Lana and Lois spent much of the 1950s and 1960s competing over who would become Superman's wife" (Fetters). While this incarnation of Lois can be described as "flighty" or "frivolous" compared to the image of a modern woman today, even these less-than-desirable versions of Lois can be interesting characters to analyze. In the 2006 film, *Superman Returns*, Kate Bosworth's youth seemed to turn off fans, and in a ranking on *What Culture*, Bosworth's Lois is last, claiming this portrait is best described as "cool or aloof" (Fisher). However, *Superman Returns* was also the first cinematic portrayal of Lois as a mother, so the flat reception of both the film and Lois's character can still be valuable for study.

In the end, Lois serves as a mirror for how society can, does, or might aspire to view women. Amy Adams will not be the last actor to play Lois Lane on screen, and *Fallout*, while a new way to bring Lois's character front and center, will most certainly not be the last book to feature *The Daily Planet*'s spunky reporter as the protagonist. Each reimagining of Lois will allow audiences to reflect on not just a new construction of a character first created in 1938, but also new paths and new possibilities for all of that generation's women as well.

WORKS CITED

"And the Answer Is…" *Lois & Clark: The New Adventures of Superman*, written by Tony Blake and Paul Jackson, directed by Alan J. Levi, Warner Bros., 1995.
Bennett, Marguerite. "Nostalgia." *Superman: Lois Lane #1*, DC Comics, April 2014.
Bond, Gwenda. *Fallout*. Switch Press, 2015.
"Combat." *Smallville*, written Turi Meyer and Al Septien, directed James Marshall, Warner Bros., 2007.
"Crimson." *Smallville*, written by Kelly Souders and Brian Wayne Peterson, directed by Glen Winter, Warner Bros., 2007.
Ellsworth, Whitney. "Lois Lane, Girl Reporter: The Foiled Frame Up." *Lois Lane: A Celebration of 75 Years*, DC Comics, 2013, pp. 56–59.
Esposito, Joey. "Hero Worship: Revisiting *Lois & Clark: The New Adventures of Superman*." IGN, 23 June 2013, www.ign.com/articles/2013/06/22/hero-worship-revisiting-lois-and-clark-the-new-adventures-of-superman.
Fetters, Ashley. "*Man of Steel*'s Lois Lane Is a Modern Heroine—Just Like the Lois Lanes Before Her." *The Atlantic*, 17 June 2013, www.theatlantic.com/entertainment/archive/2013/06/-i-man-of-steel-i-s-lois-lane-is-a-modern-heroine-just-like-the-lois-lanes-before/276928/.
Fisher, Matthew. "Ranking All of the Lois Lane Performances—Worst to Best." *What Culture*, 6 May 2014, http://whatculture.com/film/superman-ranking-lois-lane-performances-worst-best. Accessed December 31, 2015.
Fleisher, Michael. *The Great Superman Book*. Warner Bros., 1988.
Freeman, Matthew. "Woman on Top: Postfeminism and the Transformation Narrative in *Lois & Clark: The New Adventures of Superman*." *Examining Lois Lane: The Scoop on Superman's Sweetheart*, edited by Nadine Farghaly, pp. 189–210. Scarecrow Press, 2013.
Hirmer, Karin. "*Smallville*'s Lois Lane: From New Woman to Female Hero." *Examining Lois Lane: The Scoop on Superman's Sweetheart*, edited by Nadine Farghaly, pp. 235–260. Scarecrow Press, 2013.
Jurgens, Dan. "Arrival: Part 1." *Superman: Lois and Clark*. DC Comics, 2015.
Look, Up in the Sky! The Amazing Story of Superman. Directed by Kevin Burns. Warner Bros., 2006.

Man of Steel. Directed by Zach Snyder, performed by Henry Cavill, Russell Crowe, and Amy Adams, Warner Bros., 2013.

"Part I: 1938–1956 Girl Reporter." *Lois Lane: A Celebration of 75 Years,* DC Comics, 2013, p. 6.

Ramos, James. "Superman: 5 Reasons Why Erica Durance Is the Best Lois Lane Ever." *What Culture,* http://whatculture.com/tv/superman-5-reasons-why-erica-durance-is-the-best-lois-lane-ever. Accessed 31 Dec. 2015.

Siegel, Jerry, and Joe Shuster. *Lois Lane: A Celebration of 75 Years,* DC Comics, 2013.

_____. "Man or Superman?" *Superman #1,* DC Comics, 1942.

_____. "The Man Who Sold Superman." *Lois Lane: A Celebration of 75 Years,* DC Comics, 2013, pp. 35–47.

_____. "Superman, Champion of the Oppressed." *Lois Lane: A Celebration of 75 Years,* DC Comics, 2013, pp. 8–34.

Stern, Roger. "Secrets in the Night." *Lois Lane: A Celebration of 75 Years,* DC Comics, 2013, pp. 164–185.

Superman: The Movie. Directed by Richard Donner, performed by Christopher Reeve, Gene Hackman, and Margot Kidder, Warner Bros., 1978.

"The Secret of Superman." *The Adventures of Superman,* written by Wells Root, directed by Thomas Carr, Warner Bros., 1952.

Tresca, Don. "The Evolution of Lois Lane in Film and Television." *Examining Lois Lane: The Scoop on Superman's Sweetheart,* edited by Nadine Farghaly, pp. 11–38. Scarecrow Press, 2013.

"We Have a Lot to Talk About." *Lois & Clark: The New Adventures of Superman,* written by John McNamara, directed by Philip Sgriccia, Warner Bros., 1995.

Williams, Jeanne Pauline. *"The Evolution of Social Norms and the Life of Lois Lane: A Rhetorical Analysis of Popular Culture."* Dissertation. Ohio State University, 1986.

Alternate, Not Arrested Development

Bryan Fuller's Female Protagonists

TRINIDAD LINARES

"Most female heroines are oddities: adventuresses and orig-
inals notable less for the importance of their acts than for
the singularity of their fates"
— Simone De Beauvoir

Introduction

In most traditional tales, the woman could be either the damsel in distress who must be saved by the hero from a supernatural being or the prize
at the end of a supernatural journey. Second-wave feminism encompassed
criticisms about the representation of women and stressed that women had
a right to their own agency. Television shows during the second wave, like
Bionic Woman and *Wonder Woman*, showed women with supernatural power
under their control instead of the supernatural forces controlling the women.
If second-wave feminism was a call to arms to embrace the power and potential of women in society, then third-wave feminism is not only about the
struggle to fulfill that potential and achieve that power, but also the difficulty
of accessing and maintaining that power and finding the need to live up to
that potential daunting. Third-wave feminism's iconic show *Buffy the Vampire
Slayer* illustrates these issues. After 9/11, there was a slight push back to traditional gender roles for women as fears of the instability of societal structures grew. Bryan Fuller was the creator, writer, and executive producer of
three television series *Dead Like Me* (Showtime, 2003–2004, 29 episodes
and a direct to dvd movie; Fuller left the show after the first season but was

129

a consultant on the second), *Wonderfalls* (Fox, 2004, 13 episodes), and *Pushing Daisies* (ABC, 2007–2009, 22 episodes). All three have more women than men in their main and recurrent casts. The female protagonists of these series show how subversive third-wave feminism has become post–9/11 because although supernatural forces wreak havoc on their lives in ways they cannot control or even explain, they do not turn into passive victims. Instead, the ways that George, Jaye, and Chuck deal with the supernatural forces that they have no control over shows how third-wave feminism critiques "power structures while it also acknowledges and makes use of the pleasure, danger, and defining power of those structures" (Heywood and Drake 3).

Unlike the postfeminists, third-wave feminists do not believe in setting themselves apart from the second-wave feminists. Rather, they choose to build upon what the second-wave feminists have created, discussing oppressions in addition to the one of gender, while disregarding the idea that femininity isn't necessarily feminist and that there is only one way to be a feminist. Fuller's female protagonists are spurred on to adventures and acts of service that empower them in spite of supernatural occurrences. Chuck (*Pushing Daisies*) and George (*Dead Like Me*) live after they are supposed to be dead, while Jaye (*Wonderfalls*) starts to hear voices. In each episode, like a hero story, they must solve a task, which is often in the form of a riddle (Propp 60). George has to figure out how the person died. Chuck has to figure out who killed the person and why. Jaye has to figure out what task she must do to help someone. They are young women, but their stories are not a metaphor for adolescence. They are dealing with the difficult challenges and choices made in adulthood. These women challenge not only the traditional idea that the only goal for women is to get married and have children, but also a second-wave feminist idea that a woman gains power by rejecting domesticity and having a career. George, Jaye, and Chuck are not focused on choosing either of these paths or feel downtrodden trying to conflate them. Instead, they've created a niche where they are seeking and finding self-fulfillment on their own terms. This, along with their disregard for boundaries and acceptance of contradictions, makes them clearly third-wave feminists. Their accomplishments show that a feminist hero does not have to follow any prescribed path to success.

George in Dead Like Me

College dropout George ("Georgia") Lass, eighteen, is killed by a falling toilet seat from a Russian space station after just starting a job found through Happy Time, a work placement agency. Instead of descending or ascending after death, she becomes part of a grim reaper crew. Grim reapers help detach souls from the bodies of people right before they die so the souls can cross over to the other side. The grim reapers are dead people who have not crossed over yet. However, after they help a certain number of people, the grim reapers will then have the opportunity to cross over themselves. George's reaper work involves figuring out who will die and how. Her only clue is a post-it that has the person's initials, the location, and estimated time of death. Unfortunately, reapers do not know how many people they have to help in order to cross over until they help their last person. George's specific grim reaper crew is assigned to handle accidental, homicidal, and violent deaths.

When George is first visually introduced to the audience, she states (in the voiceover): "I'd say I'm sorry to disappoint you, but I'm not. I excel at not giving a shit. Experience has taught me that interest begets expectation, and expectation begets disappointment, so the key to avoiding disappointment is to avoid interest. A equals B equals C equals A, or whatever. I also don't have a lot of interest in being a good person or a bad person" ("Pilot"). In the beginning, George tries to resist this mission or destiny to care for the dead souls because she had no idea what she wanted to do with her life before she died and dying didn't resolve anything for her. Now as a grim reaper, she has a job she must perform, but isn't given any information as to why she must perform this job. She is forced to deal with people in a sympathetic manner, which she managed avoid living at home where her mother took care of everything. George's air of cynicism and lack of interest in anything can be seen as the conundrum attitude of the third wave of feminism that has benefited from previous waves, but is unsure on how to progress (White and Walker 88). The other female reapers, Daisy, Betty, and Roxy, can be seen as the representative of their earlier waves of feminism because they lived and died during those time periods. Daisy and Betty were first-wave feminists who saw themselves as "independent-minded women … in a world of men" (White and Walker 87). Daisy and Betty never saw themselves as equal to or independent from men, but rather were interested in how their relationships with men could benefit them. While first-wave feminists may have had many more objectives, they are known mainly for getting women the right to vote and this wave dissipated after voting rights were garnered. Roxy is a second-wave feminist who combines the struggle for "civil rights" with an "independent and self-sufficient nature," and yet she also seeks to "educate and liberate [other] women" (White and Walker 87). Roxy inadvertently becomes a mother figure to George in the reaper group by stressing self-sufficiency to her.

Just before George died, her mother, Joy, told her, "You will get out of bed and you will go to work. You will collect a paycheck and you will move out of this house" ("Dead Girl Walking"). As Joy wished for her when she was alive, George must leave home and assert her independence by not only working as a reaper, but seeking additional employment at Happy Time. Reapers get new bodies and personas, but not financial compensation for their work. While she was a slacker in life, George cannot regress back to her old ways because she must care for herself and her job as a reaper is mandatory. George must become self-reliant and responsible because the other reapers will not carry her like George's mother has done in the past. George was able to go home after deciding to leave college, but death proves a more complicated barrier. If George did not die, she would have been more of a postfeminist because of the privilege afforded to her by her parents' socioeconomic status and her antagonistic relationship with her mother. Because it relies on the second wave and is not in opposition to it, third-wave feminism has an awareness of privilege and oppression that postfeminism does not. George's death, which separated her from her family, also causes her to reconsider her relationship to them as part of her emotional growth.

Jaye in Wonderfalls

Jaye Tyler, at twenty-four, has the college education that George never finished, but she hasn't gotten any further professionally. Jaye chooses to be apathetic in the face of her highly ambitious and successful family. She works a low-level retail job, even though she graduated from Brown University. Jaye's father Darrin is a doctor, her mother Karen is a best-selling author, her sister Sharon is a lawyer, and her brother Aaron is a graduate student on a scholarship. As she's discussing her family with her friend Mahandra, Jaye comments, "Well, just look at them. They all work really hard every day and they're dissatisfied. I can be dissatisfied without hardly working at all" ("Wax Lion"). Jaye rejects the need to compete for prestige. Jaye definitely fulfills the description of a slacker: She's highly educated, of the upper-middle class, and has no interest in succeeding at her job (Ostler 203). Conversely, unlike her high school classmate Gretchen Speck, Jaye's not interested in finding the perfect man who will marry and take care of her. Gretchen plans the ten-year reunion high school three years early to show her classmates how well she married and show her husband how popular she was in high school ("Pink Flamingos"). Gretchen spends her time flaunting her new marriage to everyone, even though she's really miserable.

Like George, Jaye seems to exemplify not striving for anything:

JAYE: I'm a non-winner
BIANCA: By choice. You're the prototypical Gen Yer. You represent a generation of young people who've been blessed with education and opportunity who don't just fall through the cracks, but jump through ["Karma Charmeleon"].

Bianca, another graduate of Brown, is incapacitated by fears of not amounting to anything in her life. She admires that Jaye is disinterested in trying to be successful or even faking success. Bianca is so jealous that Jaye feels no such pressure to rack up achievements that she tries to copy Jaye:

> BIANCA: You've shown me a new way. I can live in a pressureless, expectation-free zone.
> JAYE. That's my zone! You're parked in my zone!
> BIANCA: And it's the only place I'll ever be able to breathe ["Karma Chameleon"].

Jaye's consternation at Bianca's attempts to mimic her contradicts the disinterested impression she tries to give. Furthermore, Jaye's discomfort with Bianca's discipleship calls into question her own narcissism.

When Jaye suddenly starts hearing the muses (voices coming from inanimate objects, mainly stuffed animals) talking to her to give her missions with cryptic messages, she isn't cut off from her old life or her family, which happens to George as a reaper. Rather, the muses force Jaye to draw upon the connections of community and family that she and the living George had eschewed. Jaye, who values isolation and is very noncommittal, must not only interact with strangers, friends, and family, but also create and strengthen relationships in order to complete her missions.

Chuck in Pushing Daisies

While the protagonist of *Pushing Daisies* is supposed to be Ned, the show starts when Chuck ("Charlotte") Charles comes back into his life. His flashbacks often include her and we learn as much about her history as his. After Ned brings her back to life, Chuck helps to save Ned from the man who killed her. The series narrator describes Ned's grateful moment as a "delight. The girl he rescued from death had returned the favor" ("Pie-lette"). Chuck coming back into Ned's life doesn't result in her just saving him physically from death in one instance, but helping him find meaning is his own life again. Before he brought back Chuck into his life, Ned was emotionally closed off and not really interacting with people. Chuck is the girl who lived after being fated to die, similar in a way to George. In her second chance at life, Chuck joins Ned and Emerson, the private investigator who uses Ned to wake the dead, in investigating murders.

At twenty-eight, Chuck is the oldest and least formally educated of the three women. She is self-taught, garnering her post–high school education by books, audiotapes, materials from her aunts (Lily and Vivian), and volunteering. Unlike George or Jaye, Chuck is not formally employed because her relationship with Ned gives her some financial stability. However, she asserts her agency by helping out in the Pie Hole, Ned's restaurant, and helping solve murder cases. Even though her death resulted from a vacation to get away from her family, Chuck is very close to her family and she, like George, finds ways to maintain a connection with them after her death.

Not Queen Bee, Not Even Buffy

Different from the powerful female protagonists in the second wave, the special third-wave state of George, Jaye, and Chuck doesn't grant them any privileges over the other members of their community or group. At certain times, they can become more isolated or are forced into uncomfortable situations: "[The] superpowers within these series serve as a mechanism of marginalization more so than they do of empowerment; in other words, superpowers become a narrative technique to disenfranchise these characters both socially and culturally" (O'Reilly 2). Unlike superheroes, these women are hampered by the supernatural instead of it being a power they possess. George becomes just another reaper so she does not get the chance to revel in her special gift. She starts off at a disadvantage as the new person in her reaper group and she also has very little life experience to draw upon because she died so young: "I mean do you know what it's like to be on the cusp of adulthood and not know who you are? What you want to be? Or even if you want to be? It's ten shades of suck is what it is" ("Pilot"). Because she was so unsure of herself in life, George is reluctant to assume her job as reaper. She tries more than once to get out of her duties. Each time George tries to avoid reaping someone, that person suffers more or others suffer because that death didn't occur. One man ends up witnessing his own autopsy because George didn't take his soul and many people die from a faulty product because George keeps the company owner from going to his appointed death ("Dead Girl Walking"; "Reapercussions"). Realizing the removal of souls before death is a service so people don't suffer any pain at point of death and that death is necessary, George assumes her duty. Still, her work is rarely smooth sailing. George encounters client who flashes her before he dies and one who can't acknowledge death because she has Alzheimer's ("Death Defying"; "Always"). Her unavoidable responsibility situates George in adulthood, as shown in this conversation with another reaper:

> GEORGE: I don't think I'm supposed to be doing this.
> RUBE: If somebody else was supposed to be doing this, I'd be talking to somebody else.
> GEORGE: But I don't know anything about anything.
> RUBE: You think I do?..When I'm supposed to know something I'll know it. When you're supposed to know something, you'll know it…. You're learning ["Dead Girl Walking"].

Although George's job is supernatural, it calls on her to perform actions she doesn't want to do and may expect knowledge from her that she doesn't have, an experience that women entering the workforce at any given time or taking on certain jobs have had to face in real life.

In addition, while they have the ability to take souls, reapers still must find a way to get food and shelter like the living: "Even with this seemingly divine power that I have, I don't get paid a cent, I can't disappear or fly or walk through walls" ("Dead Girl Walking"). As a result, George has to win over Delores, her boss at Happy Time, again (this time as Millie, her new identity after death) to get a job at Happy Time in order to survive. When she was alive, her interview with Delores was so caustic that Delores supposedly gave George her first job as punishment ("Pilot"). Often, the consequences of her reaping job single her out. George frequently has to miss work at Happy Time or come in looking disheveled because of her reaping. She also has to keep up the pretense of being a recovering alcoholic to make it to reaping appointments which occur during work hours. George's situation, having to work two jobs and struggling to get them both done, shows how society's view of slackers may not be accurate. Her experiences also negate the myth of meritocracy, which promises success for hard work, because in the real world "identities, job securities, and family structures are no longer stable" (Paule 89). Showing the intersections of identity and questioning the myths of society, especially how they apply to women, is a third-wave perspective.

Like George, the muses mess with Jaye's work and social life. The muses force her to interact with people and be nice to them, especially to her family. Jaye asks the muses, "Is that supposed to mean something? Is that a metaphor?" ("Wax Lion"). Jaye struggles against these acts of politeness and selfless service to others as innate feminine traits. She will not unquestioningly be what the world expects of women: "Jaye's cynicism is a reflection of a capitalist, dog-eat-dog world where acts of kindness are not recognized as such" (K. Beeler 95). Her experiences reinforce her skeptical view of the world. In fact, the first person Jaye helps accuses her of pulling a scam and hits her ("Wax Lion"). Furthermore, she has to feign excuses to get out of work, just like George. Two of her missions nearly land her in jail. She received fines twice because of one task. Sharon complains Jaye's too old to act like a "troubled teen" ("Pilot"). People view these occurrences are part of Jaye's regular shenanigans. They think what she's doing is just part of her slacker attitude.

Contrary to George or Chuck, Jaye is happy to be self-reliant. She becomes frustrated when she needs to reach out to others because of her ordeal with the muses, but no one understands her. Mahandra, her friend, thinks it's her subconscious asserting itself ("Wax Lion"). Jaye's family sends her to Dr. Ron, a psychologist, because they think she's having a mental break-down. Ironically, she learns more about the muses from the brass monkey in Dr. Ron's office than she does from Dr. Ron. Yet, Jaye ends up saving Dr. Ron's life from another patient because she became his patient ("Cocktail Bunny"). However, when Jaye avoids listening to the muses out of frustration, negative consequences result, just like in George's story. Jaye accidentally runs over her father in an attempt to block out the muses ("Pink Flamingos"). Jaye real-izes, "I find myself in unpleasant situations all the time. You know why? Because even if you have a choice it can and will be taken away from you. We're all fate's bitch" ("Caged Bird"). While Jaye is talking about the super-natural forces messing up her life, this realization that all choices that the second wave of feminism said we deserve are not necessarily possible is a third-wave conundrum. Jaye's countermove is to find another puppet for the universe. She tries to make the grandson of a Native American seer into a seer himself in order to get answers and remove her gift ("Totem Mole"). Of course, everything she does to get him anointed as a chosen one only proves that she has a gift. Her recalcitrance to being labeled as a seer herself is almost as strong as her original reluctance to listen to her muses: "I don't want to be chosen. In this instance, I'm anti-choice" ("Totem Mole"). Jaye's comment here has two points. Part of her comment references the feminist fight for reproductive choice. Clearly, Jaye is for reproductive choice because she says "[i]n this instance" ("Totem Mole"). The main thrust of her comment though is that she no longer wants to do the bidding of the muses. Her refusal to listen to muses is not an anti-feminist move to be passive. Instead, her "refusal is essentially a refusal to give up what one takes to be one's own interest" (Campbell 59–60). Jaye, like the prototypical hero, rejects the obligation of being a hero before she accepts it. She is asserting her independence, not choosing to be powerless. She rejects the supernatural force trying to control her life until she realizes that she can use the power to help others and herself: "You know I'm not sure if my burden is a burden or not. I mean, other people seem to want it. And that should always make you pause before you give something up" ("Totem Mole"). Ironically, Jaye, who has viewed herself and been viewed by others as only self-centered, must take further interest in her own life in order to help others because of her gift. She's not self-less or self-sacrificing like a damsel, but has a sense of self like a hero.

Even though Chuck's resurrection did not come with guidelines, there are limiting factors for her as well. She cannot touch the man she loves because to do so would be to die permanently. In addition, she must not show herself to her family or community, concealing or disguising herself so people won't recognize her as the woman who died. Chuck feels lost in this position of invisibility: "What if we've interrupted the natural transition between life and the afterlife? I didn't move on to where mom and dad are and I didn't return to where I was either. I'm just stuck. I'm stuck and I'm absolutely alone and I don't if I can go one like this or if I want to" ("Bad Habits"). Unable to establish solid connections with her family in the past or present, Chuck doubts her place in the world. Chuck becomes as disheartened as George because she too has to limit her contact with family members after her death. In adulthood, people often feel like they are in limbo between their inability to stay at home and the loneliness that comes with independence.

After her death, Chuck finds a caring partner in Ned, but she has to work through the complicated aspects of being in a relationship. Ned's attempts to protect Chuck diminish her power and objectify her. While Chuck likes the tropes of fairytales and romance, she does not like being told what to do. Before meeting with Ned after her death, Chuck was mothering her aunts and helping out in her community. So, even though she didn't often socialize outside, she was very much in charge of her own life. Chuck decides to force Ned to open up and thwart Ned's overprotective nature so they can have a real relationship:

> CHUCK: I hate having secrets. Now I am one. All these disguises. Hiding in your apartment all the time.
> NED: I hate secrets too.
> CHUCK: What? You love secrets. You want to marry secrets and have half-secrets, half-human babies ["Dummy"].

As Jaye helps the hesitant Bianca to get her words out, Chuck consistently labors to get Ned's emotions and words out. Ned buries his feelings through negative words and Chuck is the only one who can draw positive feelings and words out of him (Parmiter 162). She asks him, "Am I seriously the first person to question your aversion to change?" ("Smell of Success"). Chuck's relationship with Ned shows that relationships, even loving ones, are not perfect, but women do not have to become powerless in a relationship.

Chuck does have the option to escape these restrictions to her freedom by leaving the area where she was known and assuming a new identity elsewhere. When her father comes back into her life, he encourages her to leave town with him and make a fresh new start, saying he can protect her:

> CHUCK: He promised me an adventure like the ones he told me about when I was a kid…. He's trying to be the dad I always dreamed of. Someone who could keep his little girl safe and happy. Except I'm not a little girl ["The Legend of Merle McQuoddy"].

Chuck rejects her father's offer because of her independent nature, not out of fear of leaving. She doesn't want to be infantilized. She sees herself as an adult woman. Chuck tells Ned that he is a "good man" ("The Legend of Merle McQuoddy"). She has always had the ability to make a new life for herself, but she is staying because she wants an adult relationship with Ned and to care for her aunts. Although Chuck performs traditional female gender roles by enjoying acts of domesticity (e.g., cooking, cleaning), is in a heterosexual relationship, and dresses in a very feminine manner, she has a strong sense of self and refuses to be entirely dependent on Ned.

Various reviewers commented on how unfriendly Jaye and George were when *Dead Like Me* and *Wonderfalls* were reviewed. Robert MacDonald called Jaye "unlikeable" and mentioned that she rarely smiles; Rob Owen says George's gaze "depressive" makes it difficult for the audience "to embrace her"; and Tom Jicha points out that George "actually smiles" briefly in one episode as if this was a major achievement (MacDonald; Owen; Jicha). Oddly enough, their attitude fits in with their disaffected youth style that the critics acknowledged that they were representing in their shows. Scott Moore calls George a "slacker," while Joy Press, Joanne Ostrow, and Alex Strahan all call Jaye a "slacker" (Moore; Press, Ostrow; Strachan). A male hero does not receive criticism for not smiling and acting surly. In fact, critics gave praise to George's reaper boss, Rube, for showing that very demeanor. Tim Goodman described Rube as a "fatherly figure to George without being to sugary"; Margo Jefferson calls Rube's attitude "tough-love"; and Alisa Cohen's says Rube's style is "deadpan" (Goodman; Jefferson; Cohen). Laura Mulvey's seminal article, *Visual Pleasure and Narrative Cinema* discusses how the gaze of the camera is male and objectifies women: "Unchallenged, mainstream film coded the erotic into the language of the dominant patriarchal order" (343–344). Regardless of the gender of the reviewer, their criticism of Jaye and George involves imposing the male gaze, and expecting George and Jaye to smile as the object of the camera's attention. Because "surveillance of women's bodies constitutes perhaps the largest type of media content across all genres and media forms," by rejecting the gaze, George and Jaye perform a transgression the minute the camera views them (R. Gill 149). They defy societal expectations, thus creating a space between public and private not generally afforded to women. In *The Contingent Smile: A Meta-Analysis of Sex Differences in Smiling*, researchers' "results [showed] … that there are gender display rules that call for women and adolescent girls to smile more than men and adolescent boys" (LaFrance et al. 325). Because of the multimedia society we live in, there has been an overlap in the viewing women in media and viewing them in real life, which has turned this expectation into a standard. From the press critiques of Serena Williams and Hillary Clinton not smiling during their interviews to women harassed by men on the street expecting them to smile, there is the patriarchal belief that part of your job as a female is to smile. Recently, there has been a backlash against this imposition on women, from street artist Tatyana Fazlalizadeh, who started a project called *Stop Telling Women to Smile* in 2012, to online media like the *Huffington Post*

(Fazlalizadeh; Lindlar). Therefore, Jaye and George have been engaging in a feminist act before there was a large feminist response to it in society.

Chuck's feminine style and breezy manner make her seem different from Jaye and Chuck, but she too wants to transgress from the rules and regulations that were created by her resurrection. For the most part, she's hiding from her aunts, but she also defies Ned's and Emerson's directives regarding concealment. Even when she's supposed to be disguised, Chuck wears statement pieces, which can be an "article of clothing or an entire outfit that somehow stands out and grabs the attention of onlookers" (Goettel and Everette). Chuck's clothing stands out because she is protesting the invisibility required of her. Her clothing is unabashedly feminine, referential to the past, and rarely understated: "Through this critical engagement with 1950s styles, Chuck is also negotiating her own identity, her status as 'alive again,' and her place within the microcosm of The Pie Hole and the context of the larger world" (Burger 188). Outside she wears bright colors, distinctive prints and eye-catching styles, but there isn't more than a hint of flesh underneath. Chuck's clothing communicates the contradiction between her desire to be seen and the rules that require her to stay hidden. When Ned gets jealous because Chuck is very sympathetic to a man whose apartment is invaded by a plane, Chuck responds, "I'm not saying he isn't guilty and I'm not saying I am. I'm just saying it's not about him" ("Pigeon"). Chuck has stressed to him that her friendliness is not an open invitation to men. Chuck can also use her friendliness to accomplish things. Instead of the roundabout way that Emerson uses to get a key card, Chuck just uses her affectionate hug to lift one from the security guard ("Dummy"). Like her vintage clothing, Chuck's friendly decorum conceals as much as it reveals.

Slacker Girl Skills

As their names suggest, George, Jaye, and Chuck will not be confined to traditional gender roles. Although George and Jaye do not present a friendly demeanor, they are sympathetic to the people they help. Chuck refers to Ned in heroic terms (e.g., hero, knight), but she enjoys going on adventures as much as doing domestic chores. Their skills are across the board, often combining abilities gendered as masculine or feminine, and although their professional lives seem stagnant, they are performing heroic duties outside of them.

As an adult in the world of the living, George learns to understand Delores's personality and negotiate with her so she can reap souls and still keep her job at Happy Time. While George doesn't truly have much in common with Delores, she curbs her sarcastic behavior and she listens to Delores' tales of Murray, her cat, and her life outside work. Delores becomes the only living person George reaches out to and counts on. George also becomes a true friend to Delores. She stays by Delores when Murray gets sick, even trying to ward off the reaper who takes pets' souls ("Rest in Peace"); rounds up everyone at the office and makes them work to impress an efficiency expert on Delores' behalf ("Hurry"); and tackles co-worker Brian when she catches him stealing Delores' wallet ("Last Call"). In her relationship with Delores, George learns to care about someone outside her family who is different from her. In addition, her acquired office skills, like data entry, prove useful to her and the other reapers at Happy Time when they need to catch up on the paperwork of the dead who were reaped ("Vacation"). In this way, George's work with the living provides more than simply financial support to her work with the dying.

Jaye's evasive attitude toward personal involvement and work belies the fact that she is clearly a person who has agency and can easily perform actions for herself or in service to others. Jaye can act decisively, without any sense of embarrassment or concern about what other people might think. This willingness to do almost anything is what the muses exploit. In order to get the monkey to answer her question about her gift, Jaye licks the light switch ("Cocktail Bunny"). Although she chooses to pretend to be a delinquent, she is clearly book smart as well as street smart. She graduated with a degree in Philosophy from Brown University and she can hotwire a car. She easily writes the magazine article about the Generation Y that stymied the supposedly "highly motivated" Bianca ("Karma Chameleon"). Then Jaye has no issues giving Bianca the glory for writing the article in order to stop Bianca from copying her life and send her on her way ("Karma Chameleon"). While she is clearly capable of attracting men or using her intellect to obtain fame, Jaye is fine with her life existing in what Eric, her love interest, termed the "creative non-permanence" ("Wound-up Penguin"). She can fly by the seat of her pants and improvise as needed. When Jaye is asked to describe her life, she calls it "a work in progress" ("Karma Chameleon"). Admitting she has no set plan, makes Jaye more honest and realistic than some of her contemporaries.

Although she has the least formal education, Chuck has the most varied skill set, mostly from volunteer work. She was a beekeeper and used the sales of her honey to help the homeless ("Pie-lette"). Her knowledge of marble allows her to lift prints from a crime scene ("Bitter Sweets"). Chuck speaks different languages because she learned them through language courses on tape ("Dummy"). She's able to speak Mandarin to a murder victim ("Dim Sum Lose Sum"). She also knows about different types of insurance claims because she had helped a judge by phone ("Pigeon"). Chuck also performs femininity with her motherly attitude and domestic skills like baking and decorating.

Unlike George or Jaye, who tried to run away or ignore the supernatural force in their lives, Chuck uses the event to start her life again: "I can't be alive again for no reason" ("Dummy"). Unfazed by the aspect of dying, Chuck jumps right into the act of solving murders, starting with her own. As Ned cautions her about the danger, since she already died once, Chuck replies, "Luck pushed me first," as she looks straight into the camera without fear ("Pie-lette"). Chuck is not scared away by the thought of imminent death. When Ned refuses to work on a case, Chuck sells herself to Emerson: "I may not be Superman, but I'm smart and helpful. Maybe I could be your sidekick. I could be the Alive-Again Avenger who came back from the dead to solve her own murder and stayed back from the dead to bring justice to murder victims everywhere with the help of a crusty unflappable streetwise gumshoe" ("Window Dressed to Kill"). Chuck knows she doesn't have supernatural power like Ned or investigative experience like Ned's partner Emerson, but she believes in her ability to help others. During the Dickerson Department Store case, she renames herself the "Alive-Again Avenger" ("Window Dressed to Kill"). This is important, not only because she is presenting herself as a female superhero, but also because the "power of naming is one of the most decisive human activities in constituting the world as experienced. The power has been an almost exclusive male prerogative throughout most of human history" (King 44). Chuck does not see herself as diminutive to anyone, whether its her romantic relationship with Ned or her investigative partnership with Ned and Emerson.

While Chuck does enact femininity often by playing the caregiver, she has no qualms becoming aggressive if she feels the situation calls for it (Farr 143). And like a hero, she can do it to defend the rights of others, not just her own. When the Pie Hole is attacked by a competitor, Chuck fights back on Ned's behalf by breaking into a competitor's store with Olive:

> OLIVE: I didn't think you'd go for this. I thought you were all goody-goody, apple pie, and baseball.
> CHUCK: Well so far as I know how to use a baseball bat to make someone's face look like apple pie ["Bitter Sweets"].

Chuck's warm personality doesn't make her a pushover. She only feels guilty about breaking into the other store when Ned goes over to the store to clean up and is jailed as a result. However, she doesn't spend time second-guessing her actions. Instead, she promptly gets working on the case with Emerson in order to free Ned. While she dresses in nostalgic highly feminine clothing and her romance is originally presented in terms of a fairy tale, Chuck's incongruities make her a part of third-wave feminism as much as Jaye or George.

Out of Bounds Families

Antithetical to the detached persona of the slacker, all three female protagonists maintain ties with their family. For Chuck and George, contact is indirect because they're dead. George mothers her younger sister, Reggie, from afar. She often understands the needs of Reggie better than their parents. Early on, Rube cautioned George to cut her ties, which is often expected of a hero. Joseph Campbell in *The Hero with a Thousand Faces* equates the hero's call to adventure with the Freudian "separation from mother" (52). Through her death, George enters adulthood, experiences actual separation from her family, and her afterlife journey keeps her from returning home. In her own time, George builds an auxiliary family with the other reapers and Delores, but she keeps a distant watch on her family. In contrast to her father, Clancy, who uses George's death as an excuse to extricate himself from his family, George never forfeits her family ties.

Jaye's family is loving, but they have no concept of personal boundaries and are overly concerned with professional and social success. Her father Darrin tries to encourage Jaye with the myth of meritocracy and stories of slow starters while her mother Karen is always on the lookout for men to match up with Jaye and Sharon. When Aaron, her brother, and Sharon joke about Jaye's retail job and her trailer park home, she responds, "Those things are all facts. Should I be ashamed?" ("Karma Chameleon"). Jaye doesn't care because she believes herself more independent than Aaron who lives at home and she doesn't feel the constant need to seek for parental approval like Sharon. Jaye's assignments continually force her to communicate with her family from whom she had sought to maintain a distance. In a way, the muses can be seen as encouraging her familial obligations by their challenges. When Jaye pours a drink on former classmate Gretchen at the reunion because of the muses, Karen views it as Jaye competing for her affection ("Pink Flamingos"). She reassures her daughter that she doesn't want her to be anyone else. Jaye running over her father leads him to get further tests in the hospital, which helps them detect a dangerous blood clot ("Pink Flamingos"). As a result, he is thankful to Jaye for having saved his life. We see in this instance that it's not only Jaye's submission to the muses, but also her defiance of them leads to a benefit. Aaron, who is studying comparative religions, witnesses Jaye's power and her actions suddenly make him think that there's meaning in the world ("Muffin Buffalo"). This helps them reconnect as siblings. After the muses encourage Jaye to get her sister a date, Jaye is moved to be kinder to Sharon:

JAYE: I love you.
SHARON: I love you too.
JAYE: I don't feel dirty. I thought I was gonna feel dirty.... I don't feel dirty at all

which is surprising. You know maybe we could say it again sometime. But not for a while and not often ["Wax Lion"].

Jaye expresses sisterly love and finds that she's okay with it. This is a surprise to her because she's never been close to Sharon. She learns to listen to Sharon, thus learning that Sharon's a lesbian ("Wax Lion"). As Jaye deals with helping people who are isolated in one way or another, Jaye becomes more willing to let her family in and they become more willing to try to understand her behavior instead of simply judging her, which is how family relationships are often negotiated in adulthood.

Chuck, like George, tries to help out her family from afar. Early on after her death, Chuck finds a way of covertly taking "responsibility for Lily and Vivian's happiness and took action" ("Fun in Funeral"). She sends them pies baked with mood enhancers to relieve their emotional problems. Like a hero, she acquired a magical agent and used it (Propp 43). Although this may seem like an assault on the aunts, Chuck had been in charge of their medication and maintenance when they were alive. She learned that since her death, they were not maintaining themselves. Later, she directs Olive on how to nudge her aunts back to swimming as a way of coping with their grief over Chuck's death ("Smell of Success"). As the aunts' mental health gets better, the mood enhancers are phased out and just the ritual of giving the aunts pie is maintained. While Chuck won't allow her father to forbid her from seeing Ned and will not return to being a little girl for him to make up for lost time, Chuck considers leaving Ned when he helps her aunts make plans to leave town for a European tour ("The Legend of Merle McQuoddy"; "Kerplunk"). What Chuck faces in trying to resolve her romantic and familial love is "the contradiction that feminism's third wave has to face: an often conscious knowledge of the ways we are compelled and constructed by the very things that undermine us" (Heywood and Drake 11). She is trying to sustain both familial and romantic love instead of sacrificing one for the other. Chuck may love others, but she won't be defined solely through her relationships with them.

Love Is a Many Splintered Thing

In traditional studies, women are generally required to remain virginal and untouched until the hero kisses them, while the heroes can have a variety of romantic experiences. The female characters are often the bride that the hero starts the journey for or part of the prize package along with the kingdom (Propp 35, 63). Women are not meant to have romantic experiences as well as heroic adventures. As heroes themselves, Chuck, Jaye, and George change the dynamic.

During her life, George remained a virgin because she kept her distance from people. Even though it happened after death for her, losing her virginity was still a coming of age moment. George's intellect couldn't prepare her for her first sexual experience or how vulnerable it made her feel. George's awakening isn't a punishment for having sex that generally happens to female protagonists, like Buffy in *Buffy the Vampire Slayer* ("Innocence"). Even after multiple waves of feminism, there are very few stories where a girl losing virginity is treated like as a part of growing up, like it is for boys, rather than a tragedy about the loss of virginity (Fetters). For George, it does become a rite of passage, but one that occurs only after death: "Losing your virginity is supposed to be one of the steps to being really alive. For me, it was one of the ways, I finally realized that it was over" ("Death Defying"). George learns having sex doesn't guarantee a relationship with someone and she realizes she can't even be in a relationship because she was already dead. George just had to go through the emotions and the consequences of venting those emotions as an adult.

Jaye's journey is about being adult enough to enter into a meaningful relationship. Jaye is not a romantic. She compares getting into a relationship to "heaving after bad fish" and love to "an open wound" ("Lovesick Ass"). For Jaye, it's not about getting Eric to fall in love with her. Even though she's had more dating experiences than George, Jaye has also kept an emotional distance between herself and other people. She has a track record of dumping people when the relationship starts to get serious. Jaye has to learn to value potential romantic interest Eric as a person, not just a trophy, and risk emotional vulnerability so she can have a fuller relationship than she has had before. The marriage of George's former classmate Gretchen was an example of considering a partner as a trophy to show off ("Pink Flamingos"). Gretchen married a man who fulfilled the requirements of a list she created and she becomes unhappy because she spends so much time trying to prove her husband loves her instead of contemplating if she really loves her husband. By being separated from Eric, Jaye is able to admit to her friend Mahandra and sister Sharon her true feelings for him ("Cocktail Bunny"; "Caged Bird"). Jaye actually has the time to look inward and decide that she wants to be in a committed relationship, even if it is an emotional risk. After she accepts that the gift is a part of her, she is able to understand the journey she took to being with Eric ("Caged Bird"). She realizes that the tasks she had to accomplish, even the ones that were difficult to carry out, all served a purpose in starting her relationship with Eric.

Chuck's level of sexual experience, like her education, is never fully divulged. Although, she may have more knowledge through books and her Aunt Lily's pornographic materials than actual practice, she puts herself on equal footing with Ned ("Dummy"). She finds it cute when Ned doesn't know what a key party is and he keeps guessing incorrectly ("Robbing Hood"). Since on skin contact of any kind would lead to Chuck's death, they struggle with negotiating a relationship, similar to people with physical disabilities who must "explore an alternative sex culture on the artfulness of the disability" (Seibers 46). At first, Ned is fixated on the physicality of their relationship because he wants to keep Chuck alive. When he gets jealous of another man touching Chuck, she informs him their relationship is more than physical obstacles: "See isn't this neat? Here we were thinking we have one big problem when in actual fact we have hundreds of little problems we've to sort out before we even get to the big problem, which means we're like everyone else in the world" ("Pigeon"). As they grow as a couple, they continually try to find ways to show each other affection and attraction. They use plastic wrap to kiss, gloves to hold hands, and beekeeper outfits to dance with each other. In this way, "they represent disability, not as a defect that needs to be overcome to have sex, but as a complex embodiment that embraces sexual activities and pleasure" (Seibers 46). They add spice to their relationship by using safety precautions as ways to turn each other on or using safe types of contact. By doing this, Chuck and Ned's relationship shows how third wave's "[p]ro-sex feminism [which] offers a more nuanced analysis of sex, power, and fantasy and is consistently more interested in sex as *it is* rather than as it should be" (italics hers) (Johnson 261). Chuck and Ned's relationship presents a contrast to most able-bodied romantic stories and shows how physical acts that differ from the prevalent representations can still be meaningful.

In the Service Sector

These women go about resolving their tasks without expecting the prizes or acclaim of the traditional male hero. Chuck, George, and Jaye use their skills serving others, both in traditional and nontraditional sense. Their traditional work involves service occupations: George works for a temp agency, Chuck volunteered when she was alive and waitresses after her death, and Jaye is a retail clerk. Their experiences mirror the lives of many real American women who work in the service industry, often at low-wage jobs (Iversen et al.). By presenting his female protagonists in service jobs, Fuller is giving a face to and empowering the image of the service worker, indicating that their lives are worth examining and these sectors are also sites of important human connections. George and Jaye occupy positions in the service sector where smiling to appease others is required and the fact that they don't provides another site of resistance to their gendered and socioeconomic roles (Hecht 1334). Acting surly in these low-power position shifts the power balance as well as expectations on women.

In *On a Pale Horse*, the book that is the inspiration for *Dead Like Me*, the protagonist Zane learns he was chosen because he would rebel against the rules (Jicha; Anthony). It is this quality to question the status quo that George also embodies as a reaper and as Millie as well. Her ability to think for herself is how George manages the souls in her care and copes with being undead: "In fact, what makes George a deeply human character is the reluctance with which she comes to accept these rules and the way in which she reflects on them" (P. Gill 119). In contrast to Zane's main rebellion, which is really just a traditional quest that ends saving a damsel in distress, George questions situations from her sense of right and wrong, yet is willing to acknowledge there are gray areas. As she ponders the group dynamics of her reaper group and office co-workers, she disparagingly remarks, "Hey, you have ten fingers. I have ten fingers. Let's be friends. We'll make rules and slogans. Then if we find someone with nine fingers we can beat the crap out of them" ("Curious George"). Even though she says she doesn't care, George will pick what she feels is right over what is popular. In a flashback, we see that George may have been chosen to be a reaper because as a child she accepted being the patsy instead of hurting another girl for the amusement of the popular kids ("The Shallow End"). George's resistance to joining a group in order to belong somewhere bucks society's perception that women are so innately sociable that they would be unable to exist in solitude. George would rather have the right to think for herself than go along with the crowd. It doesn't mean that George isn't lonely, but rather that she is capable of the independent power that her mother wanted for her.

The supernatural in their lives doesn't present them as saviors, but rather allows them to be servers. For instance, "Jaye does not have the comforting presence of an angel, a pillar of fire, or even a burning bush. Jaye's contact with the divine is completely in keeping with the mundane situation of contemporary humanity" (S. Beeler 327). The point of these acts is not to elevate Jaye, but rather humanize her. While the muses guide her behavior at times, Jaye also finds herself helping others, like getting Pat, who is shut-in, a social life, without supernatural intervention ("Muffin Buffalo"). The fact that "Jaye's community ties become richer and deeper, small in scale though they are, and they are just as important to Jaye's power as a visionary as being able to save a city or the world" does question how society belittles service occupations (Howell 90). Jaye proves that heroic work doesn't have to be massive in scale to be impactful. Yet, because women are stereotyped as naturally caring and helpful, their work in the service industry is considered of lower value than men's (Miller). Jaye's promotion loss to co-worker Alec, who she had trained and who was also a slacker as a sales clerk, mirrors the experiences of women in real life jobs.

Chuck's ability to empathize with witnesses and listen to them helps the investigative team gather information on their cases. When Ned and Emerson's mockery of witness Jeanine's eating habits, Chuck rebukes them, "That's not funny.... The girl's got a whole secret life in the bathroom" ("Dummy"). She realizes that Jeanine has bulimia and explains it to Ned and Emerson so they will quit making fun of her. Chuck has true compassion for others and uses it to keep Ned and Emerson in line. Ned adjusts his attitude to be more empathetic easily, but Emerson is more resistant. Chuck argues with Emerson about returning objects that had been stolen from dead bodies back to their families ("Fun in Funeral"). However, by the end of the series, Emerson admits, "I choose to affiliate myself with the both of you [Chuck and Ned].... Because your moral compass is always pointed due—the right thing" ("Kerplunk"). While Emerson is not as sympathetic as Chuck, he recognizes the importance of her ability to be sympathetic.

In *Outlaw Culture: Resisting Representations*, bell hooks discusses how service is a meaningful occupation: "A love ethic emphasizes the importance of service to others. Within the value system of the United States any task or job that is related to 'service' is devalued. Service strengthens our capacity to know compassion and deepens our insight. To serve another I cannot see them as an object, I must see their subjecthood" (249). All three women have gained insight into their own lives (and deaths) by their experience aiding others. They also help bring meaning back into the lives of others. George helps a woman with Alzheimer's connect to her life so she can understand that she is dead ("Always"). Jaye restores a wayward nun's faith by bringing a father to a daughter he never knew he had ("Wound-up Penguin"). Chuck reassures many clients that their loved ones truly cared for them. For instance, she tells Jeanine that Bernard loved her ("Dummy"). Therefore, regardless of their demeanor during (or reluctance at times to perform) their tasks, the effort it takes to accomplish them provides a service to those they aid as well as enobles George, Jaye, and Chuck. In their low-key ways, George, Jaye, and Chuck are making a difference.

Fate's Bitch?

The journey for these women is not specifically geared toward a career or domestic bliss, which may make their development seem arrested on the surface, but rather it is a spiritual one. Not spiritual in the sense of deciphering the supernatural aspects of their world or the various religions they encounter. Rather, for George, Jaye, and Chuck, "[s]pirituality can be described as a process of transformation and growth, an organic and dynamic part of human development, of both individual and society" (King 5). The magical occurrences don't cleave them from their path or deny them their search, but are a part of it. Therefore, the supernatural occurrences and gifts trigger an all-encompassing search for self. The fact that the spiritual search is a difficult one highlights their agency in changing themselves and the lives of others around them.

George would probably not have grown up if she stayed alive. She would have been able to shirk responsibilities and stay emotionally stunted. Her mother, although she would have complained about it, would still have done George's laundry and cleaned up after her as she is still doing with her younger sister Reggie. Her father would have continued hiding his secrets and pretending everything was all right. Only after George died, did her family start dealing with their inability to express and handle their emotions. A living George would have made a very isolated and unfinished adult, but undead George matures a substantial amount. Delores unknowingly makes this distinction when she rewrites George's original evaluation in order to make it more palatable for Joy:

> DELORES: I know exactly what to write. I know what will make her mother proud.
> GEORGE: What?
> DELORES: I'm gonna base her on you.
> GEORGE: I thought we wanted to make her seem impressive.
> DELORES: You are impressive. I've watched you. In one short year, you've grown into a fine young woman. I'm sure George's mom will be pleased ["Always"].

Delores was loath to give Joy the original evaluation because she viewed George then as full of potential, but troubled. Therefore, even though she thinks she's basing it on Millie, she's really giving a proper assessment of George's progression after death. George achievement wasn't a compulsory part of being a reaper. Daisy and Mason, two other reapers who died at older ages and have been dead for many more years, illustrate a significant lack of mental and emotional development compared to George.

Jaye is highly privileged because of her intelligence and her well-off family. So although she didn't suffer the same depth of loss as Chuck and George, she also has to learn to deal with the challenges the muses present and open up to people, even if pain is involved. Jaye realizes in her supernatural adventures that "there's no wrong way to do it" ("Totem Mole"). Much like the ways third-wave feminism works, Jaye learns there isn't one specific method that works for everyone, but acknowledges that the work has to be done. In addition, she can see the successful careers of her mother and sister, which would be praised by second-wave feminism, don't compensate for everything. Although the muses put Jaye through awkward situations, she learns to value her experiences and her own path. In the process, she develops more meaningful relationships with her boyfriend and family, but her sense of self is very much intact.

Even though she was murdered, Chuck refutes the role of victim:

CHUCK: I'm not who you think I am. [Ned and Emerson turn to see Chuck standing in the kitchen]
EMERSON: Who does we think you are?
CHUCK: The small town girl who never saw the world only to have her first time out be her last—well, that is who I am, but I was hoisted by my own petard!
NED: What's a petard?
CHUCK: In my case, the petard is that Tahitian getaway: it was a devil's bargain ["Pie-lette"].

She believed that by choosing to go on the getaway, she was complicit in her death. Yet, Chuck doesn't pick on herself for making a poor choice because it resulted in her death. Chuck's desire for adventure was only held at bay by her responsibility to her aunts. After she dies, she sees the possibility in starting over: "I could be anybody, anybody I want. I like that" ("Fun in Funeral"). Chuck didn't want to abandon her aunts, but she relishes independence from home. She is both the traditional female who is comfortable in the domestic sphere and the hero who longs for a journey. Chuck's death gives her the chance to explore the world in ways she hadn't before. She admits to Ned that in the life she lived before she died, she was "terrified of change" ("Circus, Circus"). Caring for her aunts kept her from caring about herself. Chuck applies for her first job, has a relationship, and learns more about her family after death. Like George, she has to leave home. For Chuck, it isn't about responsibility as much as it is about carving out a space for herself in her relationship with Ned and the world. Before she died, she "[n]ever strayed from far home. She read about people she could never be on adventures she could never have" ("Pie-lette"). Dying was the impetus for Chuck to challenge herself to take more risks and be a main character in her life. This second chance and her association with Ned and Emerson allowed her to play at multiple personas and go on different adventures while enlarging their detective work to aid people, not just their own pockets. While Ned's gift provided Emerson with a chance to increase his monetary gain, Chuck guiding it gives meaning to Ned's life and those of their clients.

Conclusion

In *Prime-time Feminism: Television, Media Culture, and the Women's Movement Since 1970*, Bonnie J. Dow notes, "Celebrating individual choice and achievement is satisfying and necessary: it shows what is possible for some women and what feminism wants to make available to all women" (213). By having no definitive career path or plans to marry and settle down, Jaye, George, and Chuck could be considered underdeveloped underachievers. However, the fact that they can delay or bypass these restrictive roles enforced on most female protagonists, truly shows that they are enjoying the undefined path that is the luxury of male protagonists. Yet, they tread on this path with their femininity, their sexuality, and critical feminist eye intact. After all, when they are taking care of their clients it requires a nurturing aspect like motherhood, when they are engaging in partnerships or relationships they can use skills like one would need for marriage, and their ability to work with others is the kind of experience needed for success in a career. At the same time, they are asserting their agency in ways that don't fit the standards for success as a woman shows how narrow those standards are and that the narrative of women needed to be more diverse, which is a goal of third-wave feminism. George, Jaye, and Chuck show that women in adulthood may be as or more conflicted than in adolescence. They may be young and dealing with supernatural forces, but their experiences can be read as the responsibilities women have to take on as adults, even if they feel ill-prepared. Bryan Fuller's female protagonists show that asserting one's agency does not have to be a tragedy, but a place of personal growth, even if adulthood is full of complicated, unsettling intersections that the third wave is still trying to sort out.

WORKS CITED

Anderson, Sarah. "Always." *Dead Like Me: The Complete Second Season*. Santa Monica, CA: Metro Goldwyn Mayer Home Entertainment, 2005. DVD.
_____. "The Shallow End." *Dead Like Me: The Complete Second Season*. Santa Monica, CA: Metro Goldwyn Mayer Home Entertainment, 2005. DVD.
Anthony, Piers. *On a Pale Horse*. Ballantine, 1983.
Beauvoir, Simone. *The Second Sex*. Knopf, 1953.
Beeler, Karin E. *Seers, Witches and Psychics on Screen: An Analysis of Women Visionary Characters in Recent Television and Film*. McFarland, 2008.
Beeler, Stan. "Wonderfalls." In *The Essential Cult TV Reader*, edited David Lavery, 322–328. University Press of Kentucky, 2010.
Beers, Steve. "Last Call." *Dead Like Me: The Complete Second Season*. Santa Monica, CA: Metro Goldwyn Mayer Home Entertainment, 2005. DVD.
"The Benefits of Raising the Minimum Wage for America's Women." *The White House*. Web. Accessed April 4, 2014.
Burger, Alissa Burger. "Fashion, Femininity and the 1950s: Costume and Identity Negotiation in Pushing Daisies." In *The Television World of Pushing Daisies: Critical Essays on the Bryan Fuller Series*, edited by Alissa Burger, 174–192. McFarland, 2011.
Campbell, Joseph. *The Hero with a Thousand Faces*. Princeton University Press, 1972.
Cohen, Alisa. "Dead Like Me: The Complete First Season (Film)." *Entertainment Weekly* 770 (2004): 70. *Academic Search Complete*. Web. Accessed 12 May 2016.
Dow, Bonnie J. *Prime-Time Feminism: Television, Media Culture, and the Women's Movement Since 1970*. University of Pennsylvania Press, 1996.
Dowling, Kevin. "Dead Girl Walking." *Dead Like Me: The Complete First Season*. Santa Monica, CA: Metro Goldwyn Mayer Home Entertainment, 2004. DVD.
Edwards, Paul. "The Fun in Funeral." *Pushing Daisies: The Complete First Season*. Burbank, CA: Warner Home Video, 2008. DVD.
Farr, Daniel. "The Queer, Quirky World of Pushing Daisies." In *The Television World of Pushing Daisies: Critical Essays on the Bryan Fuller Series*, edited by Alissa Burger, 137–154. McFarland, 2011.

Fazlalizadeh, Tatyana. "Stop Telling Women to Smile." *Tatyana Fazlalizadeh.* Accessed 20 May 2016. http://www.tlynnfaz.com/Stop-Telling-Women-to-Smile.

Fetters, Ashley. "The To Do List's Radically Practical Message About Virginity." *The Atlantic,* 26 July 2013. https://www.theatlantic.com/entertainment/archive/2013/07/-i-the-to-do-list-i-s-radically-practical-message-about-virginity/278124/.

Gill, Patrick. "It's a Destiny Thing—Enjoy It." In *The Television World of Pushing Daisies: Critical Essays on the Bryan Fuller Series,* edited by Alissa Burger, 115–136. McFarland, 2011.

Gill, Rosalind. "Postfeminist Media Culture: Elements of a Sensibility." *European Journal of Cultural Studies* 10, no. 2 (2007): 147–66. Accessed 8 April 2014. https://journals.sagepub.com/doi/abs/10.1177/1367549407075898.

Goettel, Diane, and W. Everett. "What Is a Fashion Statement?" *WiseGeek.* Accessed 12 May 2016. https://www.wisegeek.com/what-is-a-fashion-statement.htm.

Goodman, Tim. "There's Plenty of Life and Insight in 'Dead Like Me,' Showtime's Snarky but Smart Response to 'Six Feet Under': FINAL Edition." *San Francisco Chronicle,* 27 June 2003. https://www.sfgate.com/entertainment/article/There-s-plenty-of-life-and-insight-in-Dead-Like-2606814.php.

Grabiak, Marita. "Karma Chameleon." *Wonderfalls: The Complete Series.* Twentieth Century–Fox, 2005. DVD.

Grossman, David. "Death Defying." *Dead Like Me: The Complete Second Season.* Santa Monica, CA: Metro Goldwyn Mayer Home Entertainment, 2005. DVD.

_____. "Vacation." *Dead Like Me: The Complete First Season.* Santa Monica, CA: Metro Goldwyn Mayer Home Entertainment, 2004. DVD.

Hecht, Marvin A., and Marianne LaFrance. "License or Obligation to Smile: The Effect of Power and Sex on Amount and Type of Smiling." *Personality and Social Psychology Bulletin* 24, no. 12 (1998): 1332–42. https://journals.sagepub.com/doi/10.1177/0146167298 2412007.

Heywood, Leslie, and Jennifer Drake, eds. *Third Wave Agenda: Being Feminist, Doing Feminism.* University of Minnesota Press, 1997.

Holland, Todd. "Cocktail Bunny." *Wonderfalls: The Complete Series.* Los Angeles: Twentieth Century–Fox, 2005. DVD.

_____. "Lovesick Ass." *Wonderfalls: The Complete Series.* Twentieth Century–Fox, 2005. DVD.

_____. "Pink Flamingoes." *Wonderfalls: The Complete Series.* Twentieth Century–Fox, 2005. DVD.

_____. "Wax Lion" *Wonderfalls: The Complete Series.* Twentieth Century–Fox, 2005. DVD.

_____. "Wound-Up Penguin." *Wonderfalls: The Complete Series.* Twentieth Century–Fox, 2005. DVD.

hooks, bell. *Outlaw Culture: Resisting Representations.* Routledge, 1994.

Howell, Charlotte E. "Prophets in the Margins: Fantastic, Feminist Religion in Contemporary American Telefantasy." MA Thesis. University of Texas, 2011.

"Hurry." *Dead Like Me: The Complete Second Season.* Santa Monica, CA: Metro Goldwyn Mayer Home Entertainment, 2005. DVD.

Iversen, Torben, et al. "Women and the Service Sector." Memo. Wealth and Power in the Post-Industrial Age Working Group Meeting, UCLA, Los Angeles, CA. 16 April 2004.

Jefferson, Margo. "The Grim Reapers, Killing Time in a Waffle Shop." *New York Times,* 27 June 2003. https://www.nytimes.com/2003/06/27/movies/television-review-the-grim-reapers-killing-time-in-a-waffle-shop.html.

Jicha, Tom. "Life Begins with Death in Showtime's 'Dead Like Me.'" *South Florida Sun-Sentinel,* 26 June 2003. https://www.sun-sentinel.com/news/fl-xpm-2003–06–26–0306250196-story.html.

Johnson, Meri Lisa. "Pro-Sex Feminism." In *The Women's Movement Today: An Encyclopedia of Third-Wave Feminism,* edited by Leslie Heywood, 259–61. Greenwood, 2006.

Kane, Adam. "Pigeon." *Pushing Daisies: The Complete First Season.* Burbank, CA: Warner Home Video, 2008. DVD.

King, Ursula. *Women and Spirituality: Voices of Protest and Promise.* Macmillan, 1993.

Kroeker, Allan. "Bitter Sweets." *Pushing Daisies: The Complete First Season.* Burbank, CA: Warner Home Video, 2008. DVD.

LaFrance, Marianne, Marvin A. Hecht and Elizabeth Levy Paluck. "The Contingent Smile: A Meta-Analysis of Sex Differences in Smiling." *Psychological Bulletin* 129, no. 2 (2003): 305–34. https://www.ncbi.nlm.nih.gov/pubmed/12696842.

Lauer, Peter. "Curious George." *Dead Like Me: The Complete First Season*. Santa Monica, CA: Metro Goldwyn Mayer Home Entertainment, 2004. DVD.

_____. "Reapercussions." *Dead Like Me: The Complete First Season*. Santa Monica, CA: Metro Goldwyn Mayer Home Entertainment, 2004. DVD.

Lehmann, Michael. "Caged Bird." *Wonderfalls: The Complete Series*. Los Angeles: Twentieth Century–Fox, 2005. DVD.

Lindlar, Daisy. "Why We Should Stop Telling Women to Smile." *The Huffington Post UK*, 15 June 2014.

McDonald, Robert. "*Wonderfalls*: The Best TV Show You Haven't Seen." *Metro* (Melbourne) 146/147 01 Jan 2005: 202. Association of Teachers of Film and Video. Web. Accessed 19 March 2014.

Miller, Claire Cain. "As Women Take Over a Male-Dominated Field, the Pay Drops." *New York Times*, 19 March 2016. https://www.nytimes.com/2016/03/20/upshot/as-women-take-over-a-male-dominated-field-the-pay-drops.html.

Moore, Scott. "Ellen Muth Is Reaping Life's Rewards." *Washington Post*, 22 Aug. 2004. https://www.washingtonpost.com/archive/lifestyle/tv/2004/08/22/ellen-muth-is-reaping-lifes-rewards/5d4423ea-361e-46b8-8b90-e98c19d25703/?noredirect=on&utm_term=.b8f5cb139eae.

Mulvey, Laura. "Visual Pleasure and Narrative Cinema." In *Media and Cultural Studies: Keyworks*, edited by Meenakshi G. Durham and Douglas Kellner. Blackwell, 2006.

O'Fallon, Peter. "Bad Habits." *Pushing Daisies: The Complete Second Season*. Burbank, CA: Warner Home Video, 2009. DVD.

O'Reilly, Julie Dianne. "Power Versus Empowerment: A Textual Analysis of Television's Superpowered Women, 1996–2005." Dissertation, Bowling Green State University, 2005.

Ostler, Rosemarie. *Dewdroppers, Waldos, and Slackers: A Decade-by-Decade Guide to the Vanishing Vocabulary of the Twentieth Century*. Oxford University Press, 2003.

Ostrow, Joanne. "*Wonderfalls* Gushing with Promise on Fox." *Denver Post*, 11 March 2004. Web. Accessed 13 March 2014.

Owen, Rob. "Mandy Patinkin and Ellen Muth Are the Reapers in Showtime's 'Dead Like Me.'" *Pittsburgh Post-Gazette*: 41. 27 Jun 2003. ProQuest. Web. Accessed 11 May 2016.

Parmiter, Tara. "Sweet Talk in the Pie Hole: Language, Intimacy, and Public Space." In *The Television World of Pushing Daisies: Critical Essays on the Bryan Fuller Series*, edited by Alissa Burger, 155–173. McFarland, 2011.

Paule, Michele. "Super Slacker Girls: Dropping Out but Divinely Inspired." In *Geek Chic: Smart Women in Popular Culture*, edited by Sherrie A. Inness, 85–102. Palgrave Macmillan, 2007.

Podeswa, Jeremy. "Totem Mole." *Wonderfalls: The Complete Series*. Twentieth Century–Fox, 2005. DVD.

Press, Joy. "Voice Choices: TV: Guided by Voices: Freaks and Mystiques: Not Just Another Drama About a Girl Who Talks to Stuffed Animals." *The Village Voice* 49 (2004). Web. Accessed 24 March 2014.

Propp, V. *Morphology of the Folktale*. University of Texas Press, 1968.

Robinson, Julie. "Window Dressed to Kill." *Pushing Daisies: The Complete Second Season*. Burbank, CA: Warner Home Video, 2009. DVD.

Seibers, Tobin. "A Sexual Culture for Disabled People." In *Sex and Disability*, edited by Robert McRuer and Anna Mollow, 37–53. Duke University Press, 2012.

Shapiro, Paul. "Robbing Hood." *Pushing Daisies: The Complete Second Season*. Burbank, CA: Warner Home Video, 2009. DVD.

Shaver, Helen. "Rest in Peace." *Dead Like Me: The Complete First Season*. Santa Monica, CA: Metro Goldwyn Mayer Home Entertainment, 2004. DVD.

Sonnenfeld, Barry. "Dummy." *Pushing Daisies: The Complete First Season*. Burbank, CA: Warner Home Video, 2008. DVD.

_____. "Pie-Lette." *Pushing Daisies: The Complete First Season*. Burbank, CA: Warner Home Video, 2008. DVD.

Trilling, Lawrence. "Circus, Circus." *Pushing Daisies: The Complete Second Season*. Burbank, CA: Warner Home Video, 2009. DVD.

_____. "Dim Sum Lose Sum." *Pushing Daisies: The Complete Second Season*. Burbank, CA: Warner Home Video, 2009. DVD.

_____. "Kerplunk." *Pushing Daisies: The Complete Second Season*. Burbank, CA: Warner Home Video, 2009. DVD.

_____. "The Legend of Merle Mcquoddy." *Pushing Daisies: The Complete Second Season*. Burbank, CA: Warner Home Video, 2009. DVD.

_____. "Smell of Success." *Pushing Daisies: The Complete First Season*. Burbank, CA: Warner Home Video, 2008. DVD.

Strachan, Alex. "Wonderful *Wonderfalls*: Final Edition." *The Gazette*, 11 March 2004. Web.

Whedon, Joss. "Innocence." *Buffy the Vampire Slayer: Complete Second Season*. United States: Twentieth Century–Fox, 2002. DVD.

White, Cameron, and Trenia Walker. *Tooning In: Essays on Popular Culture and Education*. Rowman & Littlefield, 2008.

Winant, Scott. "Pilot." *Dead Like Me: The Complete First Season*. Metro Goldwyn Mayer Home Entertainment, 2004. DVD.

Zisk, Craig. "Muffin Buffalo." *Wonderfalls: The Complete Series*. Twentieth Century–Fox, 2005. DVD.

Re-Framing and
Re-Forming Gender Roles

Vampires Who Go to High School

Everyday Women's Culture
in Twilight, Dracula
and Fifty Shades of Grey

CAOLAN MADDEN

One of the most interesting things about *Twilight* is how boring it is.

During the peak years of the *Twilight* franchise's popularity—from about 2007 until the end of 2012, when the final movie came out—the novels and films became the targets for significant criticism in both the mainstream media and the science-fiction and fantasy communities. Many complaints centered on the banality of the story: it's a vampire story with literally no stakes. Several commentators seemed irritated that despite their limited narrative scope, the *Twilight* books and movies were able to rival the commercial success of huge science-fiction and fantasy franchises like *Star Wars*, *Lord of the Rings*, and *Harry Potter*. The threat *Twilight* seemed to pose to scifi and fantasy communities is neatly articulated in a 2011 video recorded by George Takei, in which Takei urges *Star Trek* and *Star Wars* fans to unite against *Twilight*, "an ominous mutual threat to all science fiction," adding that in *Twilight*, "gone is any sense of heroism, camaraderie, or epic battle. In its place, we have vampires that sparkle, and moan, and go to high school ... the only message that rings through loud and clear is 'Does my boyfriend like me?'"

Takei's call for "star peace" is tongue-in-cheek, but it articulates a set of highly gendered values that are no laughing matter, values that we can detect behind most of the negative press surrounding *Twilight* in the mainstream media as well as in the blogosphere. According to these values, *Twilight* is inane—or, as Takei puts it, "really, really bad"—because of its investment in experiences and aesthetics that have been historically coded as feminine. The vampires are ludicrous because they "sparkle," a quality we associate with little girls' glittery toys, as well as with the highly performative femininity of adolescent girls, divas, and drag queens; they're also ludicrous because they "moan," which means they express suffering, vulnerability, and desire rather than (merely) anger, violence, and stoicism. At first glance, Takei's privileging of "camaraderie and epic battle" over going to high school and worrying about boyfriends may seem slightly less gendered: he's valuing friendship over romance and high-stakes, world-changing events over petty personal concerns. But historically "camaraderie" and "battle"—not to mention the literary genre of "the epic"—have been experiences open almost exclusively to men, particularly male soldiers. To dismiss "does my boyfriend like me" as a ludicrous concern is to dismiss the value of the depiction of adolescent female subjectivity. To privilege "epic battle" over "high school" is to privilege historically masculine fields of exceptional adventure and accomplishment over the everyday, a concept that has long been associated with the domestic and the feminine. As Henri Lefebvre argues, "everyday life weighs heaviest on women ... they are the subject of everyday life and its victims or objects and substitutes" (73). Expanding on Lefebvre's point, Rita Felski explains that "the disdain for the everyday as it is conventionally lived often relies on a disparagement of domestic activities and skills associated with women. It is women above all who embody repetitive time, whether equated with the mindless instinctual rhythms of biological life or the standardized soul-destroying routines of capitalism" (613). Compared to the excitement of "epic battle"—or the excitement of exploration and innovation implied by the name of *Star Trek*'s starship *Enterprise*—the unvarying daily routines associated with domestic labor can often seem boring, valueless, and invisible.

Most feminist analyses of the *Twilight* franchise tend to agree with Takei that *Twilight* is "really, really bad" for women. For many feminist critics, Bella Swan's helpless idolatry of teenaged vampire Edward Cullen is a bad example for adolescent girls, and the traditionally feminine elements mentioned above—sparkling, moaning, a narrow focus on romance and on everyday, domestic life—serve merely to reinforce insidious gender stereotypes. These critiques are valid, but, as Anne Helen Petersen argues, they risk underestimating women readers' ability to engage thoughtfully and critically with the texts they read; the assumption that reading a novel or watching a film will transform young women into versions of its heroine, Petersen writes in response to similar critiques of the *Fifty Shades of Grey* film, "harkens back to old, thoroughly disabused theories that a film, book, or song is a hypodermic needle that, once injected in its viewer, reproduced its values in its new host" ("Sly Capitalist"). In recent years, some feminist critics and bloggers have begun to contest the explicit and implicit misogyny in the vitriolic attacks on *Twi-*

light and its female fan base, and even to identify the ways in which the series might be empowering for young girls. While these analyses tend to focus on Bella's frank sexual desire and determination to make her own life choices, almost none have investigated the very banality that so many of *Twilight*'s critics and defenders—both feminist and antifeminist—find problematic. But what if *Twilight* is appealing to women readers not *despite* the fact that it's boring, but precisely because of its investments in the feminine everyday?

This essay considers the feminist implications of the mundane and the "boring" in the *Twilight* novels and films, implications often missed by critics who seek to explain the fascination *Twilight* offers to female audiences, as well as by readers and viewers who expect fantasy and horror genres to provide primarily novelty and excitement. The first section of this essay reads *Twilight* alongside the 1975 feminist film *Jeanne Dielman, 23 quai du Commerce, 1080 Bruxelles* in order to demonstrate that *Twilight*'s banality participates in a tradition of feminist attention to everyday life. The essay then traces a brief history of the everyday, the banal, and the boring in modern vampire fiction, beginning with *Dracula* (1897). Finally, the essay's focus turns to the *Fifty Shades of Grey* franchise, a series of novels and films that began as *Twilight* fan fiction, to examine what happens to *Twilight*'s model of everyday life when its supernatural elements are stripped away: in the absence of vampires, it becomes clearer how the categories of the "boring" and the "everyday" become the site of a struggle within both texts between an acknowledgment of the gendered violence of everyday life, on the one hand, and a utopian fantasy of "everyday" social harmony, erotic satisfaction, and personal fulfillment on the other.

Attending to the use of the "everyday" and the "boring" in *Twilight* reveals the ways in which the text insists upon the value of everyday women's culture, exposes the threat of masculine violence that is inextricable from that culture, and opens up possibilities for cultural critique. Attending to the everyday also changes how we think about *Twilight* and genre. Taking Takei's lighthearted critique seriously raises the question of whether, given the fact that *Twilight* is not necessarily "hard" science fiction like *Star Trek*, it makes sense to include the *Twilight* novels and films within the broader category of speculative fiction—or if the boring, everyday aspects of these texts exclude them from a category we associate strongly with novelty, suspense, and surprise.

The Value of Doing the Dishes: The Feminine Everyday in Vampire Fiction

Arguments that cast *Twilight* as an antifeminist text commonly cite Bella Swan's domestic qualities as evidence; after she moves in with her divorced dad Charlie, Bella immediately takes over the role of housekeeper and cook. Here's a passage from the first *Twilight* novel (2005) in which Bella describes a typical day at home:

> When I got home, I unloaded all the groceries, stuffing them in wherever I could find an open space. I hoped Charlie wouldn't mind. I wrapped potatoes in foil and stuck them in the oven to bake, covered a steak in marinade and balanced it on top of a carton of eggs in the fridge. When I was finished with that, I took my book bag upstairs. Before starting my homework, I changed into a pair of dry sweats, pulled my damp hair up into a ponytail, and checked my e-mail for the first time [Meyer 2005, 33].

Twilight is full of passages like this, in which readers get unnecessary details about Bella cooking dinner, Bella getting dressed, Bella checking her email. Readers also get long, laborious descriptions of how the office at Bella's high school is furnished—"padded folding chairs, orange-flecked commercial carpet, notices and awards cluttering the walls, a big clock ticking loudly. Plants grew everywhere" (13)—and what Bella's truck looks like after Charlie adds snow chains to the tires—"There were thin chains crisscrossed in diamond shapes around them" (55). If at the beginning of *Twilight* we suspect that these mundane details serve as a foil for the thrilling, sparkling vampires who are hiding in plain sight in this ordinary-seeming world, we soon discover that the world of the vampires, too, is full of mundane details: in *Breaking Dawn*, the last book in the series, we get similarly laborious descriptions of the decorations for Bella and Edward's wedding, of what Bella cooks herself for a snack right before she realizes she's pregnant with a half-vampire baby. These details aren't really necessary to the narrative—they don't advance the plot, they don't tell us much about character, they don't hold obvious symbolic value. In this sense, they contribute to what Roland Barthes has described as a "reality effect"—an accretion of material details that have no symbolic significance except as a marker of "realism." The particular reality depicted in *Twilight* is a kind of middle-class, adolescent female everydayness, one that includes cooking and housework, but also the everyday activities of driving to and attending high school.

In the context of Chantal Akerman's 1975 film *Jeanne Dielman, 23 quai du Commerce, 1080 Bruxelles*, however, *Twilight*'s "boring" passages take on a more political, and specifically feminist, function. A classic of minimalist and feminist cinema, *Jeanne Dielman* presents the mundane details of the heroine's everyday life. Over nearly four hours, the viewer watches Jeanne, a single mother of a teenaged son, make coffee; turn off the light when she leaves a room; dredge a veal cutlet in flour; crack an egg into ground beef; wash the dishes; shop for groceries. While there are some cuts, much of Jeanne's daily activity is presented in real time. The viewer learns exactly how long each household duty takes to perform; if viewers wanted to use the film as a tutorial for making meat loaf, they could. For most of the film, there's no dialogue; the only sounds are the ambient noises produced by Jeanne as she moves through the house doing her chores. Spoiler: once a day, the viewer also watches Jeanne have sex in her bedroom for money, and the film ends with a sensational act of violence. This sensational ending makes it possible to read *Jeanne Dielman* as slowed-down melodrama: the titillating psychological horror of a B-movie, drawn out and dilated by the everyday.

In this way, *Jeanne Dielman* is an overlooked but crucial antecedent not only for *Twilight*'s boring domestic passages and for the corresponding scenes in the movie adaptations, but for the *Twilight* franchise as a whole, whose admirers appreciate it for its "slow burn" (Petersen 57). *Jeanne Dielman*'s drawn-out form is inseparable from its feminist politics: according to Akerman, this was "the only way ... to shoot that film" in order "to avoid cutting the woman in a hundred pieces ... cutting the action in a hundred pieces, to look carefully and be respectful" (Akerman 119). In an interview, Akerman explains that the film works against "the hierarchy of images" in which dramatically violent or erotic acts such as "a car accident or a kiss in close-up" are "more valued in the hierarchy than doing dishes.... This is not by chance, but exactly in relation to the place that women hold in society's hierarchy" (quoted in Yervasi 397). Akerman seeks to upend this hierarchy through experimental filmmaking techniques, eschewing many of the storytelling conventions of mainstream cinema in favor of *Jeanne Dielman*'s single-shot scenes that unfold in real time, the film's use of ambient sound, and what Carina Yervasi describes as the "non-narrative ritual abstraction" produced by the "banal gestures" of Jeanne's "monotonous housework" (389). For Yervasi, such "non-hierarchal images, slow tempo, and real time set apart the practices of feminist cinema from mainstream ... cinema" (387). The blockbuster *Twilight* films, of course, are undeniably mainstream cinema, and the *Twilight* novels are not strikingly experimental in form. Like *Jeanne Dielman*, however, *Twilight* "include[s] images ... that mainstream cinema would have cut out in the editing process" (Yervasi 388–89). And although the *Twilight* films and novels are full of sex and violence, these acts, like those in *Jeanne Dielman,* are located in and among a host of mundane details that many readers find "boring." In addition, as the "slow burn" of Edward and Bella's romance unfolds across *Twilight*'s four novels and five corresponding films, those cinematic "kiss[es] in close-up" begin to appear with the same regularity, the same predictability, as shopping and cooking. Longing looks, stuttering hearts, and the intense guitar solos that fill the movies' soundtrack are themselves part of the everyday fabric of adolescence. In the *Twilight* saga, the boring stuff of women's lives—shopping, cooking, cleaning, and sitting—has exactly the same weight as, if not more weight than, the exciting stuff we go to the movies to see women do or have done to them—kissing, suffering, killing.

Where do the vampires come in, then? Is it possible that *Twilight* is not fantasy or science fiction at all, but realism? As I will explain below, to some degree the vampires in *Twilight* are almost beside the point. At the same time, the mundane details of modern life have played an important role in the formation of vampire literature as a genre. Another important source text for *Twilight*, as it is for all twentieth- and twentieth-century vampire novels, is Bram Stoker's *Dracula*, originally published in 1897. As many critics have pointed out, the narrative of *Dracula* is inseparable from the detritus of nineteenth-century mass media and information technology, including newspaper journalism, phonography, photography, the telegraph, shorthand, and typing—technologies that were new and modern in 1890s England, but that were also beginning to become ubiquitous, banal, and everyday. A "note" at the end of the novel, purportedly written by the lawyer Jonathan Harker seven years after the events of the novel, reveals that the text the reader has just read is a typescript produced by Jonathan's wife Mina, transcribed from a multimedia hodgepodge of shorthand diary entries, phonograph records, newspaper clippings, and letters.

In *Dracula*, the characters' preoccupations with and daily practice of such technologies take up as much space in the narrative as, if not more space than, the supernatural elements. Mina's own commitment to the daily practice of tedious-sounding activities such as "practising shorthand very assiduously," "practising very hard" on the typewriter, and "keep[ing] a diary" in order to improve her memory—"I am told that, with a little practice, one can remember all that goes on or that one hears said during a day," she writes to her doomed friend Lucy (86)—becomes immensely useful to the "little band of men," including Harker, who go hunting for Dracula (419). Jennifer Wicke points out that *Dracula*, like many vampire texts, might seem to be primarily occupied with the exotic, the spectacular, the bizarre, but behind the sensationalistic supernatural horrors of monstrous brides, exoticized "gypsies," runaway wolves, murdered ship's crews, and Dracula's bloody feasts—not to mention the showy modern technologies that many critics cite as a marker of the novel's self-conscious modernity—lie the boring elements of the feminine everyday: the "feminiz[ed]" banality of Mina's office work, of middle-class domestic space, of the ubiquitous, disposable newspaper clippings, Kodak snapshots, and cheap novels that women readers consume and produce (Wicke 471). While the novel positions many of these everyday, modern elements in opposition to the ancient and extraordinary Dracula, Wicke shows that the modern media and technology that facilitates Dracula's downfall display their own "vampiric powers" of reproduction, dissemination, and consumption (476). Dracula himself, with his need to "consume on a daily basis" (Wicke 479) might in turn be a figure for the interchangeable, endless days of a domestic life like Jeanne Dielman's. Another day, another dinner.

Similar affinities—between vampires and the everyday, but also between vampires and boredom, between vampires and mass culture—are at work in *Twilight,* of course; they're also visible in many of *Twilight'*s late twentieth- and early twenty-first-century precursors, including Anne Rice's Vampire Chronicles (1976–2003), the television show *Buffy the Vampire Slayer* (1997–2003), and Charlaine Harris's Sookie Stackhouse novels (2001–2013). In Rice's *Interview with the Vampire* (1976), the everyday makes itself most felt in the tedium of immortality, in which a family of vampires spend day upon day together, desperate for amusement or distraction, condemned to never change or develop. *Buffy the Vampire Slayer,* like *Twilight,* locates its supernatural creatures in and around a high school; as Rhonda Nichol argues, *Twilight* and *Buffy* have more in common than critical narratives that dismiss *Twilight* as anti-feminist and celebrate *Buffy* as uncomplicatedly feminist might suggest. On the one hand, one of the pleasures of *Buffy* is the contrast between the characters' everyday teenage problems and their high-stakes battles against vampires and other monsters. The irony of the show's title comes from the same sly denigration of the feminine everyday that motivates Takei's video: the joke is that it's absurd to imagine a young woman with a perky, Valley-Girl name like Buffy, who lives in a town called Sunnydale, doing something as serious as slaying vampires. At the same time, however, *Buffy* takes Buffy's power very seriously, and the seemingly banal high-school setting and the supernatural evil of the vampires turn out to have more in common than we might initially assume.As Becca Klaver puts it in her poem "Southern California Gothic," Buffy is "slayed by the weight of/the world's perfect metaphor,/high school as hellmouth (19–21).

Like Bella Swan, Harris's Sookie Stackhouse is a human woman with a vampire lover and a narrative tendency to dwell on boring domestic details of dressing, eating, housework, and sleeping arrangements. Early on in the first novel, Sookie describes her bedtime ritual after an exhausting day spent waitressing, meeting her first vampire, and rescuing him from vampire hunters:

> I turned on my own light and shut the door and began taking off my clothes. I had at least five pair of black shorts and many, many white T-shirts, since those tended to get stained so easily. No telling how many pairs of white socks were rolled up in my drawer. So I didn't have to do the wash tonight. I was too tired for a shower. I did brush my teeth and wash the makeup off my face, slap on some moisturizer, and take the band out of my hair [Harris 14–15].

This passage resembles similar passages from *Twilight* in which Bella recounts the events of her day with the same procedural precision and excessive level of detail, establishing the heroine's allegiance to the world of the boring feminine everyday. And Harris, like Meyer, extends that banality to her vampires: Sookie's first vampire lover, Bill, uses Herbal Essences shampoo and maintains an Internet vampire database (Harris *Club Dead*). At the same time, however,

Harris makes it very clear that Bill, despite his enthusiasm for everyday human grooming products and affection for an everyday human woman, is inhuman; by the end of the thirteen-book series, Sookie has had enough of the vampires' amoral universe and commits to life with a warm-blooded, mortal lover.

De-Fanged Vampires, Dangerous Boyfriends: Transferring Danger from the Supernatural to the Everyday

With the exception of *Twilight*, each of the vampire texts discussed here emphasizes the unbridgeable gap between vampires and humans. Vampires may move in and out of the everyday spaces of London or New Orleans or Sunnydale or Bon Temps, Louisiana; they may form close relationships with human beings; they may serve as metaphors for the everyday threats that haunt those humans' lives. But if vampires are *in* the everyday, they are never *of* it. Humans and vampires can't really be together, and vampires—even those who smell like Herbal Essences—always pose a genuine threat to their human companions.

In *Twilight*, however, the fact that Edward Cullen is a vampire poses no significant obstacle to his relationship with Bella; his vampirism is almost beside the point. Unlike their literary predecessors, Stephenie Meyer's vampires are both harmless and unambitious. The members of the Cullen family refrain from drinking human blood and, as Anne Rice observed in a 2011 Facebook post, "choose to spend an eternity going to high school over and over again in a small town." So, while the premise of *Twilight*—a human girl falls in love with an immortal vampire boy who wants to drink all her blood—suggests that Bella and Edward's romance is doomed, through the course of the novels Meyer is careful to remove every problem that Edward's vampirism might cause for Bella, so that in the end Bella doesn't have to make any compromises when she chooses to stay with Edward forever, ultimately becoming a vampire herself. In the scene where Bella first discovers Edward's true identity, Edward responds to Bella's questions about vampire life by explaining that most of what Bella has heard about vampires is a myth:

> "Don't laugh—but how can you come out during the daytime?"
> He laughed anyway. "Myth."
> "Burned by the sun?"
> "Myth."
> "Sleeping in coffins?"
> "Myth." He hesitated for a moment, and a peculiar tone entered his voice. "I can't sleep" [Meyer 2005, 185–86].

From the beginning, then, Edward and his vampire family are free from the disadvantages conventionally attributed to becoming a vampire. They're not confined to the darkness, and they're able to survive happily enough without harming humans: drinking animal blood, Edward explains, is like "living on tofu and soy milk" (188). Edward's face takes on a "wistful expression" over his inability to sleep (186), but this wistfulness disappears once Bella becomes a vampire and can joyfully share Edward's long nights as his partner. There are still some drawbacks to dating or becoming a vampire, many of them familiar from earlier vampire literature. Over the course of the series, Meyer establishes that Edward finds the scent of Bella's blood irresistible; becoming a vampire makes you lose your humanity and become a "monster"; new vampires have to suffer through years of uncontrollable bloodlust; vampires can't have children of their own. By the end of the *Twilight* series, however, even these drawbacks are revealed to be myths, or at least misconceptions. Edward has incredible self-control and has no problem restraining his lust for Bella's blood. It turns out that vampires, even though their bodies are dead, can still have and enjoy sex, and human women and their vampire boyfriends can even conceive healthy, adorable, nearly immortal children together. In Meyer's world, becoming a vampire doesn't damage your relationship to your existing family, or stand in the way of your creating lasting ties with a nearly-immortal family of your own; Bella and Edward and their daughter and Bella's friend Jacob will get to spend several joyful lifetimes together, never feeling lonely or abandoned or afraid. Additionally, it turns out that Bella loses none of her humanity when she becomes a vampire; instead, Bella retains all of her positive human characteristics and gains beauty, grace, and the power to magically shield the people she loves from harm. As the vampire wife of her vampire husband, Bella becomes her best self.

Compared to Buffy and her vampire boyfriend Angel, who can't achieve sexual intimacy without Angel losing his soul and becoming a monster, Bella and Edward seem to have it easy. (Don't even mention Mina Murray and Dracula. Although the characters' highly sexualized intimacy in the novel has prompted some adaptations—most notably Francis Ford Coppola's 1992 film—to depict Mina and Dracula as star-crossed lovers, such romance squares uncomfortably with the violent, nonconsensual encounter in which Dracula forces Mina to drink his blood and the unwanted, traumatic nature of Mina's subsequent ability to hear Dracula's thoughts. Yet perhaps Coppola's adaptation—in which Gary Oldman's handsome, sensual Dracula is drawn to Winona Ryder's Mina because of her resemblance to his centuries-dead Transylvanian beloved—is another literary source for *Twilight*'s vulnerable, lovesick vampire boyfriend.)

The difference between *Twilight* and most other vampire fiction lies in the fact that vampires are usually metaphors. As Nina Auerbach explains, "every age embraces the vampire it needs" (145), and throughout history vampires have reflected current cultural anxieties about uncontrollable forces, including female sexuality, same-sex desire, immigration, sexually-transmitted disease, childbirth and pregnancy, and modern technology and medicine. Initially, Edward's thirst for Bella's blood is a very clear metaphor for male desire of women's bodies, a desire that through much of Western literature has been figured as violently destructive: like *Jane Eyre*'s Edward Rochester and the other nineteenth-century antiheroes on whom Meyer modeled her vampire's character, Edward is conflicted between a tender, respectful love for Bella and a desire that could easily destroy her. For Tracy L. Bealer, the "cold, solid, inflexible … male vampiric bodies" in the *Twilight* saga are in many ways a literalization and intensification" of "toxic masculinity" (165); in first rejecting and then reimagining his vampirism in terms of a loving and egalitarian partnership with Bella, Bealer argues, Edward "challenges normative masculinity" (164) and "models one way for men to live empathetically" (177). Whatever Edward's private struggles might be, however, Meyer almost immediately removes the possibility that his vampirism might pose a threat to Bella: even though *Edward* continues to insist that he's still dangerous to Bella, neither Bella nor the reader ever seriously believes that he could drink her blood. Although *Midnight Sun*, a fragment by Stephenie Meyer written from Edward's point of view, purports to reveal that Edward posed a real danger to Bella, it doesn't change the fact that *Twilight* itself is narrated exclusively by Bella, who is never really afraid of Edward. She's lovestruck, confused, and frustrated, but she never seems to doubt his ability to control his vampiric appetites.

In *Twilight*, then, the metaphor of bloodlust for sexual lust dissolves as the vehicle merges with the tenor; Edward's desire for Bella rapidly becomes not a metaphor for a boy's sexual desire for a girl, but *merely* a boy's sexual desire for a girl—or rather a boy's romantic love for a girl, since Edward's sexual desire for Bella is inseparable from his desire to be her husband and companion. It *is* entirely ordinary, as is Bella's desire for Edward. Their entire relationship is ordinary. They meet in high school, they fall in love, they have some misunderstandings, they break up for a while, they get back together, they get married, Bella has a difficult pregnancy, they have a baby. The baby falls in love with a werewolf. Okay, their lives do take some unusual turns, but in general, these are experiences that a lot of people have.

This returns us to the question: Why vampires? The answer is that the vampires are there to mark the everydayness of *Twilight* as important. If this vampirism is entirely decorative, with no structural function in the narrative, the vampires still play an important role as sparkling beacons pointing to the everyday as worthy of our attention. And they're vampires, not unicorns, because the everyday is in fact dangerous. The fact that Meyer has carefully removed the threat Edward poses *as a vampire* doesn't mean he poses no threat to Bella as a boyfriend. Countless critics of *Twilight* have pointed out that Edward can be disturbingly controlling, even abusive: he sneaks into Bella's house at night and watches her sleep, he abandons her, he sabotages her car so that he can drive her to school himself, he withholds sex—all for her own good. He tries to force her to terminate a pregnancy she desperately wants to bring to term. The pregnancy itself is incredibly, almost fatally, dangerous, and while Bella's pregnancy is not the result of abuse or coercion it functions as a reminder of yet another danger that contact with men can pose to women's bodies—a danger that haunts so many of the Victorian novels that inspired *Twilight*. These threats are especially visible and especially powerful in the films, perhaps because we get to see the anxiety and doubt on the actor Kristen Stewart's face as she walks down the aisle or as she changes into sexy lingerie on her wedding night. We get to see Bella's bruised, wasted pregnant body and the graphic horror of her labor and delivery.

It's important to note here that this study does not necessarily argue that Stephenie Meyer explicitly wrote the *Twilight* novels as a critique of patriarchal control of women's minds and bodies; at the same time, however, it's crucial to note that a text can portray cultural problems and values without subscribing to those values or condemning them. Just as the banal details of *Twilight* direct us to the importance of the everyday, of the boring and the feminine, the presence of the vampires marks everyday life for women as violent and dangerous—just as it is in *Jeanne Dielman*. Even in normal, non-supernatural everyday life, men's bodies and men's desire can destroy young women. That this idea is not a Victorian anachronism should be painfully clear to anyone who has engaged in contemporary debates about rape culture or women's reproductive rights. Today's young women still have to navigate between sexual desire and their own safety, between loyalty to family, to a partner, and to a child. Sex can, in fact, kill you; so can pregnancy.

The banality of *Twilight*'s vampires, then, directs our attention away from the threat posed by fantastic monsters and toward the threat posed by everyday life under patriarchy. At the same time, Meyer's systematic efforts to domesticate and de-fang her vampire hero register a desire to dismantle that patriarchal control. The threat posed by Edward's patriarchal masculinity is always present in *Twilight,* but it coexists with the possibility of the alternative models for masculinity that Bealer detects in Edward's character. The everyday depicted in *Twilight* is always dangerous for women, but it coexists with another version of the everyday that is always a fantasy of wish fulfillment. The *Twilight* series ends, after all, with Bella and Edward as perfect equals, moving forward into the "forever and forever and forever" of unending domestic bliss—the unchanging everyday implied by the last chapter's title, "Happily Ever After" (Meyer *Breaking Dawn*).

In order to further illuminate the relationship between fantasy and reality in *Twilight*, the remainder of this essay focuses on a text that amplifies many of *Twilight*'s fantasies and anxieties about gender, desire, and violence: E.L. James's 2011 novel *Fifty Shades of Grey*. First, however, since *Fifty Shades*, even more than *Twilight*, has become synonymous with a much-ridiculed strain of female heterosexual eroticism—if the teenage girls who loved *Twilight* were "Twihards," the presumably middle-aged women who read *Fifty Shades of Grey* are consuming "mommy porn"—it seems important to acknowledge the heteronormative focus of *Twilight*, *Fifty Shades of Grey*, and by extension, this essay. One reason Bella and Edward's romance seems so boring, so everyday—and, for many commentators, so antifeminist—is that as a white, cisgender, heterosexual couple they inhabit unmarked or "default" racial, sexual, and gender identities. Just as the unearthliness of the vampires in texts such as Sheridan Le Fanu's 1872 novella *Carmilla* and Rice's *Interview with the Vampire* serves to heighten the queer eroticism of same-sex encounters between an ordinary human and his or her vampire lover, the heteronormativity of Edward and Bella's vampire relationship seems to be a marker of its ordinariness. In this sense, as in many others, a world in which Edward and Bella's relationship is "boring" and "everyday" is both the stuff of fantasy and painfully realistic. Insofar as *Twilight* assumes whiteness and heterosexuality as the default in its depiction of the feminine everyday, marginalizing and even erasing the existence of queer women and women of color, it depicts an unrealistic world—or perhaps it accurately reflects a culture that has systematically centered white, heteronormative experience. Meyer's portrayal of the Quileute tribe to which Bella's werewolf friend and love interest Jacob Black belongs is highly exoticized, as are her accounts of the few vampires of color who occasionally visit throughout the series.

At the same time, *Twilight*'s heteronormativity, if not its whiteness, is a function of the text's efforts to grapple with the very real threat of male violence against women, including trans women, and nonbinary people—an everyday violence that is so common as to be almost unremarkable, even "boring." The heteronormative relationship between a male vampire and a human woman, then, allows Meyer to dramatize both the everyday threat of violence and the romance-novel fantasy in which that violence is converted to companionship and mutual pleasure. Even if we read that fantasy, as Bealer does, as imagining the male vampire in terms of a non-normative, potentially queer masculinity, he is still a male vampire with a female partner. In tracing the ways in which *Twilight* and *Fifty Shades of Grey* struggle to reconcile these often-incompatible versions of the everyday, then, I necessarily focus upon the heteronormative relationships they depict, with the acknowledgment that readers of *Twilight* and *Fifty Shades of Grey* are by no means all straight, cis women.

Happily Ever After: Everyday Fantasy in Twilight *and* Fifty Shades of Grey

The *Fifty Shades* series, a trilogy of erotic novels that began as *Twilight* fan fiction, converts the character of Edward Cullen from a rich, handsome, teenaged vampire into Christian Grey, a rich, handsome human man who may or may not be a sadist. In James's original version of the story, which she posted serially on fanfiction.net in 2009 under the title *Master of the Universe*, Christian actually *was* Edward—following common fan fiction practice, *Masters of the Universe* used existing *Twilight* characters to explore new situations and relationships. Although James changed the characters' names and other details for copyright reasons in order to publish her story as *Fifty Shades of Grey*, the relationship between the fabulously wealthy and powerful Christian and the young, beautiful, but seemingly "ordinary" narrator Anastasia Steele is strikingly similar to the relationship between superhuman Edward and klutzy mortal Bella. As was the case with *Twilight*, feminist activists and antifeminist pundits found common ground in their dislike of James's novels, which have been criticized for their inane dialogue, their misrepresentation of the BDSM community, and, most seriously, for their glorification of violence against women.

Like *Twilight*, the *Fifty Shades* series is fruitful ground for thinking through the relationship between gender, violence, and the everyday. In *Fifty Shades of Grey*, Christian's violence and his eroticism are both unremarkable and boring. Perhaps surprisingly, however, given the novel's association with sadomasochism, Christian's violence and sexuality are presented as separate, and incompatible, versions of everyday experience. Charting the changing meanings of Christian's everydayness demonstrates how the everyday is recruited in *Twilight* and *Fifty Shades* as both the index of a violent reality and the object of an exuberantly utopian, if still very boring, fantasy life.

Edward's vampirism does very little metaphorical work in *Twilight*, since the threat Edward poses to Bella comes not from his vampiric thirst but from ordinary, everyday "toxic masculinity." In this sense, *Fifty Shades* takes *Twilight*'s representation of masculine violence to its logical conclusion by dispensing with the metaphor altogether. Instead of a monster whose appetite for human blood might serve as a metaphor for masculine sexual violence, Christian Grey is a man with a taste for sexual violence who serves as a metaphor for men with a taste for sexual violence. At the same time, Christian, like Edward, is a figure of erotic fantasy, an idealized lover whose primary function is to provide pleasure for Ana, the female narrator and stand-in for Bella Swan, as well as for the novels' heterosexual women readers. The novels continually open up the possibility that Christian's "sadism," like Edward's vampirism, is merely decorative, a detail that adds excitement to an idealized consensual erotic relationship. As Salam Al-Mahadin argues, Christian is not really a sadist "since the latter can only enjoy an unwilling victim," while Christian is "an 'element' and an 'essential subject' in a masochistic … context of pleasure" centered on Ana's desires (568).

Throughout the *Fifty Shades* novels, it's almost impossible to determine which of these interpretations is correct: are the necktie and handcuffs that appear on the covers of two of the *Fifty Shades* books innocently pleasurable sex toys, or symbols of patriarchal violence? As a character, Christian Grey oscillates between, on the one hand, an abusive boyfriend with control issues, "stalkerish" tendencies, and a genuine desire to inflict physical violence on Ana and, on the other hand, an instrument for the fulfillment of Ana's (and the reader's) every desire. In neither case, however, is Christian really a Dominant in the sense that the term carries in the BDSM community—just as Edward Cullen is never really a vampire. Critics well-versed in literary erotica often find *Fifty Shades of Grey* lacking not only because it misrepresents the BDSM lifestyle, particularly the emphasis the BDSM community places on mutual consent and respect, but because the sex it does represent is unoriginal and boring. These critics may be correct, but they may also be missing the point: *Fifty Shades of Grey* is not interested in accurately documenting a subculture, nor is it interested in erotic innovation. Instead, in *Twilight* and *Fifty Shades of Grey*, BDSM and vampirism, along with the gothic allure of their attendant counter-cultures and subcultures, serve as a hinge mediating between two opposing, but equally boring, versions of the everyday: the everyday threat of patriarchal violence against women and the fantasy of a never-ending loving, monogamous, companionate marriage hinted at by the phrase "happily ever after."

Despite his famous (and much-lampooned) claim early on in the first *Fifty Shades* novel that "I don't make love. I fuck … hard" (96), Christian implies over and over throughout the series that what he most desires is "vanilla" sex in the context of a loving, monogamous relationship. Christian's wondering enthusiasm over every traditional romantic activity he pursues with Ana—"another first," he comments over and over, after they sleep in the same bed, have sex in the missionary position, eat dinner with his family— implies that although he has only experienced sex in the context of Dominant/Submissive relationships, conventional monogamy is the sexual and romantic milieu he really wants to be part of. Here, again, is the boring, the everyday: not only the domestic everyday of *Twilight*, but the sexual everyday of vanilla heterosexual sex. In *Fifty Shades*, however, ordinary, everyday sex is always incredible. Just as the heart-stopping kisses in *Twilight* come to be as predictable and as boring as meals and school schedules, Ana's "intense, body-shattering orgasm[s]" (276) punctuate the three *Fifty Shades* novels at regular intervals. And as many commentators have noted, this predictable sexual ecstasy takes place in an atmosphere of material luxury: Christian's fantastic wealth generates a palatial apartment, private jets, helicopters, an endless supply of beautiful clothes and high-end electronics and Thomas Hardy first editions for Ana. The everyday of *Fifty Shades of Grey* is, to some degree, the everyday of a glossy lifestyle magazine; like pornography, but also like "world-building" speculative fiction, the novels deemphasize the exceptional events that structure conventional novelistic plotting in favor of an endless, glamorous new version of everyday life.

The novels' materialist excesses serve as an important indication of Christian's attentiveness to Ana's desires. Of all the moments of fantasy consumerism in the three novels, Ana is most moved by the fact that Christian notices the brand and variety of tea she likes best. During an early encounter, Ana notes that Christian has provided "a Twinings English breakfast teabag. Jeez, he remembers how I like my tea" (71). In fact, Christian not only remembers how Ana likes her tea, he seems to have intuited it before she ever told him her preference. During a coffee date earlier in the novel, he hands Ana "a cup and a saucer, a small teapot, and a side plate bearing a lone teabag labeled TWININGS ENGLISH BREAKFAST—my favorite" (41). As a three-hundred-year-old British brand, Twinings invokes the old-fashioned values of Ana's beloved nineteenth-century novels as well as the capitalist excesses of the British Empire; at the same time, Twinings tea bags are a relatively accessible, everyday grocery-store staple in both the United States, where the novels are set, and the United Kingdom, where James lives and writes. In choosing a Twinings tea bag for Ana, Christian situates their relationship within a consumerist culture in which brand preferences do much to construct identity; at the same time, he demonstrates that his function in the novels is to understand Ana's (boring, everyday) desires. This perfect understanding forecasts the possibility of the fantasy that underlies both *Twilight* and *Fifty Shades*: the perfect fusion of partners into a (boringly harmonious) companionate marriage.

The novel's structure, then, demands that Christian be boring. For Christian is not only sexually boring, but also boring as a literary character. Framed as psychologically complex—"I'm fifty shades of fucked up, Anastasia," he admits at a vulnerable moment in the first novel (269)—with deep, dark secrets, Christian is in fact strikingly shallow: his thoughts and feelings are nearly always on the surface. For this reason, *Grey,* James's 2015 retelling of *Fifty Shades* from Christian Grey's perspective, is almost unbearably boring: Grey's inner monologue adds almost no new information to the narrative. In one telling passage, Christian and Ana are exchanging flirtatious emails— emails that have already appeared verbatim in *Fifty Shades of Grey*. Flirtation for Ana and Christian involves making light of Christian's "stalker tendencies":

"Have you sought therapy for your stalker tendencies?" Ana writes. In his role as first-person narrator, Christian tells us, "I smother my laugh. She's funny"; in his email, he tells Ana, "I pay the eminent Dr. Flynn a small fortune with regard to my stalker and other tendencies." Ana's reply has the subject line "Expensive Charlatans," which leads Christian-as-narrator to tell us "Damn, this woman is funny ... and intuitive; Flynn charges me a small fortune for his advice" (James *Grey*, 280–1).

As readers, we know that Ana has intuited nothing: Ana knows Flynn is expensive because Christian told her that in a previous email. Why does Christian think Ana is intuitive? Why does he repeat the phrase he used in his email, "small fortune," in his narrative voice as if the phrase is just occurring to him? The simplest explanation is that James, in the hasty process of converting *Fifty Shades of Grey* to Christian's perspective for the publication of *Grey*, forgot that Christian's remark about the "small fortune" he pays Dr. Flynn was already in the email to Ana. This oversight, however, was made possible, even likely, by the fact that the fantasy produced by the novel demands that Christian have no inner life, no secret thoughts or desires that he does not reveal to Ana. The fact that Christian himself seems unable to tell the difference between the language he uses to ingratiate himself to Ana and the language of his most private thoughts is emblematic of Christian's total lack of depth, but also of Christian and Ana's total compatibility as a couple. The exact content of Christian and Ana's flirtatious email conversation is irrelevant; what is important is the fusion of their opinions, their sexual appetites, their brand preferences. Yet, as Ana's lighthearted remark about Christian's "stalker tendencies" reminds us, such a fusion of identities can come about through manipulation and coercion as well as through equal and affectionate partnership. The everyday patriarchal violence that makes "stalker tendencies" something to joke about (when in fact Christian has certainly stalked Ana) is present in Christian and Ana's email exchange alongside the possibility of the companionate marriage of equals that both *Twilight* and *Fifty Shades of Grey* present as alternatives to that violence.

What *Fifty Shades* does more spectacularly than *Twilight*, perhaps because both its status as fantasy and its threat of violence are more overt than that of *Twilight*'s, is to reveal this double-sided, highly gendered version of the everyday. As we have seen, however, that double-sided everyday is present in multiple texts. Wicke argues that *Dracula* "is not a coherent text" but one that "refracts hysterical images of modernity" (469), simultaneously exposing the threat underlying the everyday technologies of modern life and proposing those very technologies as the weapons that might defeat evil. *Twilight* and *Fifty Shades* create an even more profound divide within the imagery of everyday life. The everyday is simultaneously a safe, harmonious place (vampires and sadists don't really exist; there are only kind and loving boyfriends) and the site of ordinary, unremarkable violence (boyfriends don't need to be vampires or sadists in order to hurt women). If we acknowledge, along with critics of both novels, that this everyday gendered violence reflects our own reality, it becomes possible to understand the ways in which the vision of the everyday as safe and harmonious is a vision of fantastic optimism—or optimistic fantasy. In *Twilight* and *Fifty Shades,* this fantasy is much more powerful than it is in *Dracula:* while in *Dracula* the best the everyday can do is produce weapons to fight against the vampire, pitting the cool light of reason against Dracula's dark magic, in *Twilight* the everyday transforms the vampire into a lover and an ally. As Bealer argues, toxic masculinity becomes enlightened masculinity. Dracula becomes a wiser, smarter, more loving, more understanding, more passionate version of Jonathan Harker.

In this way, the everydayness of *Twilight* and *Fifty Shades of Grey* is inextricable from their status as "fantasy" not only in the erotic sense, but in the speculative fiction sense as well. *Twilight* is like *Jeanne Dielman* in its commitment to representing the boring everyday life of young women, with its mundane pleasures and its equally mundane threats. At the same time, *Twilight* produces a fantasy of an everyday life that is boring precisely because it is so safe and so happy: the same satisfying boredom, in fact, that often pervades the utopian spirit of *Star Trek.* The boredom of *Twilight* is simultaneously the haunted monotony of *Jeanne Dielman* and, to return to Takei's video, the enlightened tedium of true Star Peace. *Twilight* and *Fifty Shades of Grey* both yearn for the boredom of whatever is left after epic battles are no longer necessary. But both *Twilight* and *Fifty Shades of Grey* know that young women live in our world, where neither Star Wars nor Star Peace prevail. What we have in these texts are not extraordinary choices, not epic battles. We have merely the battles young women fight every day, moaning and sparkling all through high school.

Acknowledgments

I would like to thank Jennifer L. Knox, Shanna Compton, Marisa Crawford, Becca Klaver, Paul Hughes, Rory Madden, Alison McDonough, Logan Hughes, Rebecca Onion, Anne Helen Petersen, Sam Frank and Lizzie Oldfather for their help and encouragement as I developed this essay.

Works Cited

Akerman, Chantal. "Chantal Akerman on *Jeanne Dielman.*" *Camera Obscura* 1, no. 2 (1977): 119.
Akerman, Chantal, dir. *Jeanne Dielman, 23, Quai du Commerce, 1080 Bruxelles.* New York: The Criterion Collection, 1975. DVD.
Al-Mahadin, Salam. "Is Christian a Sadist? *Fifty Shades of Grey* in Popular Imagination." *Feminist Media Studies* 13, no. 3 (2013): 566–570. Accessed 15 Dec. 2015. https://doi.org/10.1080/14680777.2013.786271.

Auerbach, Nina. *Our Vampires, Ourselves.* University of Chicago Press, 2012.
Barthes, Roland. "The Reality Effect." In *The Rustle of Language.* Translated by Richard Howard, 141–8. University of California Press, 1989.
Bealer, Tracy L. "Of Monsters and Men: Toxic Masculinity and the Twenty-First Century Vampire in the *Twilight* Saga." In *Bringing Light to* Twilight: *Perspectives on a Pop Culture Phenomenon,* edited by Giselle Liza Anatol, 163–180. Palgrave Macmillan, 2011. Google E-Book. Web. 1 Dec. 2015.
Felski, Rita. "Introduction to Special Issue: Everyday Life." *New Literary History* 33, no. 4 (2002): 607–622. Web. 14 April 2016.
Harris, Charlaine. *Club Dead: A Sookie Stackhouse Novel.* Penguin Group, 2003. Kindle file.
_____. *Dead Until Dark: A Sookie Stackhouse Novel.* Penguin Group, 2001. Kindle file.
James, E.L. *Fifty Shades of Grey.* Vintage Books, 2012. Kindle file.
_____. *Grey.* Vintage Books, 2011, 2015. Kindle file.
Le Fanu, J.S. *Carmilla.* Wildside Press, 2001.
Lefebvre, Henri. *Everyday Life in the Modern World.* Translated by Sacha Rabinovich. Continuum, 2002.
Meyer, Stephenie. *Breaking Dawn.* Little, Brown, and Company, 2008. Kindle file.
_____. *Midnight Sun* [unpublished]. Available at: https://stepheniemeyer.com/wp-content/uploads/archive/pdf/midnightsun_partial_draft4.pdf.
_____. *Twilight.* Little, Brown, and Company, 2005.
Nichol, Rhonda. "When You Kiss Me, I Want to Die: Arrested Feminism in *Buffy the Vampire Slayer* and the *Twilight* Series." In *Bringing Light to* Twilight: *Perspectives on a Pop Culture Phenomenon,* edited by Giselle Liza Anatol, 133–147. Palgrave Macmillan, 2011. *Google E-Book.* Web. 1 Dec. 2015.
Petersen, Anne Helen. "The Sly Capitalist Seduction of *Fifty Shades of Grey.*" *Buzzfeednews,* 15 Feb. 2015. https://www.buzzfeednews.com/article/annehelenpetersen/submit-to-capitalism.
_____. "That Teenage Feeling: *Twilight,* Fantasy, and Feminist Readers." *Feminist Media Studies* 12, no. 1 (2012): 51–67. Web. 17 March 2013.
Rice, Anne. *Interview with the Vampire.* Knopf, 1976.
_____. "Lestat and Louie Feel Sorry for Vampires That Sparkle in the Sun..." Facebook post. 28 Oct. 2011. Web. 2 Jan. 2016.
Stoker, Bram. *Dracula.* Broadview Press, 1997.
Takei, George. "George Takei Is the Broker of Star Peace." 10 Dec. 2011. YouTube video. https://www.youtube.com/watch?v=mvTCr5Z-0lA.
Whedon, Joss, creator. *Buffy the Vampire Slayer.* Mutant Enemy Productions, 1997–2003.
Wicker, Jennifer. "Vampiric Typewriting: Dracula and Its Media." *ELH* 59, no. 2 (1992): 467–493.
Yervasi, Carina. "Dislocating the Domestic in Chantal Akerman's Jeanne Dielman." *The Journal of Twentieth-Century/Contemporary French Studies* 4, no. 2 (2000): 385–398.

Using the Animator's Tools to Dismantle the Master's House?

Gender, Race, Sexuality and Disability in Cartoon Network's Adventure Time and Steven Universe

AL VALENTÍN

Introduction

While the situations in cartoons may be fictional, they often touch on topics or lessons that reflect reality. They make us laugh and we learn important lessons in the process; we gain a sense of who we are as individuals, where we belong in the world and how to navigate interpersonal relationships with others. Cartoons and other forms of media that children view or use engage them in a process of socialization in which their media consumption impacts their concepts of societal norms (Freeman, Giroux, Arnett) which, as many researchers have indicated, includes concepts of race (Fuster Burguera), health (Brown and Witherspoon), politics (Bennett), war/peace (Staub), religion (Barry, Padilla-Walker and Nelson), body image (Lopez, Corona and Halford), sexuality (Marshall and Sensoy) and gender roles (Zuckerman, Singer and Singer) in both positive and negative ways. This essay looks at two popular Cartoon Network animated shows to analyze the ways that they depict gender, sexuality, race and ability to ask whether cartoons can work to chip away at structures of sexism, heterosexism, cissexism, racism and ableism through creating new, more expansive models of being and social interaction. If the media plays a pivotal role in socializing children to understand the way that they "should" present their gender and conceive of their gendered, raced, and disabled bodies, cartoons with characters that depict gender norms, race or disability in novel ways may be an important force in reshaping the ways that children and society at large approach gender by moving away from binaries and toward more inclusive representations of gender and sexuality. While some scholarly research has looked specifically at how a cartoon like *Adventure Time* can impact a child's concepts and performance of gender roles, this essay aims to expand the conversation to also include questions on race and disability. Furthermore, rather than focusing just on *Adventure Time,* this essay will also look at *Steven Universe,* another popular Cartoon Network show that has had its own unique approach to these topics.

Adventure Time is a fifteen-minute-long, weekly show that airs on Cartoon Network. The show originally aired on April 5, 2010, and had ten seasons. This show is wildly successful and has spawned a video game, comic book series, toys and apparel, as well as garnering Emmy and Annie (an American award for achievement in animation) nominations. While the show has fans of a wide variety of ages, Common Sense Media, a nonprofit organization dedicated to helping parents make informed media choices, rates the show as being appropriate for ages ten and up. They advocate a bit more caution for children ages six to nine on their website due to soft but present depictions of violence, romance and swearing ("*Adventure Time* with Finn and Jake"). *Adventure Time* is a children's cartoon that is set in a post-apocalyptic Earth, sometime after a nuclear war which has reshaped society into various kingdoms and has likely exterminated all but one of the humans. That last human is named Finn, a young male adventurer who was raised by a family of magic dogs ever since he was an infant. Finn and his magic dog brother, Jake, work together to keep all of the kingdoms and the various princesses that rule them safe from evil entities like the Lich King and the Ice King. Though this cartoon follows a very traditional and familiar story of male adventurers or heroes fighting to save princesses from male villains, the way that they handle gender in the cartoon often gives the characters non-normative characteristics that can work to challenge the binary and help children to express themselves in less restrictive ways.

Steven Universe is another animated series on Cartoon Network that aired in 2013 and is currently in its fifth season. Since its inception, the show has gained a large and dedicated fanbase, also spawning its own video game, comic books, toys and apparel. Similarly, the show has also been nominated for both Emmy and Annie awards. Created by Rebecca Sugar, a former writer and storyboard artist for *Adventure Time,* her new series, *Steven Universe,* centers around another young boy on a quest to save the world. This time, our hero takes the form of Steven Universe, a half-human, half-alien child and a member of the Crystal Gems living in a fictional beachside locale, aptly named Beach City. The Crystal Gems are a group of humanoid aliens who have gone rogue against their own kind in order to save the Earth from their home planet's plans to colonize Earth and destroy humanity. The other members of the Crystal Gems, Garnet, Pearl, and Amethyst were friends and allies of Steven's mother and the former leader of the Gem Rebellion, Rose Quartz, who gave up her physical form in order to give birth to Steven. They are dedicated both to saving the Earth and protecting Steven who has gone from being their ward to being just as integral to saving the world as they are. The Crystal Gems function as friends, parents and guides to intergalactic warfare. Much like *Adventure Time,* this show does a lot to push past the traditionally normative depictions of gender in animated series. But before we get into a deeper analysis of either cartoon, we must first look at the literature surrounding cartoons as well as gender theory.

Sex, Gender and Socialization Through Media

Mainstream understandings of sex and gender often collapse the two terms into one seemingly biological category that we are born into, with one of two rigid definitions and rules to go along with our categorization. The concept of gender performativity confounds that conflation and allows us to think about gender differently. In "Performative Acts and Gender Constitution: An Essay in Phenomenology and Feminist Theory," Judith Butler argues against the essentialist notions of gender that seek to locate gender in biology and nature. Butler writes, "gender is in no way a stable identity or locus of agency from which various acts proceed; rather, it is an identity tenuously constituted in time-an identity instituted through a stylized repetition of acts" (519). Gender is not a function of nature nor is it something intuitive; it's taught. Gender is not something innate that our actions come from but something that our actions produce. Considering this, if gender is produced, what are the acts that produce it? According to Butler, "gender is instituted through the stylization of the body and, hence, must be understood as the mundane way in which bodily gestures, movements, and enactments of various kinds constitute the illusion of an abiding gendered self" ("Performative Acts" 519). A simple example would be the idea that women wear dresses and makeup because they are women. Butler would disagree and say that women have repeatedly worn dresses or makeup throughout time and so the wearing of dresses and makeup have become signifiers for "woman" through that repetition. This may not be true for men because they have not repeated the act enough for it to gain cultural weight or legibility as a male signifier. This repetition obscures the constructed nature of gender. The actions become "natural" through repetition because we've seen them so many times and assume them to be true in a biological or absolute sense.

It is in this way that Butler makes a distinction between biological sex and gender, which is defined culturally and loaded with meaning and implications. As Butler writes:

> To be female is, according to that distinction, a facticity which has no meaning, but to be a woman is to have become a woman, to compel the body to conform to an historical idea of 'woman,' to induce the body to become a cultural sign, to materialize oneself in obedience to an historically delimited possibility, and to do this as a sustained and repeated corporeal project ["Performative Acts" 522].

While it may be a biological fact that there exists a set of genitals that we've labeled female and male, these are categories that are distinct from, but dependent upon, gender. Gender is a cultural concept; a synthesis of movements and actions stylized in ways that we can read because we've written the script together. But it is important to note that work by writers such as Anne Fausto-Sterling in *Sexing the Body* have shown that even biological sex has been shaped by hegemonic conceptions of gender and may not be as "neutral" as one might have believed before. Thus, saying that sex is biological while gender is cultural is too simplistic of a binary; there is an interplay between the two categories.

In "Doing Gender," Candace West and Don H. Zimmerman echo this social constructionist concept of gender. The authors write, "Rather than as a property of individuals, we conceive of gender as an emergent feature of social situations: as both an outcome of and a rationale for various social arrangements and as a means of legitimating one of the most fundamental divisions of society" (1). According to the authors, gender is not something that we know or feel inherently from birth but a collection of behaviors and actions that we learn through various means of socialization. We learn what gender is and how to perform it because it stands to determine our privileges and disadvantages. Therefore, we learn what is expected of us in terms of our behaviors, actions and dress and try to adhere to those standards to avoid social sanctions. This teaching of gender happens through various institutions of socialization that range from our educational system, religion or families. However, another important learning context is the media, including children's cartoons.

In "Equally Super? Gender-Role Stereotyping of Superheroes in Children's Animated Programs," Kaysee Baker and Arthur A. Raney discuss the significance of cartoons in this process of socialization. Baker and Raney write, "Kids love cartoons. Studies consistently demonstrate that animated programs are the preferred format for children starting at 18 to 24 months of age" (25). Not only are animated cartoons the preferred television format for children, they also watch an incredible amount of television weekly. In "The Influence of Television on Children's Gender Role Socialization," Susan D. Witt and Kathleen G. Burriss note that preschoolers watch about 30 hours of television weekly (322). Witt and Burriss also reference a Nielsen Media Research study in 1992 which found that by the time a child reaches sixteen, sleep is the only activity that has consumed more time of their life than watching television (322). These statistics are incredible because they show that watching television consumes a considerably large portion of children's time. If sleeping is the only thing that outweighs the time spent watching television and cartoons are children's preferred television format, it is safe to say that they are an extremely powerful cultural force in children's lives.

Still, many adults might argue that cartoons are obviously fantastical, unrealistic, and therefore inconsequential to children's understandings of reality. The research evidence is to the contrary. As Swan writes, "Television provides all people with a window on the larger world, but the view through that window has a far greater influence on children's sense of it, simply because their individual worlds are so constricted, their experience so limited, and their perception of social reality so plastic" (1). Another study by Hui Li, Katherine Boguszewski and Angeline S. Lillard, found that children at age four were fairly good at determining whether or not a "fantastical" event depicted in television was real. As their age increased, they got better at determining the difference. But much like Swan, Li, Boguszewski and Lillard noted that having experience with which to juxtapose the "fantastic" events is one important factor in children's ability to differentiate between reality and fiction. While we may recognize the distinction between fantasy and reality as adults, it is a bit more difficult for children. Still, even if children are able to differentiate between fantasy and reality at a relatively young age, this doesn't mean that they aren't being socialized into particular beliefs about sex, gender, race and disability. This makes it all the more important to analyze how cartoons can affect children.

Gender in Media and Animated Television

In "Television Viewing and the Learning of Sex-Role Stereotypes," Paul E. McGhee and Terry Frueh analyze children in grades 1, 3, 5 and 7 to determine the extent that heavy television viewing affects children's stereotyped sex-role beliefs. In the study, the authors found that "heavy viewers were significantly more likely than light viewers to attribute to each sex the psychological characteristics typically associated with males and females by adults" (183). Children that watch more television have more gender stereotypical understandings of what men and women are. And if studies have consistently proven that cartoons are the preferred format, it is safe to say they get much of these stereotypical understandings from cartoons. McGhee and Frueh show that heavy television viewing plays a tremendous role in socializing children into having stereotyped beliefs about gender. Similarly, Witt and Burriss write: "young children will imitate and repeat behaviors they see on television. Consequently, children may exhibit these gender-biased attitudes that they see modeled on television" (322). Thus, children won't just have stereotypical beliefs about other men or women. They will begin to model their own behaviors on those that they see in cartoons. With this in mind, what are the stereotyped beliefs or gender-biased attitudes that children learn from television and cartoons?

In "Variations in the Gender-Stereotyped Content of Children's Television Cartoons Across Genres," Perlman et al. analyze four different genres of cartoons to examine gender stereotypes. In their findings, the authors note that male characters were more aggressive while female characters were shown to be fearful more often, as well as more focused on romance. Similarly, Witt and Burriss write, "Television programming emphasizes male characters' strength, performance and skill; for women, it focuses on attractiveness and desirability" (322–323). Men are traditionally depicted as aggressive, capable and intelligent, while women are portrayed as fearful and sensitive, with an emphasis on their appearance rather than their accomplishments. The constant reiteration of these types of beliefs will begin to construct the way that gender is performed by young children. Cartoons will show boys that they are intelligent and capable while showing girls that their attractiveness and desirability are their most valuable traits. This comes to shape children's own performances of gender and can have profound effects on the child's development of which Witt and Burriss write:

> Developing autonomy, initiative and a sense of industriousness are critical to young children's positive development. Children who witness female characters on television programs who are passive, indecisive, and subordinate to men, and who see this reinforced by their environment, will likely believe that this is the appropriate way for females to behave. Female children are less likely to develop autonomy, initiative, and industriousness if they rarely see those traits modeled. Similarly, because male characters on television programs are more likely to be shown in leadership roles and exhibiting assertive, decisive behavior, children learn this is the appropriate way for male to behave [322].

This means that these unhealthy and unequal depictions of gender have a direct impact on the way that children come to perform their own gender. Young females will learn that they should depend on others rather than themselves and focus on their appearance. Young males, alternatively, will learn that they should be assertive and aggressive. This creates a handicap for girls, not allowing them to tap into skills and traits that are gendered masculine but necessary for their development as healthy, functional and successful adults. It also moves boys away from the ability to show their emotions and insecurities, which can be detrimental to their emotional development and social interactions later in life as girls and boys are socialized to express their emotions differently (Root and Denham).

Furthermore, Witt and Burriss note, "A study of Saturday morning cartoons revealed that females were pictured less often than males, were less active than males, played fewer roles than males, played fewer lead roles than males, and worked primarily in the home. Although these findings were obtained more than 25 years ago, no significant improvement is evident" (323). Female characters are usually far outnumbered by male characters in cartoons, and those that are there tend to work in the home. The implications of this are highlighted by Teresa L. Thompson and Eugenia Zerbinos' work in "Television Cartoons: Do Children Notice It's a Boy's World?" The authors point to the stereotypical depictions of male and female characters as affecting children's job preferences. The authors write, "Our results indicate that children do notice differences in the presentation of male and female characters in children's cartoons, and that noticing such differences appears to be related to reporting more stereotypical job preferences. These findings were especially strong for male respondents" (427). So, it is clear that if children are continuously viewing these very strict, normative, binary concepts of gender, they will model their decisions on everything from everyday behavior to career aspirations on what they know or believe about gender.

We can see that media in general and cartoons specifically show children that men behave one way, women behave another, and that there is little wiggle room shown in between. Understanding that gender is socially constructed and performative in nature may be the first step in making gender less restrictive. If we understand that it is a construction, we understand that it is not absolute; rather, it is malleable, subject to change. In "Performative Subversions," Judith Butler argues that attributing feminine behaviors to a masculine body or masculine behaviors to a feminine body complicates the process of gender's construction. Each person's performance becomes steeped in both masculinity and femininity which subverts the traditional ascription of male bodies as always masculine and female bodies as always feminine. Though Butler seems to be focusing on the idea of drag in the excerpt presented, this attribution of masculine traits to the female body or feminine traits to the male body is undoubtedly significant for all realms of life. Butler writes, "This perpetual displacement constitutes a fluidity of identities that suggest openness to resignification and recontextualization; parodic proliferation deprives hegemonic culture and its critics of the claim to naturalized or essentialist gender identities" ("Performative Subversions" 50). Through the displacement of the feminine onto male bodies and vice-versa, we challenge the very idea that these traits are natural to one gender or the other, which in turn challenges the culture that enforces these biological essentialist arguments. We can therefore show there is no one way to be a woman and no one way to be a man and open up room for many variations in terms of identity.

This is what makes the depictions of male and female characters so important. In "The Gender-Role Content of Children's Favorite Television Programs and Its Links to Their Gender-Related Perceptions," Jennifer Stevens Aubrey and Kristen Harrison write, "On the whole, studies of television's effect on children's gender-role learning have suggested that the medium can contribute to both traditional and nontraditional gender-role learning" (112). When children see characters with non-normative gender performances, it can be just as effective in shifting their concepts of gender as normative ones. Additionally, while Thompson and Zerbinos did find that children who notice differences between the depiction of male and female characters in cartoons do have more stereotypical job preferences, they add, "Similarly, noticing nonstereotypical behaviors in female characters appeared to be related to nontraditional female job expectations in both male and female respondents" (427). This means that cartoons with nontraditional depictions of gender can be just as effective in affecting children's concepts of gender roles as traditional ones are. It is in this way that cartoons with characters that have atypical gender expressions can be a powerful tool in changing the way that children think about and express their own gender identity. While the media is clearly not the only institution that socializes children into a "proper" gender role, I see cartoons as being an incredibly unique platform on which to fight the battle against the binary. But one thing that all of these pieces of literature leaves out is any discussion of the different factors that impact their gender identity. All of these studies disregard the impact of other forms of difference. While we have clearly seen that children's concepts of gender are shaped by television, it is important to look at whether the same can be said for two categories of difference ignored by these studies: race and disability.

Race in the Media and Animated Television

In addition to looking at the way that gender is depicted in cartoons, we also have to look at the way that race is handled in animated shows. The history of race and cartoons is a long one. As Xavier Fuster Burguera notes in his article, "Muffled Voices," the history of animation is linked to the history of vaudeville and, with it, the racist minstrel depictions of black people. He writes, "Taking advantage of the black-and-white images, earlier cartoons were designed to recall this kind of characters. Oswald the Lucky Rabbit, Felix the Cat, Bosko, Mickey Mouse, Bimbo, Foxy or Piggy are clear examples of characters modeled after blackface actors" (72). These characters, Fuster Burguera argues, have the clear signs of blackface influence through the usage of "Afro-American" accents, the frequent usage of singing as well as the heavy reliance on slapstick comedy. These influences may have been explicit, yet many of the characters that initially made use of these tropes were animals, as the list put forth by Fuster Burguera suggests. However, this would soon shift. As Fuster Burguera notes, African American characters did begin to appear in cartoons around the mid–20th century, but he agrees with those who suggest these characters represented concerns about decolonization and the loss of empires (73). This is a particularly interesting point to be made because we can see how cartoons are often shaped to reflect the larger cultural and social values of a nation. Entertainment becomes a way to work through those "anxieties" related to a shifting world, and children of each generation are there to watch it all unfold.

But the overt racism that was initially a huge part of the beginning of the animated cartoon format would soon soften. As Hugh Klein and Kenneth S. Shiffman write, "The decline in overt racism in animated cartoons began shortly after World War II, and reduced to near-zero levels in the years following the Civil Rights Movement of the 1960s. It appears to us that, as public pressures increased in our society to treat members of racial minority groups with greater equality and to discriminate less against them, animated cartoon content followed suit by greatly reducing overtly racist portrayals" (176). Since then, there has been a large shift in the depictions of race in children's cartoons. In the same paper, Klein and Shiffman put forth a content analysis of race in animated cartoons, focusing primarily on the short animated shows. The study was meant to look for instances of overt racism, as well as characteristics associated with different racial and ethnic groups. They found that, generally, in short form animated cartoons, Black people, white people, Latinos, Asian Americans and Native Americans weren't depicted much differently throughout the shows they studied. The one big exception to this rule, interestingly enough, is the depiction of African Americans as being more likely to engage in dancing and singing. They write, "we did discover that African Americans were more likely than members of other races to engage in entertainment-related activities like singing, dancing, and playing music—content which, we readily admit, is consistent with age-old stereotypes of Black minstrels and the notion of African Americans as entertainers of the dominant White culture" (176). Still, they argue that this may be tempered by another finding that Black characters were "more prosocial" and no other major changes were found among characters of different races

(176). However, it is important to note that the short nature of the shows they surveyed may limit the amount of content that fit into one episode and thus, shape the reliance on stereotyping among animators. Other scholarly works, focused primarily on longer formats, including animated films, have found that racial stereotyping still persists (Lacroix, Faherty, Lugo-Lugo and Bloodsworth-Lugo).

One thing that most researchers will agree on, however, in regard to animated shows and films, is that there is certainly a paucity of characters of color within their worlds. In 1982, Russell H. Weigel and Paul W. Howes came to a conclusion similar to that of Klein and Shiffman: while there may not be a high level of overt racial stereotyping on children's animated television shows, the severe lack of characters of color is a big problem that can effect children negatively. Klein and Shiffman found that

> African Americans, who comprised 11.8% of the U.S. population during the time period last covered by this research (U.S. Census Bureau, 2000), constituted only 3.3% of the animated cartoon characters at that time—underrepresented by nearly 4:1. Latinos, comprising 9.0% of the U.S. population, represented 1.2% of the characters shown during the 1990s—underrepresented by more than 7:1. Native Americans, who accounted for 0.72% of the U.S. population during the 1990s, were only 0.04% of the cartoon characters shown at that time—underrepresented by an 18:1 margin [177].

This shows us the extent to which most racialized populations were under-represented in animated cartoons. The only group for which this was not the case among the studied cartoons was Asian Americans. These statistics on underrepresentation are important because they can contribute to symbolic annihilation (Klein and Shiffman), a process in which certain groups are consistently represented in the media at the expense of other groups that are almost never shown. This is important because "by almost never showing certain 'types' of persons or characters, the media not only reflect social values about the goodness/badness or preferability of some groups vis-a-vis others, but they also reinforce these notions in people who are exposed to these media" (Klein and Shiffman 178). So, if children constantly get to see white males as heroes while they never or rarely get to see characters of color as heroes, they will begin to associate whiteness with bravery, virtue and good-ness while associating other groups with cowardice, badness, or at the very least mediocrity. Klein and Shiffman write:

> Much greater representation of African American characters and Latino characters and Native American characters is needed in order for viewers to construe these groups as valued and equal contributors to our culture. By showing so few of them, particularly compared with their Caucasian counterparts, animated cartoons send

the message—loud and clear—that African Americans do not count, that Latinos do not count, and that Native Americans do not count … at least not to the same extent that Caucasians do [178].

In addition to combating stereotypes, it is also important to have characters of color alongside white characters in order to give children models for healthy interracial relationships. As Weigel and Howes write, "Since children's programming rarely exposes viewers to cross-racial relationships of any type, there is little reason for enthusiasm regarding the medium's capacity to foster interracial goodwill through vicarious experience" (112). Since "difference" is determined relationally, we need to see characters of varying racial and ethnic groups in order to get the full extent to which cartoons can help reshape children's understanding of race, friendship and community. When cartoons continuously erase characters of color, they not only work to perpetuate stereotypes, but also do not provide models for healthy interracial relationships. Lastly, the lack of positive role models for young children of color is important because it has been shown to impact the self-esteem among both white and Black girls as well as Black boys. The influence is only beneficial to the white boys who are most commonly represented and valorized in media (Martins and Harrison).Thus, race is an important category of difference to consider when we begin to analyze both *Adventure Time* and *Steven Universe*. However, we must first look at the way that disability is similarly underrepresented in animated cartoons on television and is often used for humor.

Disability in the Media and Animated Television

In 2015, the Center for Disease Control and Prevention (CDC) put out a report based on 2013 figures which found that 53 million adults in the United States are living with a disability, about one out of every five adults (Courtney-Long et al.). These statistics show that disability is far more common than one might assume. Interestingly enough, however, some theorists have argued that disability, unlike other marginalized groups in the media, is overrepresented but in ways that are negative (Longmore). Rather than not seeing many disabled people in television and film, we see many but their representations are often incredibly problematic. When we think of mainstream media as a whole, there are many iconic characters that come to mind. From Tom Hanks' *Forrest Gump* to John Hurt's *Elephant Man* to the even more recent depiction of Stephen Hawking's life in *The Theory of Everything*. While there are many iconic disabled characters that one can list in mainstream media, many disability justice advocates argue that they often conform to three basic and harmful stereotypes: the victim, the hero and the villain. When it comes to the victim, characters were found to be, "depicted as 'vulnerable,' a 'victim' and/or a person worthy of pity.... Portrayals designed to elicit pity increased significantly, with the largest increases in recent years" (Pardun). As MediaSmarts points out, there are two ways that this characterization can go: either it can work to elicit sympathy or amusement in the audience. Two examples they give, respectively, are *A Christmas Carol*'s Tiny Tim and the intellectual disability of *Forrest Gump*'s protagonist of the same name (MediaSmarts). When it comes to the hero trope, characters are depicted as what Lynne Roper calls "supercrip," or "people who conform to the individual model by overcoming [their] disability and becoming more 'normal,' in a heroic way." By making disability something in opposition to normalcy, rather than a part of normalcy as the pervasiveness of disability proves it to be, it creates an image of a "good" disabled person and a "bad" disabled person. It makes those that "give in" to a life with disability bad for not "trying hard enough," whereas it rewards those that are able to push past their disability. This is a trope particularly popular in comics as any *Batman* and *Daredevil* fans would know. Similarly, *X-Men* plays on questions of difference and ability while making all the characters labelled as "freaks" into heroes as well.

Lastly, the villain trope uses disability as a marker of evil through the depiction of physical disabilities as "grotesque" or horrific (MediaSmarts). Similarly, many types of media portray people with mental illness as either evil or violent (MediaSmarts). In an ableist world that constructs certain bodies as abnormal by not allowing them access to the same resources as able-bodied people, the difference of disabled people and bodies are read as pathological, deviant, unsightly and dangerous (Kafer). Furthermore, it is important to note that the history of disability is one that is always racialized and gendered (Erevelles). The histories of racism and sexism depended on understandings of racialized bodies and "female" bodies as being both mentally and physically handicapped through an association with vulnerability and a lack of intelligence (Erevelles, Roper). Given the intimate proximity of these histories, it is interesting to note that most depictions of disabled characters in media are of white males (Roper). Still, rather than being distinct, the questions about gender, sexuality, race and disability are absolutely intertwined, subsumed around a logic of who is truly human and who is not. Consequently, there are devastating implications for these different populations, who are then doomed to live lives that will include discrimination and a lack of adequate resources from the state (Erevelles).

When we stop to consider animated cartoons specifically, however, it becomes much more difficult to think of any disabled characters. Furthermore, it becomes even more difficult to find scholarly research that focuses specifically on that topic. One might recall Porky Pig and his prominent stutter, or Gabriella, a deaf Latina mermaid and friend of the more widely known Ariel of Disney's *The Little Mermaid* animated series in the early '90s. But how many others can the average television viewer name? Writer Tim Smedley pointed out in July 2015 that in animated children's television shows there were only two disabled characters who were consistently featured on major, current television franchises: *Fireman Sam*'s Hannah Sparkes and *How to Train Your Dragon*'s protagonist Hiccup. If we expand the conversation to feature length films, one can consider the animated Disney retelling of the classic tale, *The Hunchback of Notre Dame*. For a more recent example, we might consider Pixar's *Finding Nemo,* which includes depictions of both physical and cognitive disabilities. But these, as feature length animated films, are different from that of an animated series formatted for television in terms of the way that their narrative must be constructed and what can fit in. Still, despite being a feature length film, *Finding Nemo* is, as Daniel L. Preston argues, a particularly good example for children to discuss questions around disability. He argues that, because many different characters are depicted as having physical or cognitive differences, which range from a damaged fin to memory loss to obsessive compulsive disorder to addiction, and because their difference is, on the whole, valued rather than demonized. Even though these disabilities are often used as a means for comedy, it is ultimately true that the different characters care for and accept each other's differences. Furthermore, their differences can be both disabling in one context and also useful in other contexts, an understanding of difference and disability that resists concepts of normalcy, wherein disability is always negative (Preston 2010). Thus, this model may be a good one to follow, as it mirrors showing difference in terms of race and gender in similarly accepting lights between different characters. It is important to continue analyzing disability in children's cartoons and what its representation can do to shift the ways that people think about disability and the ways that society is structured around a very narrow notion of ability.

Gender in Adventure Time

Since the initial completion of this essay in 2013, its presentation in 2014, and its subsequent publication, a handful of other academics have given some critical attention to the treatment of gender and sexuality in *Adventure Time* (Jane, Leslie). In Emma A. Jane's "'Gunter's a Woman?!'— Doing and Undoing Gender in Cartoon Network's *Adventure Time,*" the author uses *Adventure Time* as a "real world exemplar of 'gender progressive' or 'gender positive' children's entertainment might look like" (232). In framing the show this way, Jane points out a wide variety of writing and design choices that create this progressive potential within the series, with the hope that more shows will follow suit with similar choices. Some of these choices include

> the inclusion of roughly equal numbers of female and male characters in protagonist, antagonist, and minor roles; the inclusion of a significant number of characters who have multiple and/or indeterminate genders; the use of gendered "design elements" (King, 2010) such as eyelashes and facial hair to illustrate character traits rather than as blunt, gender-signaling instruments; the distribution of traits such as intelligence, courage, loyalty, power lust, sentimentality, selfishness, altruism, artistic temperament, and a "gross" sense of humor equally among characters regardless of gender; the privileging of extended or "found" families (often including members of other species) over nuclear family arrangements; the deployment of characterisations and plot devices which frame gender and identity as being fluid rather than fixed; and the inclusion of queer and transgender sub-texts [Jane 235].

Jane's concise outline of the particular choices that make the cartoon progressive in its depiction of gender is a helpful starting point. But it is also important to go a little bit deeper into the analysis of the series and how it puts these decisions into action. We will do this by analyzing a few specific episodes that haven't been covered in detail in the other literature.

Masculinity is handled in a very interesting way in the series. Finn and Jake, the two main heroes of *Adventure Time,* are both male identified characters. The two are brothers who have made it their life's mission to protect all of the citizens in the Land of Ooo. While they are shown to be incredibly brave and capable, characteristics that are common among depictions of males in cartoons, they are also depicted as emotional and sensitive. Their performance of masculinity does not follow the traditional binary or the stereotyical depiction of males in cartoons. Finn and Jake have a relationship that does not follow the traditional mold of male relationships in the media as it is deep and intimate in ways that are not traditionally shown on television. Rather than creating characters that are afraid of emotion and insensitive, the writers have created a pair of male heroes that are well-rounded, making them healthier role models than many other male cartoon characters.

Finn and Jake are open with each other and voice their feelings, emotions and vulnerabilities often. In the episode "Ocean of Fear," Finn reveals that he is terrified of the ocean and Jake tries his best to help Finn overcome his fear. Finn shows a vulnerability that is not often depicted for men in the media and he is not met with ridicule or shame by Jake. In the episode "Storytelling," Jake falls ill and needs Finn to take care of him. This involves tucking Jake in and, eventually, running around the forest in an effort to find a story to tell Jake, as Jake believes it is the only thing that will cure him. In "Freak City," Finn is turned into a giant foot by a crazed wizard named Magic Man. When Finn grows despondent with his lack of mobility and ability, he begins to cry. Jake then immediately rushes to help him. Finn questions how Jake knew that Finn needed him and Jake's response is that he can always sense when Finn is about to cry, describing it as a "mother-daughter thing." Jake is also often found cooking for the pair and tending to the house, for examples in episodes "Conquest of Cuteness," "Apple Thief," and "Burning Low." Similarly, Jake is shown to be a caring and nurturing father. In the episode "Jake the Dad," Jake and his partner, Lady Rainicorn, welcome a litter of pups. After the birth, Jake does his best to care for Lady Rainicorn and the pups by making them French toast for breakfast. Throughout the episode, he is shown to be a very nervous but involved father. He reads to them, constantly checks on the children, and wonders if he is doing things right. Jake does his best to comical results but in the end, we discover that because Rainicorns age rather rapidly, the pups can take care of themselves. While relieved, Jake is also a little bit sad that he doesn't get to "mother" them anymore.

These nurturing relationships, the willingness to take on roles that have traditionally been associated with femininity (that of caregiver and homemaker), and the lack of shame or negativity in applying those feminine descriptors to themselves show a progressive and anti-sexist brand of masculinity that encourages boys to be caring and kind without disparaging women or femininity. Finn and Jake take care of each other and nurture each other in a way that shows their love for one another without feeling guilty, ashamed or any less masculine. This is important because "appropriation of the feminine works to multiply possible sites of application of the term, to reveal the arbitrary relation between the signifier and the signified, and to destabilize and demobilize the sign" (Butler "Performance Subversions" 48). This appropriation of feminine nurturing works to show that there is no inherent biological basis for imposed gender roles. It opens up a space for young boys to feel okay being nurturers and caretakers. Additionally, Finn is shown to have a supportive and healthy relationship with Jake, who is his adoptive brother. This is important as in later episodes of the series, Finn's biological father is shown to be a criminal and a negligent parent. While this is obviously a source of confusion and sadness for Finn, he is able to come to terms with it by having such a supportive "found family," as Jane indicated in her opening list of design choices.

This appropriation of the feminine is also apparent in the style and mannerisms of Jake. In the beginning of the episode entitled "BMO Noire," Jake is seen preening in the mirror while Finn inquires about his missing sock. Jake sits nonchalantly and applies mascara, elongating his eyelashes. He then proceeds to take a tube of lipstick and draws a bright red spiral on his face. The application of makeup is an act that we've gendered as female. We have a much harder time accepting men in makeup like mascara and lipstick because the mainstream media reinforces this as a female specific activity through its constant marketing of makeup to women only (Hall, Gough and Seymour Smith). Men who do wear makeup are often assumed to be gay or transgender because we have a narrow understanding of who should wear what. But here we have a male identified character in a committed relationship with a member of the opposite sex, applying and proudly wearing makeup. Jake's enjoyment of makeup is not even made an issue or discussed in this episode, showing that it is acceptable behavior in the eyes of his peers.

A later episode of the cartoon furthers the narrative of "BMO Noire." In "Princess Potluck," it is explained that Jake was wearing this makeup to attend a potluck thrown by the Princesses of Ooo. In addition to his makeup, he's also sporting a purse. While discussing the event, Jake says to Finn, "Don't worry, man. We're gonna have a ton of fun. We'll eat some melon. I'll get some compliments on my pretty makeup." Finn responds that Jake looks "like a target," which denotes more of a concern with the style of makeup, reminiscent of a bullseye rather than the act of wearing lipstick itself. Jake retorts loudly, "I look pretty!" Not only is this a non-normative performance of gender but it is one that Jake is committed to despite the criticism that he encounters from his brother. Furthermore, when they arrive at the event, Jake is complimented by Princess Bubblegum on his makeup and told that he looks pretty. Jake is very pleased with this and the next frame shows him batting his eyelashes and clutching his face happily. Not only does Jake perform his gender however he wants, he is not harassed by others even when not fully understood and is actively praised by those who do understand.

This same gender transgression is apparent in the episode "Blood Under the Skin." After being embarrassed by a bully named Sir Slicer due to his lack of armor, Finn goes on a quest to recover the Magical Armor of Zelderon. Throughout the episode, Finn must go through a series of embarrassing trials and tribulations in order to finally get the armor. When Finn and Jake finally reach the cave and recover the armor, they discover that it is armor for a woman as its helmet has long flowing pigtails and its breast plate has visible space for breasts. Too embarrassed to deal with wearing the armor, Finn discards it. But when they need it to defeat a ghost, Jake puts it on and uses it to destroy their enemy. After they beat the ghost and confront Sir Slicer one last time, Finn gets on Jake's back to fly away thanks to the magical abilities bestowed on Jake by the armor. While flying away, Jake says, "Dude, this armor is totally (click-click)!" This is a sound that is used throughout the episode to denote something as "cool." This means that Jake does not see the armor as devalued because it is for a woman. He wears it proudly despite it not being made for him as a male. These are all powerful moments in animation that confound the binary through their proud appropriation of the feminine.

The cartoon's depiction of masculinity not only opens up space for healthier homosocial relationships or gender performances but also shows how boys will deal with their romantic interests. In the episode "Hot to the Touch," Finn is caught between his interest in Flame Princess and her own desire to set everything in her path aflame. Though Finn has feelings for her, her destructive tendencies go against his vow to keep the people of Ooo safe. At the end of the episode, Finn voices his frustrations to Flame Princess and cries. When he does so, Flame Princess comes to understand him more and says that he is a water elemental. She says that despite their attraction, they cannot be together because they are opposite elements. This is particularly interesting as fire as an element is classified as a masculine energy in many religious cosmologies, while water is classified as feminine (Molleur). Their relationship subverts those typical associations. Though Finn does try and cover up the fact that he's crying, he is not shamed by Flame Princess. She is intrigued and appreciates his honesty. In later episodes, the two enter a relationship and begin to work through the ups and downs of young love together. He is not sanctioned for his lack of being tough and stoic. He is rewarded with a partner who knows who he is fully and cares about him anyway. This opens up a path to intimacy and understanding, letting children know that rhetoric like "if this person knew I was really like this, they wouldn't like me" is untrue and unnecessary, for the right person will care about you regardless. While their relationship eventually ends, Finn and the Flame Princess maintain respect for each other and are successful on their own.

Still, the cartoon doesn't just open up space for a masculinity that is not afraid of femininity, it also actively critiques the normative conceptions of masculinity. In the episode entitled "What Was Missing," Finn and Jake, along with their friends BMO, Princess Bubblegum and Marceline the Vampire Queen, have their most precious items stolen from them by a creature called the Door Lord. In the episode, the group has to literally band together to create a song that is earnest and true in order to open the door to retrieve their personal belongings. Once Jake discovers that they must become a band, he asks if he can be the "jerk in the band." He plays up this character throughout the episode, as he plays his viola and is confrontational and pushy. He calls the rest of the group talentless hacks and storms off. When he eventually comes back, he is wearing low rise jeans with a mohawk and is sporting a taller, more muscular body. He breaks his viola in another fit of emotion. When the rest of the group goes on to argue, he storms off again. This time, he reminds the others that he is pretending. While Jake finds it fun to play this hypermasculine role, he wants to ensure that he doesn't hurt his friends. He finds the antics funny and critiques them by exaggerating them to the point of parody: he is mocking hyper masculinity more than he is valorizing it. And once Finn sings a song about how he loves his friends, Jake happily softens his appearance and goes back to his normal shape, indicating that it is fun to mock normative masculinity of aggression but more rewarding to be open and sensitive with and to your friends.

Furthermore, there is a running gag throughout the episodes about a book entitled *Mind Games*, by a character named Jay T. Doggzone. The book is supposed to enable men to pick up women and is used by the Ice King. In "Reign of Gunters," the Ice King tries to hit on Huntress Wizard who does not return his advances. The Ice King mentions Doggzone's advice to "Swing at Every Ball," meaning to flirt with as many women as possible because one of them is bound to return the advances. In another episode entitled "I Remember You," Ice King also references the idea that "ladies are drawn to bros with tortured pasts." This advises men to play up tragedy in order to get women to gravitate toward them. It simultaneously deploys the concept of women as caretakers and nurturers and the "natural" emotional unavailability of men, thus ensuring an unhealthy relationship, but Ice King thinks it is good advice. In "Reign of Gunters," Finn also mentions the idea of "future farming." This means that one should always act mysteriously around women to keep them confused about where you stand and therefore, interested. Though Finn is in a relationship with Flame Princess, he deploys this piece of advice and acts aloof and mysterious to Princess Bubblegum in case things with Flame Princess fizzle out. This is where we see the real critique. Jake worries that Finn is reading the book and tells Finn that he just keeps that book around for laughs, noting that it is actually terrible advice. It is also important to mention that the book seems to be playing on real life manuals that tell men how to attract women, notably *The Game: Penetrating the Secret Society of Pickup Artist* by Neil Strauss. This is clearly parodying the absurd, confusing and damaging lengths that men are told to go to in order to pick up women.

In these ways, Finn and Jake don't adhere to the traditional portrayal of masculinity. They appropriate "feminine" attributes and show children that it is not natural or biological for men to be logical, insensitive or lacking emotion. It shows alternatives to the normative concept of masculinity, thus disproving it as "natural." It gives young males the room to feel comfortable to go against the grain because they admire cartoon characters who do the same. Finn and Jake can be non-normatively masculine and have nurturing, caretaking aspects to their personality but they are still heroes and they still have the respect and admiration of those in all the kingdoms. They can also see that it is silly to be overly aggressive and emotionally unavailable or sneaky in order to gain the love and affection of others by seeing healthier, more open relationships between characters.

Men are obviously not the only ones that feel the effects of socialization. While men are told they must not be emotional, women are often told that they are too emotional and that it clouds their judgment. Women are told that they are the "weaker" or "fairer" sex. While men's socialization seems to be all about ascribing power and leadership to them, women's socialization is about ensuring that their power and agency are taken away. When we think about the show in the context of this, the way that the female characters are portrayed in the cartoon becomes doubly interesting. Though these female characters are often princesses, they have many non-normative characteristics that help them to stray from common understandings of femininity. Though there are princesses that sometimes need to be saved, they are all the rulers of their own kingdoms and seem to outnumber the males in the *Adventure Time* universe. They don't have a Prince or a King that they answer to. They are the leaders. They have power. Still, their behaviors outside their roles as rulers are important to consider.

Princess Bubblegum is the ruler of the Candy Kingdom and, as her name suggests, she is made entirely out of bubblegum. Though she's pink and her appearance is stereotypically feminine, she is a very well-rounded character. As evidenced in episodes like "Slumber Party Panic" and "Five Short Graybles," she's an incredibly intelligent scientist who uses science to both understand the world and better her kingdom. This is particularly apparent in "The Suitor." Peppermint Butler and the Gumball Guardian decide to find her a suitor so she can have romantic companionship. Princess Bubblegum repeatedly shows her disinterest in the best of her suitors, a gentle young man named Braco who goes out of his way to win her affections. Angered by the imposition, she makes it clear to Peppermint Butler that he is in no position to tell her she must find a suitor at all. Later, when Braco voices that he loves her so much that it hurts, Princess Bubblegum responds with logic and reason. She says, "What you're feeling is called infatuation. The pain is a product of you overvaluing a projected imaginary relationship with me." She later tells Braco that she's not interested in marriage or a relationship. Both of these sentiments stray away from the usual depictions of women as overly romantic, sensitive and emotional. Still, seeing the pain that her disinterest in romance causes Braco, she uses science to create a wife for him, allowing him to live happily ever after with a Princess Bubblegum Bot. The bot is interested in romance and her number one priority is to find somebody to spend her life with which leaves the real Princess Bubblegum free to do her work. While there is a hint of sadness that Princess Bubblegum voices at the end of the episode, her decision shows that she is committed to her work and lifestyle and not going to change that in order to please a suitor.

Aside from her commitment to science, her intellect is also shown in the fact she is multilingual. She is shown speaking German in episodes like "What Have You Done?" and "Go with Me." Additionally, we can assume she knows Korean, as she can communicate with her trusted companion, Lady Rainicorn, who speaks Korean throughout the series. She's also shown to be a more than competent ruler who continuously works to make her subjects' lives better, as shown in "Red Starved" (2013) when she charges Finn and Jake with locating the Spoon of Prosperity to ensure that starvation will never affect her kingdom. Though she does rely on Finn and Jake to help her with things that afflict and affect her kingdom, she has also saved them before and has fought off many attackers herself. In the episode "Lady and Peebles," Princess Bubblegum and Lady Rainicorn go on a mission to find Finn and Jake. The two heroes have been missing for three weeks after going to search for the Ice King. Princess Bubblegum and Lady Rainicorn track Finn and Jake on GPS to the Black Ice Cave. They are attacked but they hold their ground and though Lady Rainicorn is injured, Princess Bubblegum carries her to safety, unwilling to leave her behind. Once they find Finn and Jake, Princess Bubblegum realizes that they have been poisoned and hooked up to a machine that is powering up and creating a body for Ricardio. Her most dangerous foe, Ricardio is the heart of the Ice King who has come to life, become self-aware and is obsessed with winning Princess Bubblegum's hand.

After Ricardio reveals his evil intent to win the affection of Princess Bubblegum with his new body, he attacks Lady Rainicorn, incapacitating her and forcefully asks Princess Bubblegum to marry him. Princess Bubblegum initially appears to be willing to give into his advances by taking off her coat but then responds that she will only marry him if he can beat her in hand to hand combat. Her removal of clothing was in anticipation of battle rather than submission. Enraged, they fight and she beats Ricardio before tearing him artificial limb from limb. She warns him to never come back as he escapes. Once Ricardio is gone, Princess Bubblegum carries Finn, Jake, Lady Rainicorn and the Ice King back to the Candy Kingdom's hospital, a feat that takes two days. She synthesizes an antidote for their poison and even creates a new heart for the Ice King to replace Ricardio. Not only is Princess Bubblegum a hero that saves four other characters, but she also fights off an attacker that was not willing to take no for an answer. The broaching of the topic of consent and giving Princess Bubblegum power and respect in her acts is nothing short of revolutionary in a children's cartoon and in a world where rape culture disproportionately puts young girls at risk. It is also important to point out that at the end of that episode, Lady Rainicorn is revealed to be pregnant with Jake's children. The fact that she's pregnant doesn't disable her or prevent her from doing her duty to help Princess Bubblegum find Finn and Jake. She is strong and capable despite her being pregnant. This is a depiction of a female character that shows that women are not weak because of their biology. Child-bearing capacity does not mean that you cannot have strength, bravery and courage. You can be a hero, a woman, and a mother all at once.

In addition to Princess Bubblegum and Lady Raincorn, there are characters like Marceline the Vampire Queen. Marceline is a tough girl, a bit of a daredevil and a rocker. She has long black hair that was once shaved in an undercut, wears dark colors and despises most things pink and frilly except, perhaps, for Princess Bubblegum. In "What Was Missing," it is revealed that the two used to be quite close before they had a falling out for reasons unexplained. Marceline sings a song about how she wants to "drink the red" from an undisclosed person's "pretty pink face." When Princess Bubblegum says that the song is too distasteful, Marceline sings more about how she can't be what Princess Bubblegum wants, and even though Princess Bubblegum hurt her, she still desires to make up with her. Realizing she may be revealing too much, she becomes embarrassed, blushes wildly and stops singing before getting aggressive and hostile. By the end of the episode, we learn that Princess Bubblegum's most prized possession is an old band t-shirt that Marceline gave her. Princess Bubblegum says she wears it all the time as pajamas and this causes Marceline to blush again.

Additionally, in a weekly recap of the episode on YouTube, the writers alluded that the two may have been more than friends in the past by stating that perhaps Marceline likes Princess Bubblegum even more than Finn, who had a crush on Princess Bubblegum at the time. The narrator even asks, "What do you think about Marceline and Bubblegum … getting together? Does this leave Finn in the dust or is it just adorbz?" (Johnson). In addition, Natasha Allegri, one of the animators, has drawn many pictures of the two embracing on her personal blog (Johnson). This allusion to queer desire in the cartoon is something incredibly unique and it was expanded in the fall of 2015 through a miniseries entitled *Stakes* which focused specifically on Marceline and hinted even more that the two were once in a romantic relationship and that they still care for each other. Furthermore, it is also important to acknowledge that Marceline is also shown to have been in relationships with males. In "Memory of a Memory," Finn and Jake learn about a relationship that Marceline had with an immortal wizard named Ash. This would seem to point to a bisexual or queer identity. While the depictions of LGBTQ identified characters throughout all media is still lacking, bisexual representation is even harder to come by (GLAAD, 2012–2013). The fact that these types of relationships are even more taboo on a children's show is evidenced in the panic around characters like Spongbob SquarePants of

SpongeBob SquarePants or Tinky Winky of *Teletubbies* whose sexualities were never openly discussed (Kumar). For a young queer child, who so rarely gets to see relationships or desire like theirs on television, these episodes and images from *Adventure Time* could be powerful and affirming moments.

Further bolstering the depiction of smart, capable and complex female characters, there have been two episodes dubbed the "gender swap episodes" by fans. In "Fionna and Cake" and "Bad Little Boy," every character in the episode is now the "opposite" gender. Our heroes Finn and Jake become our heroines Fionna and Cake. All the princesses are now princes. And while one may argue that this still fits into the binary, I believe that it subverts the binary by destabilizing the understandings of man and woman, boy and girl. The heroes are strong and capable despite being feminine. The princes all need to be helped and saved. This shows gender as incidental and that you don't need to be a boy to be a hero and you don't need to be a girl to need a little help. It makes gender incidental rather than integral to achievement and ability because it shows that either possibility, needing to be helped or needing to help, can be realized regardless of one's gender identity.

There are also other princesses and characters whose bodies and personalities are not stereotypically feminine. There is a princess named Muscle Princess who, as the name suggests, has a physique that is very muscular. Even though this is a body type not typically associated with femininity, she is still considered to be one of the more beautiful princesses by the evil Ice King. One of her muscular arms is even stolen in his effort to make the perfect wife in the episode "Princess Monster Wife." There's also another character that Finn and Jake meet, named Susan Strong, who is very tall and also muscular, much like Muscle Princess. Though Susan Strong's body is not considered attractive for females, Finn develops a crush on her in the episode entitled "Susan Strong." By showing that women who are normatively feminine can also be empowered (and sometimes queer) and by also showing that females who are not normatively feminine can be desirable by both men and women, we can see that these episodes challenge the binary by rejecting the notion that there is one way to be a woman.

One of *Adventure Time*'s strengths is that it looks beyond the binary in a way that is very different from other cartoons. With the characters BMO and Princess Cookie, we can see hints of transgender identity within the cartoon. Through expanding the conversation to people with no gender and people who may feel like or want to be the opposite gender, we can reach children with differing gender identities and who rarely get to see people like them on screen.

BMO is the video game console and friend of adventurers Finn and Jake. BMO serves many functions as BMO can also play tapes, keep time, set alarms, take pictures, as well as record and edit video. BMO is a very interesting character in the cartoon because Finn and Jake commonly refer to BMO with different pronouns and gendered language. In the episode "Conquest of Cuteness," Finn refers to BMO as "M'lady." In the episode "Rainy Day Daydream," after BMO loses power and Jake tries to use the power of imagination to quell his boredom, Finn asks Jake to imagine that "he" has new batteries so that they can play a video game instead of play pretend. Though the ways that BMO's friends gender them are interesting to consider, we must also take into account the way that BMO genders themself.

In "Five Short Graybles," an episode with five mini storylines that relate to one theme, BMO spends some time home alone when Finn and Jake run off to do errands. While they are gone, BMO speaks to their reflection in the mirror. The reflection introduces itself as Football and asks if BMO is a robot. BMO replies, "Oh no, Football. I am a little living boy." Football asks to be taught about how to be a human or living person. BMO then does the things that BMO knows to be as human, such as using the bathroom, brushing one's teeth and using soap. In a later episode entitled "Five More Short Graybles," BMO's reflection, Football, identifies themself as "a real baby girl." While BMO identifies as a boy in this moment, their reflection, Football, identifies as a girl. This dual identification makes possible a read of the character as bigender, placing BMO on the transgender spectrum. This is extremely interesting and makes gender inconsequential to friendship and care. However, in the aforementioned gender swapping "Fionna and Cake" episode, BMO is shown to have no visible differences, unlike the rest of the characters who have changed gender. This might suggest that BMO has no gender and it could be argued that BMO is genderqueer. Still, though, if we are discussing gender, it makes the most sense to respect the self-identification of male, female, or bigender identity that BMO puts forth.

One other interesting component of BMO's character is BMO's sexual identity. In the episode "BMO Noire," BMO has to solve the mystery of Finn's missing sock. Along the way, BMO encounters an old flame, a chicken named Lorraine. In "BMO Lost," BMO gets lost after being picked up as food by a giant bird and ends up in the forest, far away from home. BMO then encounters a Bubble who is also lost. BMO makes a deal with Bubble that if they get back to BMO's home, BMO will get Finn and Jake to help Bubble. The two embark on an epic journey that includes reuniting a baby with its mother and making their way through the forest. Eventually, BMO and Bubble do make it back to BMO's home. When they get there, Bubble tells BMO that being with BMO felt like home. Then Bubble asks BMO to get married. After Bubble is popped by Jake, who did not know the Bubble's significance, we discover that the Bubble was actually Air that was trapped in the bubble. Now that Air surrounds BMO, Air says that they can be together forever. This is particularly interesting because Bubble is not given a gender and BMO is self-identified as both male and female. The depiction of a love or marriage where one party is bigender and the other has no gender shows that gender is merely incidental to love and marriage, and challenges the notion that it must be between a man and woman or even between two same-sexed people only. It completely removes gender from the equation.

Even more interesting is the character of Baby Snaps or Princess Cookie in the episode "Princess Cookie." The episode begins with Finn and Jake showing up at a local supermarket in the Candy Kingdom to help with a hostage situation. The hostage taker, named Baby Snaps, is a giant cookie and is demanding Princess Bubblegum's crown. Finn and Jake are sent in to neutralize the threat while in costume. Jake wants to be disguised as a mail-man but Princess Bubblegum tells him that a milkman is more believable, much to Jake's dismay. When Jake goes in and tries to talk to Baby Snaps, he discovers that Baby Snaps was an orphan in the Candy Orphanage. While a child, Baby Snaps was saddened by the conditions in the orphanage and the lack of energy and happiness from the fellow children until Princess Bub-blegum came to visit. She played with the children, read them stories, and told them they could be whatever they want. But when Baby Snaps, as a "male" cookie, said that they wanted to be a princess, Princess Bubblegum laughed. This humiliation left Baby Snaps with trauma and this was the reason that Baby Snaps tried to get the crown.

Feeling sad for Baby Snaps and identifying with the plight of being forced to be something that you don't want to be (because he was forced to be a milkman instead of a mailman), Jake decides to try and aid Baby Snaps. In a particularly touching moment, Jake says that he will help take Baby Snaps far away and help them start their own kingdom where everybody can be whoever and whatever they want to be. Baby Snaps is touched and agrees. Jake then morphs into a horse in order to escape Princess Bubblegum's Banana Guards. Eventually, the pair is cornered and Baby Snaps tells Jake to stop just short of them jumping the Candy Gorge and getting away. As Baby Snaps talks to Jake, it becomes apparent that Baby Snaps is going to jump off of the gorge. With their last words, Baby Snaps tells Jake that he reminds them of a mailman that they used to know and thanks Jake because, even if for a moment, Jake helped them to feel like a princess. Baby Snaps jumps off the gorge but is not killed, rather just broken apart like Humpty Dumpty. In the next scene, Baby Snaps is seen playing chess at the Candy Kingdom Mental Hospital. Jake enters the hospital dressed as a mailman and says that he has a special delivery for Princess Cookie from the Grass Kingdom. The special package is a crown made of flowers. Princess Cookie puts on the crown and is overjoyed. Her dream has finally come true. And in the background we see Finn and Princess Bubblegum while the other patients bow down to the new princess.

This episode is interesting because it can be read as a trans narrative. One could say that Baby Snaps grew up as a young male orphan and then decides that she wants to become a princess, which is a signifier for female. We can see the crowning of Princess Cookie as a metaphor for the transition necessary for her to feel comfortable in her identity and like she's living as her authentic self. Furthermore, one could see her desire to strip Princess Bubblegum of her crown as a desire to smash the system of cissexism that is perpetuated by those in power who would laugh at one's non-normative identity. She seeks to take her crown and make a space for herself; she seeks equal power and privilege.

Still, it is important to note that the association of Princess Cookie, as a gender non-conforming or trans person, to criminality can be considered problematic. Works like *Queer (In)Justice: The Criminalization of LGBT People in the United States* by authors Joey Mogul, Andrea Ritchie and Kay Whitlock, show that this criminalization is common and has real effects on the lives of queer people everywhere. Still, Jake goes out of his way to assert to Finn and Princess Bubblegum that Princess Cookie is "not a bad guy," and says that the behavior is a result of Princess Cookie just trying to be what her dreams make her want to be ("Princess Cookie"). This challenges the notion of Princess Cookie as subhuman or inherently criminal because of her identity. One might also argue that the fact that Princess Cookie is in a hospital at the end and wearing a straight jacket also suggests a negative medicalization of queer people; however, this seems to be more a result of her attempted suicide rather than her desire to be a princess. This is confirmed by her being allowed to have her own crown and the support offered by Jake, Finn and even Princess Bubblegum in the end. Her desire to transition is not denied, it is granted. This, however, does seem to speak to the gatekeepers of transition and the obstacles that trans people face in attaining necessary medical services to aid them in their transition. They must be given the ability to transition through another party and lack agency through a medical system that is paternalistic and oppressive. Even Princess Cookie's attempted suicide, while dark and somewhat disturbing, is rather emblematic of the high prevalence of suicide attempts in the transgender community whose members have far higher rates of suicide attempts than the general population (Bongar et al.). While these are not aspects that are either optimistic or positive, they are reflective of many issues that plague our community and are important to discuss.

Additionally, this episode is powerful because Jake's feeling of not being able to be his authentic self as a mailman enables him to be compassionate and kind, and to work as an ally for Princess Cookie. He can relate to her struggle and see the way that we can be boxed into categories against our will and try to help her break free of the categories that she feels uncomfortable with. Jake uses his power and privilege as an adventurer, well-known hero and friend of Princess Bubblegum to try and help Princess Cookie get away and live her dream. It is a call to cisgender (those who identify as the same gender assigned at birth) allies to understand the trans struggle. Though the explicit discussion of transition or transgender identities is not broached in the episode, I would argue that this may be a limitation of what the creators can get away with on Cartoon Network and what children will understand. Despite the fact that the episode can be read in various ways much like any piece of media, the episode may be a relatable and understandable episode for many young children who feel like they might be trans. It can give them a way to discuss and voice their identity that ultimately affirms that they can be the princess or prince that they want to be, just like Princess Cookie.

Race in Adventure Time

Despite its progressive depiction of gender, Adventure Time falls a bit short when it comes to depictions of race. While the show's central premise of Finn being the last known human on Earth makes it obvious that we cannot have a depiction of diverse types of humans, it must be acknowledged that Finn is visually coded as white due to his skin tone, long blonde hair and blue eyes. I don't think that we can easily discount this decision as being an arbitrary one. It literally renders humanity white. To be fair, throughout the land of Ooo, there are other characters who are voiced by actors of color (such as Oliva Olson who plays Marceline, Donald Faison who plays Princess Cookie, Roz Ryan who plays Fionna and Niki Yang who plays Lady Rainicorn and BMO) or who speak other languages (Korean is a particularly prevalent language in the world of Adventure Time as both Jake and Lady Rainicorn speak it). Ensuring that people of color are employed as voice actors is certainly a good decision in terms of changing the structures that often keep actors of color out of big roles. However, when Finn thought he met another human, Susan Strong as mentioned above, she was also white with blonde hair. In more recent episodes, the creators seem to have been doing a bit more to shift the representation of race in the series as other mutated humanoid members of Strong's tribe of "Hyoomans" (as they are called in the show) have been shown with a wide variety of skin tones. Similarly, in the "Stakes" miniseries, it was revealed that Marceline the Vampire Queen's mother was actually a woman of color and a human. Additionally, it was shown that there was a more diverse human population in flashbacks of Marceline's shown throughout "*Stakes*." While *Adventure Time* is a progressive example of gender representation, there are some areas where it could stand to improve. Making our protagonist Finn white while relegating the actors of color to play only non-humans, we risk perpetuating a culture that links people of color with animality, as well as denies children of color the opportunity to see themselves as heroes. Just as easily as the creators made our hero a girl in the gender swapping episode, she could have as easily been another race or ethnicity in addition to being gender swapped. But instead, we have her sidekick, Cake, whose voice acting plays up the "sassy black woman" trope that dominates representations of black women while not even having a black woman represented. This is a problem. While tolerance, compassion and kindness are clearly key themes in the series, and it may be progressive in regard to its depictions of gender and sexuality, it leaves much to be desired in terms of the ways that race is handled.

Disability in Adventure Time

Disability is another category of difference that is given some treatment throughout the series. In multiple episodes, Finn is shown glimpses into his own past lives where he's been a comet, a warrior named Shoko and a blob. And in every incarnation of Finn that we've been shown, where he is a humanoid, he has always been shown to have lost his right arm. This allusion to Finn's eventual loss of an arm went on for some time but rather than just limit Finn's disablement to his alternate lives, the creators chose to insert it into the main storyline as well. This storyline begins after Finn receives a literal blade or sword made of grass which becomes part of his body after a wizard curses him. In a later episode, Finn uses the power of his grass blade to grow his arm several sizes larger in a quest to prevent his criminal father from escaping a cosmic prison known as the Citadel by holding on to his father's ship. Once Finn's body can no longer withstand holding on to the ship, his grass arm is literally pulled off of his body. As Finn falls down into the blood of the Citadel's guardian, he grows a small flower in the place of his arm. His arm stayed like this for several episodes until an episode entitled "Breezy." This is an interesting decision made by the animators because, in all of the instances of Finn's past lives, he is shown to be wearing prosthetics. Finn initially refuses different options offered by his friends until the arm is regained later. In "Breezy," Finn's arm, through the power of love, matures into a tree. As the tree grows to huge proportions, it explodes, leaving Finn with a bit of bark that is pulled back to reveal a new arm inside, covered in sap. While Finn regained his arm, the curse of his grass blade remained. In the episode "The Comet," we learn that the arm is actually made of grass even though it is covered in skin like the rest of his body. Thus, Finn's new arm is a type of organic prosthetic. Finn is obviously shown throughout the series to be a hero and, when so few cartoons depict disabled characters, it is valuable that he is also consistently shown to be disabled. Still, one could certainly argue that this depiction of Finn "overcoming" his disability, by regaining his arm as he does in this timeline or using a prosthetic as he does in the other timelines, fits into the same stereotype of disabled people as heroes as discussed earlier in this essay. Furthermore, it feels frustrating that the writers chose to keep Finn disabled but make his disability invisible in a media landscape where so few children who are disabled get to see characters that look and live like them. It may have been more meaningful, powerful and progressive to indicate that Finn's arm was no longer his own in a more substantial or obvious way.

But physical disabilities aren't the only things that are depicted in the series. One of the central characters of the series, Ice King, is shown to be mentally ill or otherwise cognitively disabled. At the beginning of the series, Ice King's antics and "unhinged" nature were frequently used as moments of humor and comedy. He was framed as a villain initially but over time, throughout the series, he has been given a more nuanced portrayal. Rather than being treated solely as a joke or a villain, he is shown to be a tortured man who lost his mind. Originally a human archeologist named Simon Petrikov who studied ancient artifacts, he happened upon a jeweled crown. When he put it on, it gave him visions that he doesn't understand, prompting him to act in ways that he wouldn't ordinarily act. While he wore the crown, he gained strange ice powers but slowly began to lose control of his mind. The crown began to take over and slowly Simon lost his mind, becoming the Ice King. His symptoms of memory loss, alongside his visions, might be seen to mimic the descent of a person who has Alzheimer's disease and dementia. Once this was discovered by the other characters their treatment of him began to shift slightly. While they are still willing to call Simon out for his dangerous antics, they have more compassion toward him. Rather than his lack of "sanity" ostracizing him from others, it is his decision to do bad things that the other characters denounce, not him as a whole. Additionally, it is revealed that Simon cared for Marceline when she was a child, after the apocalyptic event had occurred. Marceline is shown to still have feelings for Simon, caring deeply about his wellbeing. He cares for her as well, in the ways that he can, but cannot remember her or their relationship completely. Thus, in many episodes, we see Marceline struggling to care for somebody with either mental illness or Alzheimer's/dementia, depending on which lens you chose to read Simon's story through. This compassionate approach is important as there is still stigma around mental illness, something that a depiction like this could help to combat. Although disability is a category of difference that severely lacks representation in animated children's shows, *Adventure Time* is one example of a show that at least tries to depict two characters with different disabilities that impact their lives. However, each depiction could certainly be improved.

Moving Forward: Steven Universe

As discussed in the introduction of this article, *Steven Universe* is another animated children's show which has successfully continued the important conversations about gender, sexuality, race and disability that *Adventure Time* has, arguably, started. Rebecca Sugar, originally a member of the *Adventure Time* team as a storyboard artist and writer, has gone on to change the landscape of animated cartoons by becoming the first woman to create an animated series for Cartoon Network (Amidi). Since it first aired in 2013, *Steven Universe* has developed a huge following with a devoted fanbase who passionately discuss new episodes and Crystal Gem lore with one another on social media sites like Facebook and Tumblr. The rich lore, the complex, kind and hilarious characters and the intense, emotional storylines work to draw you into the show as soon as you start. Additionally, its depictions of these many categories of difference in new, unique ways has positioned *Steven Universe* as the heir apparent to the progressive legacy of *Adventure Time*.

Steven Universe's gender parity easily rivals that of *Adventure Time* and then some: nearly all of the most important characters in the series are women or Gems. It is important to note that based on the lore of the series, the Gems are not exactly women but alien humanoids who don't ascribe to the same binary concept of gender (Dunn). While their forms may have visual cues that are traditionally ascribed to women based on a human understanding of gender, they operate under a different understanding. Even if they are genderless beings, which they are based on the lore, their voices, hair, outfits and body shapes visually code them as feminine. Some children may not be able to make this distinction and may presume that the characters are all "women," which may be further bolstered by the usage of she/her pronouns among the Gems. However children of varying ages may view the Gems' gender, it is interesting to see the way that each of their characters negotiate both femininity and masculinity in different ways. Garnet is, arguably, the least overtly feminine of the Crystal Gems. She is tall yet curvy but wears sunglasses and an outfit that is more reminiscent of body armor than the fashions that Pearl and Amethyst tend to wear. Still, it is revealed in later episodes that Garnet is actually a fusion of two distinct gems: Sapphire and Ruby. Sapphire is depicted as feminine with long, flowing hair and a long dress, whereas

Ruby wears a headband, tank top and t-shirt and has a bit more of a butch gender expression. When Gems care about each other, they can fuse, an action that has specific cultural context which will be discussed later. Together, Ruby and Sapphire make up Garnet, showing that she is a harmonious blend of both feminine and masculine attributes that make her both strong and balanced. Amethyst has an alter-ego called Purple Puma where she leads a double life as a well-known pro-wrestler. While in the form of Purple Puma, Amethyst shape shifts to become much taller, more muscular and to have very bushy chest and underarm hair (Dunn). Additionally, while in this form, Amethyst uses he/him pronouns. This shows that their "feminine" forms can shift at will making their gender expression a cognizant decision. Similarly, in the episode "Hit the Diamond" (Johnston and Liu), the Gems are shown playing baseball, with each of them wearing a different outfit and taking on a pseudonym in order to trick a group of hostile home world Gems. Amethyst chooses to go by Amy and wears shorts, a baseball jersey and a scarf. Pearl, in contrast, chooses to go by Earl and wears a more masculine, traditional baseball uniform in contrast to her usual more feminine, pastel outfit. Lapis, another new ally of the Gems, goes by Bob and wears short shorts and a crop top. Sapphire maintains her more feminine appearance, wearing a shorter, slightly more sporty dress than she usually does and sports the moniker, Sophie. Through all of these examples, we see that the gems, while genderless, negotiate different aspects of their femininity and masculinity at different points to suit their mood and context. While they may be read as female by some younger children, they remain important characters that are non-binary. Sugar allows her characters to be unique blends of femininity and masculinity that are shifting continuously, which, much like *Adventure Time*, models a gender expression that is less restrictive and more fluid. Similarly, while non-binary people are often assumed to be masculine in order to have their gender identities validated, the Crystal Gems represent genderless beings that are feminine without having their genderless mode of being invalidated, a fact that is often overlooked in a cissexist society such as ours.

These questions regarding the gender of Gems are also interesting when we look at Steven himself. If Rose Quartz, Steven's mother, gave up her form to birth Steven (Ravela), then Steven is also partly her, partly a genderless, humanoid being. Still, Steven identifies as a boy and this identification is respected by the other Gems who use he/him pronouns for Steven. Steven is shown, throughout the series, to be navigating young adulthood and romance in addition to helping wage intergalactic war against the hostile Gem homeworld. He has a close friend named Connie, a young girl of color who is brilliant and brave. While she is still a human, she is aware of the fact that Steven is a Gem and that he constantly risks his life to save the Earth. She is depicted as being the more logical, sensible of the two yet she appreciates Steven's kindness and innocence. The two appear to have strong feelings for each other throughout the seasons, with Connie even learning to sword fight using Rose's old sword in order to help protect Steven in battle. In one particularly interesting episode, "Alone Together," Steven actually fuses with Connie, becoming an older, genderqueer Stevonnie (Dunn). Stevonnie is depicted as having long hair, being quite tall and shapely. Rather than being a child-like Steven or Connie independently, they form a teenager. While fused as this genderless being, they are seen as being quite beautiful and desirable by the citizens of Beach City, framing their genderqueer identity as attractive and desirable rather than deviant or ugly. Furthermore, their ability to fuse together is indicative of their deep bond and affection for each other.

Still, Steven's life isn't all just fun and games. As mentioned above, he is locked in an intergalactic war. Even so, Steven is consistently shown to be a kind, compassionate Crystal Gem who usually tries to defuse situations to avoid fighting. Rather than breaking other Gems who are hostile, Steven tries to get them to see reason and cease fighting. He would much rather save and protect life than destroy it, a commitment that he has inherited from his mother. This is also echoed in his main weapon. Each Gem has a unique weapon dependent on their gem type and form that they can summon at will. Pearl has a long staff, Garnet has gauntlets and Amethyst has a whip. Steven has a shield. Rather than having an offensive weapon, his weapon is more about defense. As the age-old adage goes, Steven is a lover, not a fighter. Steven, much like Finn, is shown to be sensitive, kind and compassionate in ways that not all male protagonists are allowed to be. However, rather than fighting like Finn, Steven emphasizes diplomacy more than violence, which perhaps gives Steven a bit more of a gender progressive, peace focused character. War is never framed as inevitable. The show's focus on compassion, tolerance and valuing all forms of life in ways that center peace rather than conflict is unique.

Sexuality is also handled in interesting ways in the series. As mentioned before, Gems can fuse with other Gems. While Garnet was originally thought to be one Gem, we eventually learned that she was actually a fusion of Ruby and Sapphire. This is noteworthy because it is revealed that the Gems of their homeworld find fusion disgusting because it values purity and clarity of Gem lines with clear hierarchical lines set into society. Blending two Gems of two different castes was unthinkable by the Gem society's standards of class (Ravela). This was shown when Ruby, acting as Sapphire's bodyguard, in a desperate attempt to save Sapphire from an impending attack by Rose and Pearl during the early days of the Gem Rebellion, accidentally fuse together on a whim. Viewed as an abomination by the leaders of the Gems, the Diamonds, they are ordered to have their gems crushed which would prevent their ability to regenerate and, thus, effectively kill them. Ruby grabs Sapphire and runs away, leaving to Earth. The two are shown to fall in love and eventually they continuously fuse and become an even more stable bond of their two personalities. Furthermore, in the episode "Jailbreak," we learn that Ruby and Sapphire fuse to create Garnet; they are initially separated by Jasper, a homeworld Gem sent on a mission to destroy the Earth. Steven helps both Ruby and Sapphire, not knowing that he is actually speaking to the two halves of Garnet. When they are reunited, the two embrace and kiss and are fused back into Garnet (Dunn). Steven is mesmerized with his new discovery, but Garnet urges him away while she fights Jasper. During their battle, Jasper is audibly disgusted at Garnet's fused form. In retaliation, Garnet sings a song during their battle, indicating that Ruby and Sapphire's relationship, their love, is what gives her power. Thus, fusion becomes an allegory for both love across class (and perhaps racial lines as they are two different types or classes of Gem) as well as a depiction of queer love. Whereas *Adventure Time* settled for subtext in many cases, *Steven Universe* has been explicit in a way that so few cartoons have. While queerness is often used as a comedy trope, Sugar makes it a beautiful and healthy depiction of relationships at their best. She makes fusion a question of love, trust, respect and balance, making them a model for queer and straight relationships. Similarly, Pearl and Rose are shown to have been involved in a relationship and fuse together in a flashback. They had a deep relationship that Pearl felt was threatened by Greg Universe, who would eventually become Steven's father (Ravela). This is interesting because it shows that Rose has deep feelings for both people, which could be a depiction of polyamorous love. This is further bolstered by the fact that all of the Crystal Gems fuse and seem to have deep and unique bonds. This is unique for a children's show and shows a depiction of love, sexuality and relationships that is similarly expansive and fluid that centers honesty, respect and desire rather than narratives of ownership or property. Still, not all viewers were happy about these types of relationships. Indeed, portions of the show dealing with these themes have been censored ("Censorship") in other countries because they were deemed to not be "family-friendly." Still, Sugar herself has been outspoken in advocating for the continued depiction of queer love on her show. She's been quoted as saying, "You can't wait until kids have grown up to let them know that queer people exist. There's this idea that that is something that should only be discussed with adults—that is completely wrong. If you wait to tell queer youth that it matters how they feel or that they are even a person, then it's going to be too late!" (Tremeer).

But the show isn't just great in terms of its depictions of sexuality and gender. Unlike *Adventure Time*, *Steven Universe* has a wide variety of human characters and in terms of both voice actors and representation on screen, race is handled in a much more diverse way. There are a wide variety of racial and ethnic groups depicted as members of Beach City. As mentioned earlier, Connie Maheshwaran, Steven's close friend, has been confirmed to be Indian American by writers on the show and she is a very important characters in the series (Jones-Quartey "Re:@lanjq"). She is shown to be incredibly intelligent, strong and brave as she tries to manage her friendship with Steven with her somewhat strict parents' desire for her to succeed and focus on school and safety first and foremost. While her parents are initially depicted as very controlling, they have come to accept Connie's relationship with Steven much more than they initially did in the beginning. In addition, while we don't get to see a huge amount of secondary characters who are residents of Beach City, it is important to note that a significant amount of them are people of color. The Pizza family, which includes Kofi Pizza (the father), Nanefua Pizza (the grandmother) and Kiki and Jenny (sisters, daughters and granddaughters) are from Ghana (Jones-Quartey "Re:There"). Harold Smiley, a machine operator at Beach City's amusement park as well as a former singer and actor, is a tall, bald Black man, voiced by popular comedian and actor Sinbad. Two lesser known characters who are not officially denoted as being of color but are depicted with darker skin tones and voiced by actors of color, are Jamie and Kevin, voiced by Eugene Cordero, a Filipino actor and comedian, and Andrew Kishino, a Japanese Canadian actor and comedian. Similarly, almost all of the voice actresses who voice the main Crystal Gems are women of color (with the exclusion of Rose Quartz), Michaela Dietz as Amethyst, Deedee Magno-Hall as Pearl, Shelby Ann Rabara as Peridot, Estelle as Garnet and Jennifer Paz as Lapis. Thus, rather than just creating parity between male and female characters, there is far more parity between white and non-white characters on the show as well, showing the many residents interacting and getting along while creating a diverse world that doesn't rely on stereotypes. Thus, *Steven Universe* pushes past some of *Adventure Time*'s failures around race.

Moving on to the next category of difference, while disability is not explicitly discussed in *Steven Universe,* there are a few episodes and characters that seem to indicate that many of the characters have differences that render them "disabled" in the eyes of other gems. In the episode "Future Vision," Steven is shown to be stricken with anxiety and agoraphobia once he learns that Garnet has "future vision," which allows her to see the multiple routes the future may take (Abrams and Jo). Steven becomes obsessed with staying safe after learning about all the ways that he could get hurt and, thus, asks Garnet questions incessantly, in order to ensure that he doesn't harm himself. Eventually, Steven must come to terms with his intense anxiety and give in to the fact that while Garnet may have future vision, he doesn't and so he must live his life without obsessing about what could happen and instead focus on the present. In other episodes throughout the series, Steven is also shown to struggle with anxiety though it doesn't usually reach the level it did in regard to the future vision. It doesn't reach the level of a crippling disorder or disability that Steven must confront in his everyday life yet it is something that is persistent while manageable. Similarly, Pearl is shown to be a character who struggles with anxiety throughout the series. She is shown to overanalyze and worry about situations, especially when Steven is thought to be at risk. This is very different in comparison to how she is shown to be in flashbacks. When shown in the past, Pearl is depicted as being calm, stoic and fearless. It seems that once Rose Quartz, shown to be Pearl's lover, gives up her form to create Steven, Pearl is made to confront her biggest fear: the loss of Rose (Ravela). Thus, the trauma of losing Rose might be seen to mimic post-traumatic stress disorder in Pearl. She's no longer the stoic, brave person she once was. Now, she struggles with fear, especially at the thought of losing Steven, who she sees as being all that she has left of Rose. This was particularly alluded to in the episode "Sworn to the Sword," which also shows there to be a similar intense bond like Rose and Pearl's between Steven and Connie (Johnston and Liu).

Another argument can be made that some Gems can be read as disabled due to their lack of size or differing physical forms. Amethyst was grown on Earth, a product of the colonization of Earth by the leaders of the Gem home world. However, Amethyst was grown and released from her gestation in the ground before she could reach her full size ("Too Far"). Thus, Amethyst is much smaller than the typical gem of her type, akin to dwarfism in humans. Still, Amethyst is shown to be strong and accepted by Pearl, Garnet, Steven and their allies despite her difference and "deviation" from homeworld's standards for Amethysts. Similarly, Peridot, a character who was initially an enemy of the Crystal Gems but who later becomes a member of their team, uses what she calls, "limb enhancers," meant to elongate her limbs and make her taller ("Catch and Release"). The use of these enhancers seems to be similar to what we would call prosthetics. They function as a tool which allows her to do things she might not otherwise be able to do with ease. She is shown to be heavily reliant on them when we first meet her but through her growing relationship with the Crystal Gems, she abandons them. This is very different from your typical portrayal of disability in one major way: unlike Finn, Peridot isn't reunited with her "prosthetics." Instead, she learns to accept her form without them. She accepts her "natural" capabilities rather than trying to "fix" them. This is a really interesting treatment of disability because it doesn't frame Amethyst or Peridot as lacking in any way due to their differently capable forms. They are shown as capable while allowing to be the way that they are. This treatment is more akin to the social model of disability which aims to change the ways people think about and structure society around disability rather than changing the body itself (Kafer). Similarly, throughout the season, we also see "shards." Desperate to try and understand and weaponize fusion, the Gems homeworld tried to put together different gems through force. This nonconsensual fusion leaves the "shards" as body parts, stuck together. They are self-aware and yet severely disabled and unable to talk or function in the ways that other Gems are. While they initially appear as things to be feared, Steven is able to communicate with them in ways that the other Gems cannot. Thus, in "Gem Drill," the Crystal Gems learn that the "Cluster," an ominous sounding weapon being used to destroy the Earth is actually a huge number of shards nested in the core of the Earth. While the Crystal Gems were initially trying to destroy the Cluster, Steven realizes that it is alive and simply trying to form, to make itself whole out of desperation. Rather than kill them, Steven chooses to help make their home at the core of the Earth inhabitable, putting them in bubbles so they live together and find other shards with which they can communicate and form with. Rather than showing the severely disabled shards to be unworthy of life, Steven values their unique capacities and makes the Earth hospitable to them, rather than the other way around, again echoing the social model of disability mentioned before (Min).

Additionally, unlike *Adventure Time, Steven Universe* also deals explicitly with questions of colonization and colonialism. Rather than give in to the demands of the Gem homeworld, Rose Quartz, Pearl, Garnet, and Amethyst choose to fight against the draining and annihilation of Earth, its resources and its population (Gebrechirstos). Thus, *Steven Universe* itself centers on a pushback against colonialism, a topic not generally present in an animated children's show. *Steven Universe*, thus, represents a step forward, even from the progressive depictions in *Adventure Time*. It has taken some of the best parts of the *Adventure Time* and built on them, making the show more aware of difference in new and interesting ways.

Conclusion

Cartoons, while considered innocuous by many, may be one of the most powerful means through which we can reshape the socialization of children not just into healthier concepts of gender but also race and disability. While some scholarly research has focused on questions of gender and sexuality in *Adventure Time,* there has been no scholarly research on other categories of difference including race and disability. This essay aims to begin some preliminary analysis of these concepts in *Adventure Time,* while also expanding the conversation to include *Steven Universe,* another progressive cartoon that has received no scholarly analysis at the time of this publication. While *Adventure Time* has done so much to begin complex conversations about topics that are always present, *Steven Universe* has continued to push the envelope further. Not only has it expanded the conversations around gender and sexuality both on screen and off, but it has also pushed past some of *Adventure Time*'s failings around race and disability. Rather than shrinking away from forms of difference outside of gender, *Steven Universe* embraces these other categories by making them visible in ways that they rarely are for children. Thus, Rebecca Sugar heeds Audre Lorde's call in her foundational text "The Master's Tools Will Never Dismantle the Master's House." Sugar and her team of writers and animators have built a community around a cartoon that doesn't focus on just one category of difference while still perpetuating harmful hierarchies outside of that one category. This is important, especially because Sugar is the first non-binary person to have her own show on the network and because she's using her platform to ensure that she makes a difference not just for white women or girls but for children of color, queer kids and disabled kids. It isn't enough to focus on gender equality with all these other co-constitutive categories missing. Lorde made this clear in her essay, to a feminist community that was still (and is still) struggling to attend to race, sexuality, disability and indigeneity in meaningful ways. Perhaps with *Steven Universe,* we're starting to see cartoons that understand this and that do it with humor and joy. Cartoons may be the brightest, most fun and the most understandable means we have to do so to challenge racism, sexism, heterosexism, cissexism and ableism in children today. While cartoons have been considered key in socializing children into these restrictive and fundamentally violent structures, cartoons that center difference with compassion, tolerance and kindness may work to combat some of that violence. If we keep drawing and keep watching, we may be able to help dismantle the master's house using the animator's tools.

WORKS CITED

Abrams, Lamar, and Hellen Jo. "Future Vision." *Steven Universe*. Dir. Yong Seop Jeong, Elle Michalka, and Ian Jones-Quartey. Burbank, CA: Cartoon Network, 29 Jan. 2015.

"*Adventure Time* with Finn and Jake—Television Review." *Common Sense Media*, n.d. Web. 19 May 2013.

Amidi, Amid. "Rebecca Sugar Is Cartoon Network's First Solo Woman Show Creator." *Cartoon Brew* (blog), 5 Oct. 2012. http://www.cartoonbrew.com/ideas-commentary/rebecca-sugar-is-cartoon-networks-first-solo-woman-show-creator-71157.html.

Arnett, Jeffrey Jensen. "Adolescents' Uses of Media for Self-Socialization." *Journal of Youth and Adolescence* 24, no. 5 (1995): 519–33. Web.

Aubrey, Jennifer Stevens, and Kristen Harrison. "The Gender-Role Content of Children's Favorite Television Programs and Its Links to Their Gender-Related Perceptions." *Media Psychology* 6, no. 2 (2004): 111–146. *Academic Search Complete*. Web. 20 May 2013.

Baker, Kaysee, and Arthur Raney. "Equally Super?: Gender-Role Stereotyping of Superheroes in Children's Animated Programs." *Mass Communication & Society* 10, no. 1 (2007): 25–41. *EbscoHost*. Web. 2 April 2013.

Banker, Mark, Patrick McHale, Kent Osborne, Pendleton Ward, Ako Castuera, and Tom Herpich. "Go with Me." *Adventure Time*. Dir. Larry Leichliter. Burbank, CA: Cartoon Network, 28 March 2011.

Barry, Carolyn Mcnamara, Laura M. Padilla-Walker, and Larry J. Nelson. "The Role of Mothers and Media on Emerging Adults' Religious Faith and Practices by Way of Internalization of Prosocial Values." *Journal of Adult Development J Adult Dev* 19, no. 2 (2011): 66–78. Web.

Bennett, W. Lance. "Changing Citizenship in the Digital Age." In *Civic Life Online: Learning How Digital Media Can Engage Youth,* edited by W. Lance Bennett. Cambridge, MA: MIT, 2008. 1–24.

Bongar, Bruce, et al. "The Relationship Between Gender-Based Victimization and Suicide Attempts in Transgender People." *Professional Psychology: Research & Practice* 43, no. 5 (2012): 468–475. *Academic Search Complete.* Web. 21 May 2013.

Brown, Jane D., and Elizabeth M. Witherspoon. "The Mass Media and American Adolescents' Health." *Journal of Adolescent Health* 31, no. 6 (2002): 153–70. Web. 31 May 2016.

Butler, Judith. "Performative Acts and Gender Constitution: An Essay in Phenomenology and Feminist Theory." *Theatre Journal* 40, no. 4 (1988): 519–531.

_____. "Performative Subversions." *Gender: A Sociological Reader.* New York: Psychology Press, 2002, 48–50.

"Censorship in Foreign Countries." *Steven Universe Wiki.* n.d. Web. 24 May 2018. http://steven-universe.wikia.com/wiki/Censorship_in_Foreign_Countries.

"Common Portrayals of Persons with Disabilities." *MediaSmarts.* MediaSmarts: Canada's Centre for Digital and Media Literacy, n.d. Web. 16 June 2016. http://mediasmarts.ca/diversity-media/persons-disabilities/common-portrayals-persons-disabilities.

Courtney-Long, Elizabeth A., Diana D. Carroll, Qing C. Zhang, Alissa C Stevens, Shannon Griffin-Blake, Brian S. Armour, and Vincent A. Campbell. *Morbidity and Mortality Weekly Report: Prevalence of Disability and Disability Type Among Adults—United States, 2013.* Rep. no. 64 (29): 777–783. *Centers For Disease Control and Prevention,* 31 July 2015. Web. 31 May 2016. https://www.cdc.gov/mmwr/preview/mmwrhtml/mm6429a2.htm.

Dunn, Eli. "*Steven Universe,* Fusion Magic, and the Queer Cartoon Carnivalesque." *Gender Forum: An Internet Journal of Gender Studies* 56 (2016): 44–57. Web. 21 May 2018.

Erevelles, Nirmala. *Disability and Difference in Global Contexts: Enabling a Transformative Body Politic.* Palgrave Macmillan, 2011.

Faherty, Vincent E. "Is the Mouse Sensitive? A Study of Race, Gender, and Social Vulnerability in Disney Animated Films." *SIMILE: Studies in Media & Information Literacy Education* 1, no. 3 (2001). Web.

Fausto-Sterling, Anne. *Sexing the Body: Gender Politics and the Construction of Sexuality.* Basic, 2000.

Feinberg, Leslie. *Transgender Warriors, Making History from Joan of Arc to Dennis Rodman.* Beacon Press, 1996.

Freeman, Elizabeth. "Monsters, Inc.: Notes on the Neoliberal Arts Education." *New Literary History* 36, no. 1 (2005): 83–95. Web.

Fuster Burguera, Xavier. "Muffled Voices in Animation. Gender Roles and Black Stereotypes in Warner Bros. Cartoons: From Honey to Babs Bunny." *Bulletin of the Transilvania University of Brasov* IV 4.53 no. 2 (2011): 65–76. Web. 31 May 2016.

Gebrechirstos, Bemnet. "This World Looks Familiar: *Steven Universe's* Anticolonial Critique." *Bitchmedia,* 31 Oct. 2017. https://www.bitchmedia.org/article/familiar-world/steven-universes-anticolonial-critique.

Giroux, Henry A. *The Mouse That Roared: Disney and the End of Innocence.* Rowman & Littlefield, 1999.

Hall, Matthew, Brendan Gough, and Sarah Seymour Smith. "'I'm METRO, NOT Gay!': A Discursive Analysis of Men's Accounts of Makeup Use on YouTube." *The Journal of Men's Studies* 20, no. 3 (2012): 209–226.

Jane, Emma A. "'Gunter's a Woman?!'—Doing and Undoing Gender in Cartoon Network's *Adventure Time.*" *Journal of Children and Media* 9, no. 2 (2015): 231–47. Web.

Johnson, Kjerstin. "*Adventure Time* Gay Subtext: 'Spicy' or Adorbz?" *Bitch Magazine* (blog), 4 Oct. 2011. http://bitchmagazine.org/post/what-the-math.

Johnston, Joe, and Jeff Liu. "Hit the Diamond." *Steven Universe.* Dir. Joe Johnston. Cartoon Network June 2, 2016.

_____. "Sworn to the Sword." *Steven Universe.* Dir. Ki-Yong Bae, Jin-Hee Park, jasmin Lai, and Ian Jones-Quarter. Cartoon Network. 15 June 2015.

Jones-Quartey, Ian. "Re: @Ianjq we know that Connie's mom is of Indian descent, but is there any chance we can know her father's ethnicity?" Web log comment. *Ian Jq.* Twitter, 12 Sept. 2015. Web. 31 May 2016. https://twitter.com/ianjq/status/642753811820384256.

_____. "Re: There no doubt in my mind that the pizza family isn't Ghanaian and that makes me so happy." Web log comment. *IAN JQ Dot Com.* Tumblr, 30 April 2014. Web. 31 May 2016. http://ianjq.tumblr.com/post/84367436324/starheartshooter-there-no-doubt-in-my-mind-that.

Kafer, Alison. *Feminist, Queer, Crip.* Indiana UP, 2013.

Klein, Hugh, and Kenneth S. Shiffman. "Race-Related Content of Animated Cartoons." *Howard Journal of Communications* 17.3 (2006): 163–82. Web.

Kumar, Sujay. "11 Kids' Characters Who Could Come Out!" *Sexy Beast* (blog). *The Daily Beast,* 2 Nov. 2010. http://www.thedailybeast.com/articles/2010/11/02/gay-characters-on-childrens-tv-from-bert-to-spongebob.html.

Lacroix, Celeste. "Images of Animated Others: The Orientalization of Disney's Cartoon Heroines from the Little Mermaid to the Hunchback of Notre Dame." *Popular Communication* 2, no. 4 (2004): 213–29. Web.

Leslie, Carolyn. "*Adventure Time* and Gender Stereotypes." *Screen Education,* no. 78 (2015): 44–47. Web.

Li, Hui, Katherine Boguszewski, and Angeline S. Lillard. "Can That Really Happen? Children's Knowledge About the Reality Status of Fantastical Events in Television." *Journal of Experimental Child Psychology* 139 (2015): 99–114. Web.

Little, Steve, Patrick McHale, Merriweather Williams, Tom Herpich, Ako Castuera, Thurop Van Orman, and Pendleton Ward. "Storytelling." *Adventure Time.* Dir. Larry Leichliter. Burbank, CA: Cartoon Network, 8 Nov. 2010.

Longmore, Paul K. "Screening Stereotypes: Images of Disabled People in Television and Motion Pictures." *Why I Burned My Book and Other Essays on Disability.* Temple UP, 2003. 131–46.

Lopez, Vera, Rosalie Corona, and Raquel Halfond. "Effects of Gender, Media Influences, and Traditional Gender Role Orientation on Disordered Eating and Appearance Concerns Among Latino Adolescents." *Journal of Adolescence* 36, no. 4 (2013): 727–36. Web.

Lorde, Audre. "The Master's Tools Will Never Dismantle the Master's House." In *Sister Outsider: Essays and Speeches,* 110–114. Crossing Press, 2007.

Lugo-Lugo, Carmen R., and Mary K. Bloodsworth-Lugo. "'Look Out New World, Here We Come'?: Race, Racialization, and Sexuality in Four Children's Animated Films by Disney, Pixar, and DreamWorks." *Cultural Studies Critical Methodologies* 9, no. 2 (2009): 166–78. Web.

Marshall, Elizabeth, and Özlem Sensoy. "The Same Old Hocus-Pocus: Pedagogies of Gender and Sexuality in Shrek 2." *Discourse: Studies in the Cultural Politics of Education* 30, no. 2 (2009): 151–64. Web.

Martins, Nicole, and Kristen Harrison. "Racial and Gender Differences in the Relationship Between Children's Television Use: A Longitudinal Panel." *Communication Research* 39, no. 3 (June 2012): 338–57.

McGhee, Paul E., and Terry Frueh. "Television Viewing and the Learning of Sex-Role Stereotypes." *Sex Roles* 6, no. 2 (1980): 179–188. *SocINDEX with Full Text, EBSCOhost.*

McHale, Patrick, Kent Osborne, Pendleton Ward, Adam Muto, Rebecca Sugar, and Cole Sanchez. "Bad Little Boy." *Adventure Time.* Dir. Larry Leichliter. Burbank, CA: Cartoon Network, 18 Feb. 2013.

McHale, Patrick, Kent Osborne, Pendleton Ward, Adam Muto, Rebecca Sugar, and Mark Banker. "Fionna and Cake." *Adventure Time.* Dir. Larry Leichliter. Burbank, CA: Cartoon Network, 5 Sept. 2011.

McHale, Patrick, Kent Osborne, Pendleton Ward, Bert Youn, and Somvilay Xayaphone. "Princess Monster Wife." *Adventure Time.* Dir. Larry Leichliter. Burbank, CA: Cartoon Network, 28 May 2012.

McHale, Patrick, Kent Osborne, Pendleton Ward, Cole Sanchez, and Rebecca Sugar. "Lady and Peebles." *Adventure Time*. Dir. Larry Leichliter. Burbank, CA: Cartoon Network, 20 Aug. 2012.

McHale, Patrick, Kent Osborne, Pendleton Ward, Mark Banker, Adam Muto, and Rebecca Sugar. "Susan Strong." *Adventure Time*. Dir. Larry Leichliter. Burbank, CA: Cartoon Network, 7 March 2011.

McHale, Patrick, Kent Osborne, Pendleton Ward, Tom Herpich, and Steve Wolfhard. "BMO Lost." *Adventure Time*. Dir. Nate Cash and Nick Jennings. Burbank CA: Cartoon Network, 15 April 2013.

McHale, Patrick, Kent Osborne, Pendleton Ward, Tom Herpich, and Skyler Page. "Princess Cookie." *Adventure Time*. Dir. Larry Leichliter. Burbank, CA: Cartoon Network, 25 June 2012.

McHale, Patrick, Kent Osborne, Pendleton Ward, Tom Herpich, and Steve Wolfhard. "Five More Short Graybles." *Adventure Time*. Dir. Larry Leichliter. Burbank, CA: Cartoon Network, 19 Nov. 2012.

McKeon, Tim, Merriweather Williams, Adam Muto, and Elizabeth Ito. "Slumber Party Panic." *Adventure Time*. Dir. Larry Leichliter. Burbank, CA: Cartoon Network, 5 April 2010.

Min, Lilian. "*Steven Universe's* Quiet Gender Revolutions." Bitchmedia. 1 June 2016. Web. https://www.bitchmedia.org/article/steven-universe%E2%80%99s-quiet-gender-revolu tions 24 May 2018.

Molisee, Raven, and Villeco, Paul. "Gem Drill." *Steven Universe*. Dir. Ki-Yong Bae and Jin-Hee Park. Burbank, CA: Cartoon Network, 12 May 2016.

Molleur, Joseph. "Feminine and Masculine Elements." *The Wiley Blackwell Encyclopedia of Gender and Sexuality Studies*. Wiley Blackwell, n.d. Web.

Mogul, Joey L., Andrea J. Ritchie and Kay Whitlock. *Queer (In)Justice: The Criminalization of LGBT People in the United States*. Beacon, 2011.

Osborne, Kent, Patrick McHale, Pendleton Ward, Steve Little, Thomas Wellman and Jesse Moynihan. "The Suitor." *Adventure Time*. Dir. Nate Cash and Nick Jennings. Burbank, CA: Cartoon Network, 20 May 2013.

Osborne, Kent, Patrick McHale, Pendleton Ward, Tom Herpich, Skyler Page and Cole Sanchez. "Five Short Graybles." *Adventure Time*. Dir. Larry Leichliter. Burbank, CA: Cartoon Network, 9 April 2012.

Osborne, Kent, Pendleton Ward, Jack Pendarvis, Adam Muto, Ako Castuera and Jesse Moynihan. "Red Starved." *Adventure Time*. Dir. Nate Cash. Burbank, CA: Cartoon Network, 14 Oct. 2013.

Pardun, Carol J. *Changing Attitudes Changing the World: Media's Portrayal of People with Intellectual Disabilities*. Rep. no. U59/CCU3211826–03. Special Olympics/U.S. Centers for Disease Control and Prevention, 2005. Web. 31 May 2016. http://www.specialolym pics.org/uploadedFiles/LandingPage/WhatWeDo/Research_Studies_Desciption_Pages/ Policy_paper_media_portrayal.pdf.

Perlman, Carly Ann, et al. "Variations in the Gender-Stereotyped Content of Children's Television Cartoons Across Genres." *Journal of Applied Social Psychology* 32, no. 8 (2002): 1653–1662. *Academic Search Complete*. Web. 21 May 2013.

Preston, Daniel L. "Finding Difference: Nemo and Friends Opening the Door to Disability Theory." *English Journal* 100, no. 2 (2010): 56–60. Web.

Quintel, J.G., Cole Sanchez, Merriweather Williams, and Tim McKeon. "Ocean of Fear." *Adventure Time*. Dir. Larry Leichliter. Burbank, CA: Cartoon Network, 21 June 2010.

Ravela, Christian. "*Steven Universe* [TV Review]." *Queer Studies in Media & Popular Culture* 2, no. 3 (2017): 389–354.

Root, Amy Kennedy, and Susanne A. Denham. "The Role of Gender in the Socialization of Emotion: Key Concepts and Critical Issues." *New Directions for Child and Adolescent Development* 2010, no. 128 (2010): 1–9. Web.

Roper, Lynne. "Disability in Media." *The Media Education Journal* (2003). Web. 31 May 2016.

Smedley, Tim. "Children's TV Pretends Disability Doesn't Exist." *Guardian Sustainable Business* (blog). *The Guardian*, 28 July 2015. http://www.theguardian.com/sustainable-business/2015/jul/28/childrens-tv-representation-disability-nickelodoen-disney-bbc.

Staub, Ervin. "A World Without Genocide: Prevention, Reconciliation, and the Creation of Peaceful Societies." *Journal of Social Issues* 69, no. 1 (2013): 180–99. Web. 31 May 2016.

Strauss, Neil. *The Game: Penetrating the Secret Society of Pickup Artists.* Regan, 2005.

Swan, Karen. "Saturday Morning Cartoons and Children's Perceptions of Social Reality." Annual Meeting of the American Educational Research Association. San Francisco, CA. 18–22 April 1995. *ERIC: Institute of Education Sciences.* Web. 31 May 2016. http://files. eric.ed.gov/fulltext/ED390579.pdf.

Thompson, Teresa L., and Eugenia Zerbinos. "Television Cartoons: Do Children Notice It's a Boy's World?." *Sex Roles* 37, no. 5/6 (1997): 415–432. *Academic Search Complete.* Web. 21 May 2013.

Tremeer, Eleanor. "Rebecca Sugar Explains Why LGBT Representation Is So Important in *Steven Universe*." *Moviepilot* (blog). *Moviepilot Inc.*, 6 June 2016. http://Moviepilot.Com/ Posts/3954346.

Ward, Pendleton, Kent Osborne, Patrick McHale, Cole Sanchez, and Rebecca Sugar. "Burning Low." *Adventure Time.* Dir. Larry Leichliter. Burbank, CA: Cartoon Network, 30 July 2012.

Ward, Pendleton, Kent Osborne, Patrick McHale, Tom Herpich, and Skyler Page. "BMO Noire." *Adventure Time.* Dir. Larry Leichliter. Burbank, CA: Cartoon Network, 6 Aug. 2012.

Ward, Pendleton, Kent Osborne, Patrick McHale, Tom Herpich, and Steve Wolfhard. "Jake the Dad." *Adventure Time.* Dir. Larry Leichliter. Burbank, CA: Cartoon Network, 7 Jan. 2013.

Ward, Pendleton, Patrick McHale, Adam Muto, Jesse Moynihan, Kent Osborne, and Ako Castuera. "Reign of Gunters." *Adventure Time.* Dir. Larry Leichliter. Burbank, CA: Cartoon Network, 8 Oct. 2012.

Ward, Pendleton, Patrick McHale, Adam Muto, Rebecca Sugar, Kent Osborne, and Mark Banker. "What Was Missing." *Adventure Time.* Dir. Larry Leichliter. Burbank, CA: Cartoon Network, 26 Sept. 2011.

Ward, Pendleton, Patrick McHale, Cole Sanchez, Rebecca Sugar, and Kent Osborne. "Hot to the Touch." *Adventure Time.* Dir. Larry Leichliter. Burbank, CA: Cartoon Network, 2 April 2012.

Ward, Pendleton, Patrick McHale, Kent Osborne, and Cole Sanchez. "Princess Potluck." *Adventure Time.* Dir. Larry Leichliter. Burbank, CA: Cartoon Network, 22 April 2013.

Ward, Pendleton, Patrick McHale, Kent Osborne, Cole Sanchez, and Rebecca Sugar. "I Remember You." *Adventure Time.* Dir. Larry Leichliter. Burbank, CA: Cartoon Network, 15 Oct. 2012.

Ward, Pendleton, Patrick McHale, Steve Little, Cole Sanchez, Benton Connor, and Merriwether Williams. "Blood Under the Skin." *Adventure Time.* Dir. Larry Leichliter. Burbank, CA: Cartoon Network, 1 Nov. 2010.

Ward, Pendleton, Tom Herpich, Ako Castuera, Kent Osborne, Mark Banker, and Patrick McHale. "Conquest of Cuteness." *Adventure Time.* Dir. Larry Leichliter. Burbank, CA: Cartoon Network, 11 July 2011.

Ward, Pendleton, Tom Herpich, Bert Youn, Kent Osborne, Mark Banker, and Patrick Mchale. "Apple Thief." *Adventure Time.* Dir. Larry Leichliter. Burbank, CA: Cartoon Network, 3 Oct. 2011.

Weigel, Russell H., and Paul W. Howes. "Race Relations on Children's Television." *The Journal of Psychology* 111, no. 1 (1982): 109–12. Web.

West, Candace, and Don H. Zimmerman. "Doing Gender." *Gender, a Sociological Reader.* (2002): 42–47.

"Where We Are on TV Report: 2012–2013 Season." *GLAAD,* Oct. 2012. https://www.glaad. org/publications/whereweareontv12.

Williams, Merriwether, Tim McKeon, Elizabeth Ito, and Adam Muto. "What Have You Done?" *Adventure Time.* Dir. Larry Leichliter. Burbank, CA: Cartoon Network, 13 Sept. 2010.

Williams, Merriwether, Tim McKeon, and Pendleton Ward. "Rainy Day Daydream." *Adventure Time*. Dir. Larry Leichliter. Burbank, CA: Cartoon Network, 6 Sept. 2010.
Williams, Merriweather, Tim McKeon, Pendleton Ward, and Tom Herpich. "Freak City." *Adventure Time*. Dir. Larry Leichliter. Burbank, CA: Cartoon Network, 26 July 2010.
Witt, Susan D., and Kathleen G. Burriss. "The Influence of Television on Children's Gender Role Socialization." *Childhood Education* 76, no. 5 (2000): 322–24. *EbscoHost*. Web. 2 April 2013.
Zuckerman, Diana M., Dorothy G. Singer, and Jerome L. Singer. "Children's Television Viewing, Racial and Sex-Role Attitudes." *Journal of Applied Social Psychology* 10, no. 4 (1980): 281–94. Web.

"Little Geisha Dolls"

Postfeminism in Joss Whedon's Firefly

Peregrine Macdonald

Joss Whedon is often described as a feminist. His show *Buffy the Vampire Slayer* made him famous and rewrote the idea of the blond cheerleader as a weak and submissive victim, instead making her into a strong woman who wasn't to be trifled with. Another of Joss Whedon's works is the 14-episode series *Firefly*, which originally aired in 2002 and 2003 before it was canceled. *Firefly* shows us several female characters, each of them strong, or at the very least interesting, in her own way. One of the interesting things about the show is how the character of Inara Serra seems to perfectly fit the description of postfeminism, to the point where she seems to be a personification of the concept. Postfeminism can be understood to be "an active process by which feminist gains of the 1970s and 80s [came] to be undermined ... popular culture [is] perniciously effective in regard to this undoing of feminism, while simultaneously appearing to be engaging in a well-informed and well-intended response to feminism" (McRobbie 255). *Firefly* is one of those pieces of popular culture that can undo the work of feminism, through Inara. Her role on the show and how she performs her femininity exemplifies postfeminism.

Firefly is set hundreds of years in the future. Earth as we know it is now Earth-That-Was. Earth-That-Was's last great superpowers were the United States of America and China, providing the cultural backdrop of *Firefly*. The start of the series shows the end of a galactic civil war (a not terribly veiled metaphor for the American Civil War). The show's male lead, Mal Reynolds, and his army sidekick and current first mate Zoe Washburne fought for the Independents, the side of rebellion against the Alliance. The Independents, also known as "Browncoats," lost the war at the Battle of Serenity Valley, from

216

which Mal took the name for his ship, *Serenity* (a *Firefly*-class transport ship, from which the show itself gets its name). Inara is a "Companion," a high-class trained sex worker, and is stated to be one of the only respectable members of the crew of *Serenity*. She earns her living by making herself appear to be whatever her clients need. In most cases, this involves a sexual relationship. The crew is also made up of the pilot, Zoe's husband Hoban "Wash" Washburne, and the mechanic, Kaylee Frye. These two characters did not participate in the war and are coded as lower to middle class. Book is a religious Shepard whose character doesn't get explored much within the show. Jayne Cobb, is the "muscle," very low class, crass, and more criminal than much of the rest of the crew. Finally, there is the doctor Simon Tam and his sister River Tam, who came from a very high-class family, but have lost everything and become fugitives hiding from the authorities on *Serenity*.

While feminine traits used to be defined by ideas of motherhood and nurturing, in post-feminist texts, "femininity is defined as a bodily property rather than a social, structural or psychological one" (Gill 137). The idea of femininity used to be task-oriented, cooking or taking care of a family, but is now what women should be physically- women have to look the part. The women of *Firefly* are often identified by their looks. In the episode "Bush-wacked" (episode 3), when Wash is talking about his relationship with his wife, Zoe, he describes her physical properties, talking about her legs and asking the Alliance Commander if he'd "ever been with a warrior woman." With femininity being defined by societal standards of beauty, a woman's looks are constantly monitored and judged. This can be seen most strongly in the character of Inara, whose work is to be seen for her body. Unlike the other members of the crew, Inara is always impeccably dressed and ready to be seen.

Throughout the series, the physical ship *Serenity* can be seen as a reflection of its inhabitants. The same is true for Inara's shuttle, a part of *Serenity*, which she rents from Mal. In a flashback during the episode "Out of Gas" (episode 8) we see Inara's shuttle as it used to be, empty bare metal. Inara transformed the empty shuttle into a space that was warmer and more inviting to any clients she might have. The contrast is especially stark when we see her move from the main living quarters of her shuttle into its undecorated cockpit during the pilot episode "Serenity." She sits there in her beautiful clothes and speaks of missing being out on *Serenity*, indicating that the place she has created in her shuttle is not her most comfortable space and highlighting its performative nature. She has created the homelike image of the shuttle in the same way that she's created the image of herself as the feminine ideal for outside consumption. It is all about how she's viewed and how people react to her. She adorns her body and her home according to her Companion training. Like the shuttle itself, Inara is a blank space to decorate for other people's desires.

218 III. Re-Framing and Re-Forming Gender Roles

The preoccupation with women's appearances is not just limited to Inara, but can also be seen through the character of Kaylee, who is the working-class engineer of *Serenity*. In the episode "The Train Job" (episode 2), the first image of Kaylee that the show presents to us (and the first image actually aired in the original televised run of the series) consists of her sitting for Inara and getting her hair brushed. While they talk, Inara poses the idea of cleaning Kaylee's face. They discuss the idea that perhaps if Kaylee wears her hair up, she might attract the attention of the male doctor, Simon. Kaylee's desire for physical femininity is seen again in "Shindig" (episode 4) where she pines after a pink frilly dress. She explains that "the only place [she's] seen something so nice is some of the stuff Inara has." Kaylee eventually obtains the dress, and wears it to attend a high-class ball, which Inara is also attending. Kaylee aspires to be a part of a world to which Inara already belongs.

Through these interactions we see the postfeminist makeover paradigm, as enacted by Inara, the instrument of postfeminism. According to Gill, the makeover paradigm "requires people (predominantly women) to believe, first, that they or their life is lacking or flawed in some way; second, that it is amendable to reinvention or transformation by following the advice of relationship, design or lifestyle experts and practicing appropriately modified consumption habits" (Gill 142). Kaylee doesn't think that she is physically feminine enough to obtain Simon. Inara provides the idea that Kaylee could change physical aspects of her appearance. To fit in to Inara's lifestyle, Kaylee wears a dress that is very unlike her usual mechanic's overalls. When she arrives at the ball, she remarks that all the girls have "the most beautiful dresses. And so do I! How about that?" With this we see that Kaylee has at least temporarily managed to change herself to fit into a society she had thought unattainable.

The relationship between Kaylee and Inara also shows us the relationship between postfeminism and the women it influences. Kaylee is one of the youngest members of the crew, and certainly the most innocent. In "Out of Gas" (episode 8) we learn that before joining the crew of *Serenity*, she had been living with her father and had never left her planet before. Kaylee is a young woman out in the world for the first time, open to the influences that might not have existed on her home planet. Inara is postfeminism. In her we can see the societal preoccupation with beauty, and how that beauty makes her the ideal woman. Inara often indicates that acquiring a Companion is something to aspire to. When Mal asks if all the men will have bought their dates to the ball in "Shindig" (episode 4) Inara explains that she will be one of the only Companions in attendance, adding that "perhaps the other men couldn't attract one," portraying Companions as something to be desired. Not only does Inara set herself as the beautiful ideal, but the society around her does the same. She is welcomed on *Serenity* because having a Companion on board will grant Mal access to places that might not otherwise have, simply because they want to see Inara. This can be seen in "The Train Job" (episode 2), when Inara uses her respectability to rescue Mal and Zoe from potential imprisonment. When Inara enters the police station, all the locals stare at her, wanting to see the impressive woman.

This beauty is strictly maintained. Not only does Inara spend time a good amount of time maintaining her own personal grooming, to the point where she is always immaculately dressed no matter the state the ship or anyone else on board, but her role as Companion is a maintained one. She is taught to be this ideal, and trained to perform comfort to men. Inara never disparages her training as a Companion. The only time we see her less than sanguine about the requirements of being a Companion is when she does her yearly physical in "Ariel" (Season 1, episode 9), which we don't see but is described as "lots of needles and cold exam tables." This requirement is less about the performance of her gender and more about the health aspect of sex work. It is a required task, mandated by Companion Guild law, and serves to highlight the level of maintenance that goes into being a Companion— maintenance that other people may not see or even realize is required.

Inara also serves to highlight the idea of sexual difference. At no point in the series do we ever see a male Companion. There is an implication, therefore, that only women can be Companions. This would fit into postfeminist ideas that "reasserted a version of masculinity as libidinous, powerful, and, crucially, different from femininity" (Gill 143). The Companion is the height of femininity: beautiful, powerful, and able to make her own choices. Inara is surrounded by men who fit the libidinous and powerful ideas of masculinity. While in the brothel in "Heart of Gold" (episode 13), Jayne—one of the crew's main fighters and one of the most traditionally masculine characters despite his traditionally feminine name—spends the entire time sleeping with the sex workers. Closer to Inara herself, there is the non-repeating character of Atherton Wing, who thought he could use his money and power to persuade Inara to stay with him. That incident ended with a sword fight between Wing and Mal, which only enhances the idea of masculine power.

Not only that, but the sexual difference can be seen in Inara's daily life on the ship. The first aired interaction between Inara and Mal, in "The Train Job" (episode 2) shows Mal bursting into Inara's shuttle uninvited, at the same time that Inara is brushing Kaylee's hair. When Inara asks him what she'd said about entering like that, Mal responds "that it's manly and impulsive?" This is a simple way of marking sexual difference, with the implication being that only men would burst into someone else's space unasked, as well as highlighting how the two sexes might view the masculine trait of impulsiveness differently. While Inara intended it to be annoying and therefore a negative trait, Mal reframes it as "manly" and positive. Not only that, but the entrance is a display of Mal exerting his power, as *Serenity* is technically his ship to do with as he pleases, and Inara only rents from him.

The very concept of the Companion conflates the postfeminist ideas of women being "desiring, sexual subjects who choose to present themselves in a seemingly objectified manner" and of women's "individualism, choice and empowerment" (Gill, 138–9). Inara claims that she has the choice of her clients, and the show implies agency in the women who become Companions. They became Companions because they wanted to be Companions. They claim to have the power in their relationships. However, all of this is still for the pleasure of the heterosexual male gaze. Their choice was to objectify themselves for male pleasure. Gill writes that "girls and women are invited to become a particular kind of self, and are endowed with agency on condition that it is used to construct oneself as a subject closely resembling the heterosexual male fantasy around pornography" (Gill 139).

The Companion has taken this idea to the extreme. Inara is herself a construction to the point that we have very few clues as to who she is beneath her Companion identity. In "Serenity," the original pilot, a client asks Inara why she would ever want to leave her homeworld. The viewer gets to see a look of distress on Inara's face that her client doesn't get to see. To him, she merely explains that she "wanted to see the universe." This shows how conscious Inara is of her male viewer, and of her performance for him. Her backstory will destroy his illusion of her, so she stays as his ideal, albeit mysterious, woman.

Even when she is not performing heterosexual acts, both the show and Inara reinforce the heterosexual male gaze. There is only one time in the course of the series, in "War Stories" (episode 10) that we see Inara service a female client. While all her other clients come and go without the crew seeing them (or if they are seen, it is off ship for other reasons), her female client is brought onto the ship under the entire crew's watchful gaze, despite Inara's wish for privacy. While Inara greets her client, Jayne, a white heterosexual male, declares that he'll "be in [his] bunk"; the idea that he finds the two women together sexually arousing is clear. With this, the show implies that women's main role is to arouse men.

In the same episode, not only do Inara and her client provide for the male gaze, but they also reinforce sexual difference again. Inara and her client agree that "one cannot always be oneself in the company of men," implying that there is a difference in how men and women may react to things. There is also the implication again that women perform for men. Inara's client says that one can *never* be oneself in the company of men, indicating a constant performance on her part, at the very least.

One can also use Laura Mulvey's argument about the male gaze to analyze Inara's role on the ship *Serenity* and the show *Firefly*. Mulvey writes about the "silent image of woman still tied to her place as bearer of meaning, not maker of meaning" (Mulvey 59). Inara is whatever her client needs her to be, she makes herself an object for her client's consumption. In "War Stories" (episode 10), Inara's female client tells her that "there's no need for the show," implying that she was aware that Inara was not being fully herself. While Inara does create a facade to show to the world, it is the world that influences the facade that Inara puts on. While Inara may have the power to choose her clients, their gaze still controls her actions. She works and dresses to keep their gaze, to the degree that when she no longer wants it, she can't help but have it, as seen by Jayne's obvious objectification of Inara and her client. Even if the other characters, like Jayne, weren't objectifying Inara, the assumed male gaze of the camera is. One of the scenes in "Serenity" (pilot) features Inara taking a sponge bath; this includes the camera focusing on certain parts of body, with close ups of just a bare arm or shoulder. By focusing on just one body part at a time, the camera is metaphorically cutting her up, turning her into an object of pleasure for the viewer.

A part of postfeminism is the "stark and continuing inequalities and exclusions that relate to 'race' and ethnicity, class, age, sexuality and disability as well as gender" (Gill 137). As with the other aspects of postfeminism, these can be seen in *Firefly* in general and in Inara specifically. While age and disability don't appear to factor into *Firefly* at all, since the characters seem to be mostly of the same ability level and any age differences aren't addressed, race, class, and sexuality are topics which can be discussed.

There is a clear class disparity between Inara and other members of the ship. The only people who come close to meeting her class status are Dr. Simon Tam and his sister, River, who were raised with money. While different than Inara's, they had an education, connections, and are used to finer things. The Tam's class status is muddled, however, by the fact that they are fugitives and have been cut off from all their class ties. Inara's class is clearly higher, however, than that of Mal, Kaylee, and the rest of the crew, who are coded as working class at best. This only comes into play once, in the episode "Shindig." Kaylee wears her fluffy pink dress in an attempt to match Inara and to be a part of a class higher than her own. Inara's high class is the ideal for postfeminism, and something that women are supposed to aspire to without seeming as if they are trying. Kaylee's lower class is revealed by her dress, which others at the party note does not fit with the event.

In the episode, it seems briefly as though Kaylee's attempts to raise her class will fail, when another woman recognizes Kaylee's dress as something bought from a store. This is quickly turned around when an older man tells the woman off. We next see Kaylee in a crowd of men, explaining star ships

222 III. Re-Framing and Re-Forming Gender Roles

to them. She has transcended class boundaries by simply being herself, without any trouble. Kaylee is able to keep her dress, attract the male gaze, and talk about the work she loves. At the end of the episode, both Inara and Kaylee are aboard *Serenity*, being comfortable in a lower-class home. While Kaylee does keep her dress, she does not look at it with longing, but with a happy look on her face, looking at it as if remembering a nice night out, instead of a breaking of class barriers. Inara does mention that there are two different "worlds," with the implication being that she is talking of lower- and higher-class society. She mentions that perhaps she does not belong in the higher-class world to which she seems accustomed. Neither Inara nor Kaylee acknowledge that there might be a struggle that happens when someone tries to move from one class to another.

On the topic of sexuality, *Firefly* tends toward the heteronormative. The married couple aboard the ship consists of a cis-gendered male and a cis-gendered female. Kaylee's romantic attraction is to the male doctor Simon. The closest *Firefly* gets to anything other than traditional heterosexuality is Inara and her female client, a relationship which is appropriated for the pleasure of the men on the ship. Inara herself explains in "War Stories" (episode 10) that "most of [her] clientele are male." Her attraction to the masculine Mal is evident, going so far as to kiss his unconscious form when she discovers he is still alive in "Our Mrs. Reynolds" (episode 6) Even Kaylee's "boy whores" from "Heart of Gold" (episode 13) are on screen for only a moment, and exist only to highlight Kaylee's sexual frustration.

One of the major inequalities in the series comes from its dealing with race and ethnicity. *Firefly*'s mise-en-scène is heavily influenced by Chinese and other East Asian cultures. We often see Asian lettering on signs and Buddha statues on shelves, and characters will suddenly speak Chinese in the middle of their sentences. Despite the melding of Eastern and Western cultures, however, there are no Asian main characters. Occasionally there are Asian characters in the background, but they have no names and no lines. Instead, the audience seest the white characters of Simon and River, who have the common Chinese surname of Tam. These Asian influences can also be seen with Inara. Not only are Inara's costumes influenced by East Asian culture, but her Companion training is East Asian in origin as well. Viewers can see in both "Jaynestown" (episode 7) and "Trash" (episode 11) an example of a Companion's greeting ceremony, which is very reminiscent of the Japanese tea ceremony. The Companions themselves seem to be based on the geishas of Japan (Amy-Chin 179). With a lack of Asian characters, we are left with the appropriation of Asian culture for Western consumption.

This particular instance of cultural appropriation is especially problematic. JeeYeun Lee explains in "Why Suzie Wong Is Not a Lesbian" that the United States "constructs Asian women of various ethnicities as hyperfeminine, exotic, passive objects of white heterosexual male desire" (117). Lee also quotes the David Henry Hwang play *M. Butterfly*, saying "The West thinks of itself as masculine—big guns, big industry, big money—so the East is feminine—weak, delicate, poor ... but good at art, and full of inscrutable wisdom—the feminine mystique" (118). Through these quotes we can see the treatment of Asian culture in *Firefly*. With Inara representing the feminized East, Asian stereotypes are played out. Throughout the series we constantly see Inara's "inscrutable wisdom" when she gives advice and guidance, going so far as to provide absolution to a holy man in the original pilot. She is the hyperfeminine woman that white men want.

Inara is one of the only people on the crew to not participate in violence within the series. Traditionally, male characters commit acts of violence. Through this we see, again, that men are "crucially different" than women. All of Inara's strength comes from her words and her ability to use her body. Although there are two major fire fights within the series, Inara never fires a gun. When the crew mounts a rescue operation to retrieve Mal from enemy hands in "War Stories" (episode 10), Inara is nowhere around, even when the usual non-combatants take up arms, though it should be noted that Kaylee, who aspires to Inara's level of femininity, does not fire the gun she is given. When the crew protects the brothel in "Heart of Gold" (episode 13), Inara spends most of the time aiding the pregnant woman giving birth. While she does threaten a man by holding a knife to his throat, her threat is ineffective, as he easily escapes her grasp and kills another woman. The only other time Inara threatens physical violence is against another woman in "Trash." Even then, Inara does not kill, she only threatens before trapping the woman there to be found later. This incident also highlights the postfeminist paradigm of a woman's greatest enemy being another woman.

Like Inara herself, postfeminism is a pretty yet problematic concept. It is nice to think that women can have the perfect life and that feminism is done because we've achieved our goals. Postfeminism focuses on the individual woman. It celebrates her choices. It creates this perfect, idealized, hyperfeminine woman, whom all women should be like. However, it ignores constructs like race or class. It has internalized the male gaze. It does not allow for anything less than the perfect show of hyper femininity, the feminine ideal women should aspire to, pretending that it is because women want it, not men. Inara is all of this. She is the woman that postfeminism created. She is beautiful and intelligent, she makes her own choices, and she is accessible to men because she wants to be.

WORKS CITED

Amy-Chinn, Dee. "'Tis Pity She's a Whore: Post-Feminist Prostitution in Joss Whedon's Firefly?" *Feminist Media Studies* 6, no. 2 (2006): 175–189. *MLA International Bibliography.* Web. 18 Nov. 2011.

Firefly: The Complete Series, created by Joss Whedon. Twentieth Century–Fox, 2003–2003.

Gill, Rosalind. "Post-Feminist Media Culture: Elements of a Sensibility." In *The Gender and Media Reader*, edited by Mary Celeste Kearney, 136–48. Routledge, 2012.

Lee, JeeYeun. "Why Suzie Wong Is Not a Lesbian: Asian and Asian American Lesbian and Bisexual Women and Femme/Butch/Gender Identities." *Queer Studies: A Lesbian, Gay, Bisexual, and Transgender Anthology*, edited by Brett Beemyn and Mickey Eliason, 115–32. NYU Press, 1996.

McRobbie, Angela. "Post-Feminism and Popular Culture." *Feminist Media Studies* 4, no. 3 (2004): 255–264. *MLA International Bibliography*. Web. 13 June 2016.

Mulvey, Laura. "Visual Pleasure and Narrative Cinema." In *The Gender and Media Reader*, edited by Mary Celeste Kearney, 59–66. Routledge, 2012.

Beyond the Monomyth

Yuriko's Multi-Mythic Journey
in Miyabe Miyuki's The Book of Heroes

ELEANOR J. HOGAN

Heroic figures are a prominent fixture of myth and literature. Today, the hero is no longer primarily relegated to one gender as it was in ancient times. It is just as likely that the hero of a fictional work is female, such as Rey in *Star Wars: The Force Awakens* (2015), Tris in Veronica Roth's *Divergent* (novel 2011; film 2014), and Katniss in Suzanne Collins' *Hunger Games* (novel 2008; film 2012). Many female heroic characters grace the pages and screens of fictional worlds, yet labelling them is difficult. Should we refer to them as female heroes, heroines, or simply heroes? Does the gender of a hero matter, and if so, how? Since some scholars believe that the term "heroine" refers to the "side-kick" or helpmate of the male hero, or that the term is somehow lesser than or a "diminutive" of hero (Pearson and Pope vii), this essay does not use that term in its discussion of a female hero, Yuriko in Miyabe Miyuki's *The Book of Heroes*. Since gender *does* matter in terms of the language used, the various stages of the journey, and the final outcome, denoting the femaleness of the hero is important. Perhaps instead of the word "hero," gender and age could be used as modifiers, which yield phrases such as the boy hero, the girl hero, the man hero, and the woman hero. This is too cumbersome, thus "female hero" has been chosen as the appropriate term for this analysis of Yuriko.

This essay examines how Yuriko becomes not just a hero, but a Japanese hero. This discussion of a fantastic quest will concentrate on her heroic attributes, her steps taken in unison and divergent from her male and female heroic literary counterparts, and her understanding of the teachings found in Buddhist doctrine, which reflects Japanese cultural values. First, this essay

225

summarizes previous scholarship on literary heroes. Next, it examines current notions of what constitutes heroism using data gathered in recent studies and correlates this understanding with Yuriko's attributes. Finally, after synthesizing aspects of the heroic journey for male and female characters and dispelling the notion of the "monomyth," this essay illustrates that Yuriko is an exemplar of a "multi-mythic" hero, who both follows and deviates from the previously delineated "monomythic" heroic (and male) path and converges with third-wave feminism with its concentration on diversity.

Scholarship on the Hero in Literature

Several scholars have written about heroes and myths, such as Austrian psychoanalyst Otto Rank (1884–1939) in *The Myth of the Birth of the Hero: A Psychological Exploration of Myth* (1922, 2004) and Dorothy Norman in *The Hero: Myth/Image/Symbol* (1969). The most notable and frequently referenced text on this topic is *The Hero with a Thousand Faces*, written by American comparative mythologist Joseph Campbell (1904–1987) in 1949. In his monograph, referred to as a "definitive study of heroism" (Powers 3), Campbell describes the journey or archetypal adventure of the hero, noting that there really is just one story, the monomyth, which is reenacted the world over in a similar pattern, with three basic categories: Departure, Initiation, and Return (xi). Campbell defines the hero as "the man or woman who has been able to battle past his personal and local historical limitations" (19), yet his language throughout relegates women to categories such as "goddess" and "temptress (109, 120). Moreover, as with many mythic tropes that encompass the psychological aspect of Freud's "family romance," Campbell's theory purports that the hero is "made capable of enduring the full possession of the mother-destroyer, his inevitable bride" (121). Campbell draws the parallel further, noting that "the son [is] against the father for the mastery of the universe and the daughter against the mother to *be* the mastered world" (136). Campbell does not leave room for women to be the enactors of a heroic journey. Moving forward to today, manufacturers of Hasbro's *Star Wars Monopoly* game made a similar mistake: a Rey figurine was not included in their all-male character set, prompting the "#Where's Rey?" uproar on social media. As Rey is the undeniable hero(ine) of *The Force Awakens*, children and adults were furious with the lack of Rey toys, illustrating that today's younger generation does not discriminate between male and female heroes although the manufacturers do (Lawler).

Literary scholars have noted the absence of Campbell's female hero. Meredith A. Powers felt that in Campbell's "definitive study of heroism, the subliminal implication is that heroism, that innate conception of the human psyche, is possible only for men" (3). While she is correct that only men are heroes in Campbell's schema, this fact is not a "subliminal implication": it is purposeful. While one may simply write off this deficiency as typical of the times in the United States in the late 1940s, there seems to be more lurking beneath the surface. Family and women's therapist Maureen Murdock, believing that there was a connection between the women's journey and the hero's journey, interviewed Joseph Campbell in 1981. Her idea that "the focus of female spiritual development was to heal the internal split between women and her feminine nature" fell on deaf ears (2). Campbell explained that that it was unnecessary for women to make the journey because "[i]n the whole mythological tradition, the woman is *there*. All she has to do is realize that she's the place people are trying to get to. When a woman realizes what her wonderful character is, she's not going to get messed up with the notion of being pseudo-male" (Murdock 2). Murdock was both "stunned" and unsatisfied by this response as both she and the women she knew and counseled "do not want to be *there*" (2). Therefore, Murdock began her own quest to find and/or develop a "new model that understands who and what a woman is" (2), which resulted in her 1990 monograph *The Heroine's Journey: Women's Quest for Wholeness*. She states that the structure of the heroine's journey is "derived in part from Campbell's model of the heroic quest" (3), yet the terminology she employs is more reflective of women's experiences. Murdock illustrates that women's quests are to "fully embrace their feminine nature" (3), a concept that shall be explored more fully below.

Other scholars who have taken issue with masculinity or maleness as a requisite characteristic of the hero in literature have also addressed this in full-length studies. Carol Pearson and Katherine Pope in their 1981 *The Female Hero in British and American Literature* determine that "on the archetypal level, the journey to self-discovery is the same for both male and female hero" (viii), and they modify and rename Campbell's steps. Meredith A. Powers, in *The Heroines in Western Literature* (1991), focuses on the ancient role of the mythic goddess who was relegated to "the backdrop against which to better focus on the remarkable feats of the ubiquitous male" (131). More recently, Valerie Estelle Frankel's *From Girl to Goddess: The Heroine's Journey through Myth and Legend* illustrates the belief that "the heroine's true role is neither hero nor his prize" (3). Rather, her quest is to become an "archetypal, all-powerful mother," who "set[s] out on rescue missions in order to restore their shattered families" (4). Frankel envisions a cyclical pattern of the heroine's journey; she also provides a chart where she compares and contrasts her labelling of stages with Campbell's, at times, borrowing from him *in toto*, while at others rewriting them completely. In Frankel's next publication, the 2014 monograph, *Buffy and the Heroine's Journey: Vampire Slayer as Feminine Chosen One*, she critiques the "following [of] Campbell's hero's journey point by point," noting that "the girl has always had a notably different journey than the boy. She quests to rescue her loved ones, not to destroy the tyrant as Harry Potter or Luke Skywalker does" (6).

Defining Heroism

Heroism is difficult to define, but is necessary to do in order to accurately study Yuriko. The word "hero" is from the Greek and Latin term "heros," meaning protector or defender. Psychologist Philip Zimbardo created a list of twelve types of heroes: "military and civil heroes, religious figures, politico-religious figures, martyrs, political or military leaders, adventurers/explorers/discoverers, scientific (discovery) heroes, good Samaritans, odds beaters/underdogs, bureaucracy heroes and whistle-blowers" (468–471). Due to the wide range of possibilities for the label "hero," from rescuer to pop-idol, psychology professors Kinsella, Ritchie and Igou's research aims to determine the prototype or collection of representative features of a hero. They conducted seven different studies to narrow down the most salient features of heroes. The resulting data indicate that "the hero concept is made up of fuzzy sets of features organized around prototypical category members" (124). The data shows that "the most prototypical features of heroes. Identified in our research, are bravery, moral integrity, courageous, protecting, conviction, honest, altruistic, self-sacrificing, selfless, determined, saves, inspiring, and helpful" (124). Peripheral features consisted of adjectives such as "proactive, compassionate, strong, caring, humble, intelligent, talented and personable" (Table 3, 122).

There is a gender gap in notions of heroism. In 2008, professors of psychology Lindsay E. Rankin and Alice H. Eagly conducted research to determine the "cultural construal of heroism and to explore the opportunities women and men have to become heroic" (414). Modern dictionary definitions of heroism illustrate that the "consensual meaning of heroism resides in taking risks, often risks of injury or death, to benefit others" (Rankin and Early 414). While they ultimately found the term "heroism" to be "culturally androgynous" (414), their study nevertheless showed a link between heroism and maleness. The first part of their research consisted of three components: respondents were asked to define "heroic actions"; to list three heroic people; and to create a list of personally known heroes. Their results indicate that regardless of the gender of the person surveyed, the majority of known male heroes are public figures associated with traditionally male-dominated occupations such as soldiers, firefighters, and political leaders. The one exception was Mother Teresa. Women historically have not had and still do not have equal access to these kinds of positions, although Rankin and Eagly noted that over time, the connection between men and heroes may lessen as the correlation between women and heroic activities increases as equal access becomes the norm (418, 421, 422). When the definition of heroism is less strict than that of "risk plus benefit," it includes aspects such as "meeting challenges" and "family guardian" (421). The majority of participants in the study personally knew more heroic women than men, illustrating that private heroes are often women, which supports the notion that the private sphere is female dominated, while the public one is male dominated (421–422).

The second part of Rankin and Eagly's research examined how respondents perceived a story about a rescuer that saved a boy when he fell through ice into water. Their variables included changing the sex of the rescuer, changing the safety of the object used to reach the boy (plastic sled or rowboat), and the distress of the boy (exhausted from treading water or perched on a floating object.) The gender of the actor (Lisa or Gary) did not affect the perceived heroism of the rescue (419). However, the perceived risk to the rescuer and to the boy elevated the degree of heroism assessed by those in the study (421). Overall, Rankin and Eagly's work supports the hypothesis that "perceived risk to a protagonist and benefit to others underlie the social construction of heroism" (421).

The definition of heroism, then, includes risk to the protagonist and benefit to others, coupled with positive attributes such as courage, bravery, selflessness, and descriptors such as compassionate, strong, and intelligent. The next question is inevitable: since maleness is not a necessary attribute of heroism, can a male hero be replaced by a female hero in heroic stories? Scholar David Emerson believes that interchanging a female character for a male might not alter the structure of the journey, but it also does not "necessarily create a female version of the journey" (133). Emerson maintains that "a truly feminine version [of the journey] … must emphasize feminine qualities of the heroes, rather than merely than the physical fact of being female" (133). Focusing on girls who do not possess physical strength and therefore cannot easily be substituted for a male, he concludes that the qualities "for the archetypal feminine hero come from the innocent side of her spirit: love, compassion, nurturance and healing" (146).

Emerson's theory seems to be partly true; the aforementioned qualities might be considered more feminine than masculine, yet no one would agree that love, compassion, nurturance and healing are not demonstrated by men, nor are they necessarily separate from strength of body and mind. This kind of essentialism is as problematic as leaving women out of the heroic journey. It would seem that girls can be feminine heroes, but women simply become "like" male heroes, which is reminiscent of Campbell's use of the term "pseudo-male" (Murdock 2). This invalidates the role of women and girls as female and therefore as different from males. Furthermore, while physical prowess and violence can be part of a male or female hero's fate, the notion that this "macho" behavior represents "the archetypal human pattern" is incorrect as is demonstrated by many a female hero (Pearson and Pope 4.) In many cases, the hero, such as Yuriko, succeeds through appreciation and understanding and not, as clarified by Pearson and Pope, "by dominating, controlling, or owning the world or other people" (5), even if they can hold their own in a battle.

Yuriko as Hero—What's Gender Got to Do with It?

Written for the young adult audience, *The Book of Heroes* crosses genres and includes aspects of mystery, fantastic voyage, and coming-of-age. Author Miyabe Miyuki (b.1960-) is clearly well versed in archetypal myths, as her plot involves monstrous guardians, labyrinths, and descents into subterranean worlds as seen in ancient Greek and Japanese legends. In addition, she includes supernatural assistance and loyal helpers. The novel adheres to the story of the hero, while also illustrating the cultural underpinnings of Buddhist concepts. Yuriko is, without adoubt, the hero of Miyabe's *The Book of Heroes;* however, she is never called a "hero." Most importantly, she exemplifies the notion of "risk plus benefit" (Rankin and Eagly 421). She risks her life repeatedly to save her brother and to save the world from imminent destruction. Her heroic attributes are bravery, courage, compassion, strength (of mind and body), and intelligence. She is the "family guardian," as her trip to save her brother and her family makes clear. Moreover, she succeeds through understanding and appreciation, not domination or control.

The premise of Miyabe's novel is that the "monomyth" is real. There is just one story of the Hero that is copied many times over and circulated throughout the world, giving power to both the Hero and his darker side, The King in Yellow. This notion represents the Japanese belief of duality, which is prevalent in Buddhist thought. As film scholar Valerie Wee explains, in these religious traditions, "[C]onflicting forces align and hold each other in balance, serving as a foundation for stability and order" (58), as opposed to the Christian tradition's concept of 'either/or' where concepts such as good or evil are diametrically opposed and duel for supremacy. The Hero in Miyabe's novel is simultaneously both the hero *and* villain. The *Book of Heroes* within the novel is not an actual book but "a vessel" that contains the Hero and his Counterpart, keeping him/them from entering the world and causing good and evil. Yuriko must find and rescue her brother (aptly named Hiroki, pronounced Hero-key) after learning he was possessed by the dark side of the Hero. Along with magical assistance from talking books, a cape, a healing glyph, and with the guidance of few brave adults, Yuriko enters the many worlds of the stories created by "weavers," fights the forces of evil, and is able to save her brother (and many others) in an unexpected way.

The Multi-Mythic Hero's Journey

The following pages briefly list the stages included in several scholars' notions of the heroic journey, beginning with Campbell, and ending with a synthesis and relabeled framework created by the author of this essay. The bolded sections are those that are relevant to Yuriko's journey. Campbell's schema of the hero's journey is divided into three main categories with sub-categories, referred to as stages. Two-thirds of the way through *The Hero with A Thousand Faces*, Campbell includes a circular diagram of the journey with a counter-clockwise path (245). The stages are as follows:

1. **The Departure: The Call to Adventure,** The Refusal of the Call, **Supernatural Aid,** The **Crossing of the First Threshold**, and **The Belly of the Whale**.

2. **Initiation: The Road of Trials,** The Meeting with the Goddess, Woman as the Temptress, Atonement with the Father, Apotheosis and **The Ultimate Boon.**

The Return: Refusal of the Return, **The Magic Flight,** Rescue From Without, **The Crossing of the Return Threshold**, Master of the Two Worlds, **and Freedom to Live** [Campbell ix–x].

Murdock envisions the journey as cyclical and bases it on her own experience and that of "women of [her] generation who have sought validation from patriarchal systems and found them not only lacking but terribly destructive" (4). Murdock's ten stages can occur simultaneously and then begin again as a "continuous cycle of growth and learning" (4). There are four to twelve steps within each of her stages: "**Separation** from the feminine; Identification with the masculine and **gathering allies**; **Road of trials: meeting ogres and dragons**; **Finding the boon of success**; Awakening to feelings of spiritual aridity: **death**; Initiation and **descent** to the Goddess; Urgent yearning to reconnect with the feminine; **Healing** the mother/daughter split; Healing the wounded masculine; **Integration** of masculine and feminine" (4–5).

In Frankel's *Buffy and the Heroine's Journey: Vampire Slayer as Feminine Chosen One,* she lists the stages of Campbell's hero's journey alongside her formulation of heroine's journey. Frankel includes World of Common Day as her first stage and notes that it is the same for her and Campbell's work, but it is not listed in Campbell's *A Hero with a Thousand Faces*. The next two stages in *Buffy* echo or copy Campbell: ***Call to Adventure***: A Desire to Reconnect with the Feminine; and *Refusal of the Call*. The same or similar wording is italicized here; bolded words again refer to those relevant to Yuriko. The stage called Ruthless Mentor and the Bladeless Talisman is parallel to Campbell's Supernatural aid. Frankel's ***Crossing the First Threshold***: Opening Ones Senses is aligned with Campell's two stages, Crossing the First Threshold and Belly of the Whale. Frankel's **Sidekicks,** *Trials* **and Adversaries** are paired with Campell's Road of Trials. The next five stages (Wedding the Animus, Facing Bluebeard, Sensitive Man as Completion, Confronting the Powerless Father, and **Descent into Darkness)** are all pieces of Campbell's Woman as Temptress. Frankel changes Campbell's Atonement with the Father to Atonement with the Mother. Added to Campbell's Apotheosis is "**through Accepting One's Feminine Side.**" Frankel renames Campbell's The Ultimate Boon to **Reward: Winning the Family**. Lastly, Frankel pairs Campbell's The Refusal of the Return with **Torn Desires**. *Magic Flight* is the same for both. Frankel chooses the title **Reinstating the Family** to substitute for Rescue from Within. There is no parallel category in her schema for Campbell's Return. The final two stages are rewritten as **Power Over Life and Death**, which is matched with Campbell's Master of Two Worlds, while **Ascension** of the New Mother replaces Freedom to Live.

These different frameworks for the heroic journey can be consolidated into a design that allows for multiple pathways through a heroic journey. In this synthesized version of the heroic journey, the "monomyth" is replaced by the "multi-mythic journey." This multi-mythic quest is, in many ways, parallel to third-wave feminism, where choice and multiple paths to empowerment are essential. The categories within the proposed "multi-mythic" heroic framework are:

   1. Departure/Separation/Exit/Selfless Action where the long journey begins after the need to find/rescue/discover is established.
   2. Initiation/Trials, where the hero is tested mentally and physically on the path to recover or discover someone/something.
   3. Reward/Success, where the quest seems or is completed and there a reward of some kind, which is often intangible.
   4. Return/Integration/Healing, when the hero returns home, is reintegrated into society, and heals him/herself and the community.

These stages seem akin to the typical beginning, middle, end and epilogue of a traditional story, but there is a caveat: the multi-mythic journey is never ending. Within each category, steps can vary widely, and no one hero completes them all.

Yuriko's Multi-Mythic Journey

This section attempts to craft an order of Yuriko's journey; however, it would be best described with a free-flowing diagram rather than words. Using the four categories already described, this section is divided into categories with stages. Yuriko follows the circular heroic path that Murdock envisions; she does not adhere to any of the stages delineated above in a linear, or even near-linear, fashion. Yuriko's path is both circuitous *and* overlapping. This could be characterized as reflective of Helen Cixous' theory of *ecriture feminine* (women's writing) and the idea that women should not keep to "the norms that patriarchy has laid down for them" (Pamela 88) but can "circumvent and reformulate existing structures" (Sellers xxix). Yuriko's journey is also tightly connected to Frankel's schema, which illustrates the more feminine side of the journey and her connection to family.

(1) Departure/Separation/Exit/Selfless Action

THE CALL TO ADVENTURE/GATHERING ALLIES/SUPERNATURAL AID

Eleven-year-old Yuriko is jolted out of her ordinary life when her brother Hiroki kills a classmate and maims another. This uncharacteristic behavior shocks his parents, sister, and community. Moreover, after the incident, Hiroki cannot be found. Understandably, all of this sends Yuriko and her parents into despair. How does one cope with such a tragedy? Each person affected copes with their suffering differently. Yuriko's father goes out to search for him; her mother waits for calls and escapes to Hiroki's room to cry, but Yuriko is too distraught to even to cry. Yuriko's adventure begins when she tries to come to terms with her own suffering. She curls up on her brother's bed and dreams. In her dream a talking book named Aju—her ally and supernatural aid—begins speaking to Yuriko about the duality of the Hero, who also has an evil side called The King in Yellow. Ultimately, Yuriko learns that the *Book of Elem* that Hiroki recently found is a record of a Hero, which contains "a portion of the King in Yellow's hideous strength" (157). When Hiroki touched the book in anger, evil flowed through him making him kill someone. His violence enabled the dark side of the Hero to possess Hiroki; now they are one and the same (70). This dualistic aspect is a primary concept in Buddhism—the world cannot have good without evil—as "they are necessary conjoined parts of a stable whole" (Wee 66). "The meaning of each depends upon (denying) its opposite" (Loy and Goodhew 11).

YURIKO'S NON-REFUSAL OF THE CALL

Four times, at various places in all stages of the journey, Yuriko is asked if she will abandon her dangerous quest and she refuses. This stage is a deviation from all the schemas examined thus far. These opportunities allow her to reaffirm her love for her brother. The first two instances occur as she learns about the situation (38–42, 61–73). Once she fully understands the complex issues (that only a child and Hiroki's relative can succeed in this quest to rescue Hiroki; that a devastating war between good and evil will erupt due to the Hero and the King in Yellow being released; and that she may die on her mission), she firmly accepts "the call," stating, "I have to go. I have to save my brother" (72).

Rescuing her brother will also save the world, as is clarified for her by one of her allies: "Imagine a world in which a single boy, by his own free will, does not hesitate to take the life of another. This is no different from a world in which one thousand men might take the lives of another thousand, or ten thousand the lives of ten thousand" (111). Yuriko understands and replies, "My mission for one—getting back my brother—is also for many. Saving the world" (113). Japanese readers would understand this reference to saving many as a noble characteristic of a *bodhisattva* (someone who puts self above others). When asked again if she will opt out of her quest, she responds simply and with determination, "I will not run away from this" (114). Lastly, before her descent into the sunken palace, Yuriko's ally, Ash tells her she must leave if she is tricked by the voice of the King in Yellow into believing he is still her brother. Yuriko is on the precipice of failure here, and she actually feels her supernatural aid, the magical glyph, physically separating from her. Yet, she pushes it back down, and shows her strength of purpose again with the firm words, "I won't turn back. I'm an *allcaste*, and I'm going to meet the Hero" (299).

CROSSING THE FIRST THRESHOLD/OPENING ONE'S
    SENSES/THE BELLY OF THE WHALE

Passing through the threshold is, to Campbell, "a transit into a sphere of rebirth" and may give the appearance of the death of the hero (90). Yuriko does not die in the real world, but a doppelganger is necessary to replace her at home while she is on her quest. This occurs as preparation for her journey, which begins when she transports herself to the nameless land. There the real Yuriko is "reborn" as *allcaste* and chooses a new name, U-ri (or Yuuri in Japanese). Another ally tells her, "From now until your role in the story is complete, you will not be the eleven-year-old girl Yuriko Morisaki. You are the *allcaste*. You are not bound by the consideration of age, gender, or your former position in society" (122).

(2) Initiation/Trials/Descent into Darkness/Compassionate Healing

The most important events in a hero's journey are the obstacles they must overcome. Yuriko's obstacles appear throughout all the stages of her quest. Murdock refers to this category as "wandering the road of trials to discover her strength and abilities and uncover and overcome her weaknesses" (46). The first trial, which is prevalent throughout her story, even predeparture, is related to her gender. Upset upon hearing that "the Hero" was evil, Yuriko throws the dictionary against the wall and even bites it. This causes the dictionary, Aju, to taunt her, "You may have sharp teeth, but you are just a little girl. You can't save your brother. Now be good for a change. Dry your tears and blow your nose, and get to bed" (40). Aju then continues to insult Yuriko in a condescending tone by surmising that she is just trying to avoid going to school, rather than truly wanting to help her brother. This infuriates Yuriko and makes her persist in asking more questions and discovering how to help her brother.

Throughout Yuriko's quest there are many reminders of her gender and age. When Ash berates her for "drowning in [her] own emotions," the omniscient narrator states, "It would have been an unfair criticism of an elementary school girl. But she was not a little girl anymore" (264). Yet Yuriko and U-ri and the *allscaste* are one and the same; Yuriko has dual roles that exist simultaneously. Her female and childish physical attributes are the subject of questions about her suitability as a hero: "You are but a girl," the Archdevout says, "Your cheeks are soft. Your arms are thin and your legs so weak they are barely able to hold your own weight. Yet still you would go on this quest to find your brother?" (93). Yuriko responds, "I am a little girl, but that doesn't mean I'm weak" (92). She adds with certainty, "We can do everything boys can do. Sometimes better"(92). Her confidence continues during her first interaction with Ash, her primary adult ally, who peevishly goads her to do her best throughout the novel, epitomizing the "cruel to be kind" mentality. When he sees that she has turned Aju from a dictionary to a mouse, he says with scorn, "How like a girl" (191). To this she queries, "There something wrong with being a girl?" (190) Yuriko's clear and adamant acceptance of her body illustrates the stage Frankel referred to as "Accepting one's feminine side." Yuriko tells Ash, "[M]ark my words, I'm going to make you glad you had a girl for your *allcaste* by the time we're through" (196).

The slights about her gender continue throughout Yuriko's journey to the nameless land and beyond, yet these patronizing comments, while annoying, are not large obstacles. Yuriko's major trials consist of two distinct types; she needs to solve mysteries and fight physical battles, both of which include aspects of psychological duress. Her first large task is to find out why the King in Yellow was able to enter Hiroki. She is told, "You must find out what thoughts crystalized in your brother's heart in those days—they will be the clues that guide you toward him" (122). Through sleuthing and disguises she learns that Hiroki was protecting his friend from bullies and that his initial aggressive actions toward the boys came from good—from that dangerous desire to be a hero—but the King in Yellow was able to overpower him. Evil stemmed from good intentions, from his selfish desire to be viewed as a hero. Yuriko, on the other hand, never yearns to be a hero or hopes for glory; her actions focus on one goal—saving her brother (and the world). Her acts are selfless, the kind of action espoused by Buddhism.

The physical challenges faced by Yuriko range from minor to extreme and each, as noted above, cause psychological distress at varying levels. There are smaller ones—such as learning how to travel; learning about the powers of the glyph, which includes healing herself and others (190); maneuvering around a magic force field (241); healing a man possessed by an unattached story (241); and surviving a wind-wall storm (279). Hand in hand with healing is compassion, a heroic characteristic. Healing can be found twice in this framework, illustrating the "both/and" concept inherent in cyclical patterns.

The most significant trials involve violent battles with the dark side. The first is with the terrifying envoy of the King in Yellow, which is described as "a writhing darkness" (185) that turns to "a golden eyeball" with "a swarm of tentacles" and dripping acid (186). It morphs into a large mouth with a bright tongue and fangs and lashes out at Yuriko/U-ri, Sky, and Aju. With the help of her magical ally, Ash, the envoy is deflated and defeated. The second major trial is Uri's descent into the catacombs to gain information about her brother. As previously noted, this is the archetypal journey to the underworld, as seen in ancient mythologies from around the world, including Greece and Japan. Yuriko/U-ri descends with her allies. The cold, putrid smells and strange sounds petrify her—literally—as at one point she cannot move. She learns that the "black lump of foulness" and "a mass of rotten seaweed" was the new form of her uncle, ravaged by his lust for power, an illustration of giving in to his desires rather than overcoming them. His hideous form was the result of using *The Book of Elem* and trying to bring back the dead, a decidedly unnatural and evil endeavor, which is counter to Buddhist teachings that illustrate the need for "selfless renunciation or detachment" (Rahula 49). After seeing her uncle's face, U-ri screamed repeatedly and had to be carried out of the tunnel. It would seem she failed; yet she did not. Gaining this information about the change in her uncle was crucial for her development, as it prepares her for the final interaction with the Hero and the King in Yellow.

The last and "supreme ordeal" (Campbell 246) comes with a prelude of several dangerous battles. The first is with the guardians of the Hero that morph into assorted terrible shapes like a "bird of dust" that shifts into "gold and silver snakes" (304) with claws. The battles seem endless, but Yuriko and her allies prevail. After wandering through a labyrinth, they finally reach their goal and encounter "the shining Hero" in a "mist of gold" (316) whom

Ash attacked repeatedly to no effect. The Hero expanded to "giant propor-tions" (317), with incredible energy shaking the ground and flowing with light (319). Only after Yuriko sees Hiroki, who "looks at her with a tear streaked face—a look that only lasted for the space of a breath," and hears him say, "I'm sorry," and "goodbye" before "diving into the light of the Hero" (318–319) does Yuriko come to realize Sky and her brother were part of each other. This epiphany also forms part of her "reward."

Reward/Success/Reinstating the Family

After the Hero absorbs Sky, the chamber begins to crumble and the glyph transports Yuriko and company safely back to in the nameless land. Upon returning there, she still believes she can return home with Hiroki. She runs down the hill, chasing a nameless devout and vowing, "I'll search the whole place, and I'll find him! I'll drag him out of out of there, I swear it! And then we'll go home together!" (320). It is then that she is sorely disap-pointed, believing she has failed.

Yuriko learns that the purpose of her long journey, which initially began to rescue her brother, has changed. The "lies and subterfuge" of others enabled her to "purify" (328) her brother/Sky. Yuriko admits that if she had known that Sky was a part of her brother, she would have brought him back to their world. She learns that doing so would have allowed him to be the "gate" to bring in the King in Yellow, causing a long war and, ultimately, complete destruction. Nevertheless, it still takes Yuriko time to process and finally understand that she has succeeded in saving her brother by turning him (and Sky) into a nameless devout, with no memory and no real identity, "a no one, nowhere" (320). This sounds like he is able to reach Nirvana, with the attain-ment of no-self and no desires. Yet, it is more complicated. Hiroki himself has ceased to exist, only the nameless devout remains (334).

Part of Yuriko's success is related to her full understanding of the sin of wanting to be a hero. Being selfish, and concerned with the "self" counter the Buddhist belief in renunciation of the self. Desire or thirst ties human beings to the great wheel of suffering. The nameless devouts pay for the sins of all people by spinning the Great Wheels of Inculpation (toga no tairin) in the nameless land. They and the weavers who create stories are "two sides of one coin" (335) just like the Hero and the King in Yellow (335). Yuriko tries to grasp all of this difficult information in the wake of her journey. It is unimaginably difficult for anyone to lose a loved one and Yuriko is only eleven years old, yet Ash's explanation helps her come to terms with her loss of her brother and her understanding of the Buddhist unending cycle of birth, death, and rebirth. He gently tells Yuriko, "Your brother's soul rests in the great flow of stories until such a time as it will reenter the Circle inside another life.

You see? He waits for rebirth. He feels no pain. You ensured that when you purified him" (335).

Return/Integration/Healing

Yuriko's return to the nameless land and to her own world are both quick and uneventful in and of themselves. Each place affords her time to reflect on her mission and understand all the rewards gained by her journey. The serenity that accompanies the knowledge that Hiroki is at peace gave Yuriko the ability to heal her shattered family. She is able to comfort her parents with her "new found calm" which was "infectious" (340). Her "warm presence" is able to help her family "get back to the business of living" (340). Moreover, Yuriko is also able to help Hiroki's bullied friend and the teacher who tried to help them. She gives her parents the gift of knowing that Hiroki's actions stemmed from standing up against bullies.

In the epilogue, Yuriko learns that she will be able to return to the nameless land to assist future *allcastes*. Her healing prepares her to begin this new journey in the battle against the King in Yellow.

The Heroic and Endless Journey

Life is a journey. It takes various forms. Mutli-mythic journeys incorporate all kinds of heroes, patterns, and outcomes, reflecting cultural and human diversity. Buddhist teachings explain that life is a never-ending journey of suffering until one is able to escape the cycle of rebirth and attain Nirvana. Yuriko, as the female hero in a quest to make sure her brother can be reborn rather than suffer endlessly, learns a great deal about herself and the world in her battle against evil. By the end of her quest—that weaves in and out of assorted schemas of the heroic journey—Yuriko thoroughly comprehends Buddhist notions of duality and balance. Good and evil are inextricably intertwined. Desires for accolades and power through doing good deeds can lead to destruction. Yuriko demonstrates courage, bravery, compassion, mental and physical fortitude, and selflessness as she follows her path. These characteristics, along with help from magical allies, enable her to succeed in her heroic multi-mythic quest. She returns home to share and spread the inner peace gained from rescuing her brother. Then, she will set out again on another journey.

Works Cited

Campbell, Joseph. *The Hero with a Thousand Faces.* 2nd ed. Princeton University Press, 1968.
Cixous, Hélène, and Susan Sellers. Introduction to *The Hélène Cixous Reader.* Routledge, 1994.

Emerson, David. "Innocence as a Super-Power: Little Girls on the Hero's Journey." *Mythlore* 1–2 (2009): 131–147.

Frankel, Valerie Estelle. *Buffy and the Heroine's Journey: Vampire Slayer as Feminine Chosen One.* McFarland, 2012.

_____. *From Girl to Goddess: The Heroine's Journey in Myth and Legend.* McFarland, 2010.

Kinsella, Elaine L., Timothy D. Ritchie, and Eric R. Igou. "Zeroing in on Heroes: A Prototype Analysis of Hero Features/Personality Processes and Individual Differences." *Journal of Personality and Social Psychology* 108, no. 1 (2015): 114–127.

Lawler, Kelly. *USA Today.* January 5, 2016.

Loy, David, and Linda Goodhew. *The Dharma of Dragons and Daemons: Buddhist Themes in Modern Fantasy.* Wisdom Publications, 2004.

Miyabe, Miyuki. *Eiyuu No Sho* [The Book of Heroes]. Shinchōsha, 2009.

_____. *The Book of Heroes.* Translated by Alexander O. Smith. VIZ Media, 2011.

Murdock, Maureen. *The Heroine's Journey: Women's Quest for Wholeness.* Shambhala Publications, 1990.

Norman, Dorothy. *The Hero: Myth/Image/Symbol.* New American Library, 1969.

Pamela, J. "'The Laugh of the Medusa': Hélène Cixous's Theory of Écriture Feminine." *International Journal on Multicultural Literature* 4, no. 2 (2014): 88–94.

Pearson, Carol, and Katherine Pope. *The Female Hero in American and British Literature.* R.R. Bowker, 1981.

Perlich, John R. "Rethinking the Monomyth: *Pan's Labyrinth* and the Face of a New Hero(ine)." In *Millennial Mythmaking: Essays on the Power of Science Fiction and Fantasy Literature, Films and Games,* edited by John Perlich and David Whitt, 100–128. McFarland, 2010.

Powers, Meredith A. *The Heroine in Western Literature: The Archetype and Her Reemergence in Modern Prose.* McFarland, 1991.

Rank, Otto. *The Myth of the Birth of the Hero: A Psychological Exploration of Myth.* 1922. 3rd Edition. Translated by Gregory C. Richter and E. James Lieberman. Johns Hopkins University Press, 2004.

Rankin, Lindsay E., and Alice H. Eagly. "Is Heroism Hailed and Hers Hidden? Women, Men, and the Social Construction of Heroism." *Psychology of Women Quarterly* 32 (2008): 414–422.

Rahula, Walpola. *What the Buddha Taught.* 2nd ed. Grove Press, 1974.

Wee, Valerie. *Japanese Horror Films and Their American Remakes.* Routledge, 2004.

Zimbardo, Philip. *The Lucifer Effect.* Random House, 2007.

About the Contributors

Kerry **Boyles** earned an MA in English literature from Rutgers University, where she studied Victorian texts with an emphasis on the Gothic. She works as a managing editor of education journals at Taylor & Francis.

Alissa **Burger** is an assistant professor of English at Culver-Stockton College. She is the author of T*he Wizard of Oz as American Myth* (McFarland, 2014) and *Teaching Stephen King* (Palgrave, 2016).

Sandra **Eckard** is a professor of English at East Stroudsburg University of Pennsylvania. She publishes and presents not only in composition pedagogy and writing center theory, but also using popular culture in teaching.

Eleanor J. **Hogan** is an associate professor of Japanese language and literature at Gettysburg College. She teaches all levels of Japanese language, as well as Japanese popular cultural, classical Japanese literature and extraordinary fiction in Japan and the west.

Trinidad **Linares** is the assistant coordinator of Special Programs at Bowling Green State University. She has contributed to *Bitch*, *Meridians*, and *The Projector* and presented at several conference, including Pippi to Ripley, Buffy to Batgirl, and the Literature/Film Association conference, among others.

Peregrine **Macdonald** is an outreach and instruction librarian at West Texas A&M University. She co-hosts a biweekly podcast with her siblings called "No Story Is Sacred," and is a staff member at Viable Paradise Writers' Workshop.

Caolan **Madden** holds a Ph.D. in English from Rutgers University. Her areas of interest include 19th- and 20th-century women's writing and material culture, first-person modes of writing, and intersections between poetry and popular culture. She writes regularly for the blog "Weird Sister."

Stephanie **Mix** is an independent scholar with an MPA from SUNY Binghamton. Her academic writing follows the same feminist path that has led her to work in reproductive rights and victim's assistance non-profits, but with significantly more discussion of magic and superheroes.

Alice **Nuttall** completed her Ph.D. in English literature at Oxford Brookes University. She is working on several contributions to critical collections on children's literature and on her own fiction.

Shyla **Saltzman** earned her Ph.D. at Cornell University. She teaches English composition and contemporary American literature at East Stroudsburg and Kean University.

Sheila **Sandapen** is an associate teaching professor at Drexel University in Philadelphia. Her interests include cultural studies, women's studies, history and film, and she has published on on World War I aviation, Jane Austen, British cinema and *Doctor Who.*

Patricia Isabella **Schumacher** is a doctoral student of American studies at Leipzig University in Germany. Her thesis focuses on the depiction of prostitution in the American imagination. Her research interests include gender and sexuality in science fiction and popular culture, as well as Gothic narratives.

Julie M. **Still** is on the faculty of the Paul Robeson Library at Rutgers University. She has published and presented on several topics relating to librarianship, history, and literature.

Al **Valentín** is a Ph.D. candidate in women's and gender studies at Rutgers University. Their research focuses on pop culture and gender identity, sexual orientation, race, class, size and ability, with a specific emphasis on animated cartoons and video games.

Zara T. **Wilkinson** is a reference librarian at Rutgers University–Camden. In addition to her research interests in librarianship, she has published and presented on the depiction of women in science fiction television shows including *Star Trek*, *Doctor Who*, and *Orphan Black.*

Index